Public Utility Regulation

Recent Economic Thought Series

Warren J. Samuels, Editor
Michigan State University
East Lansing, Michigan, U.S.A.

Previously published books in the series:
Feiwel, G., *Samuelson and Neoclassical Economics*
Wade, L., *Political Economy: Modern Views*
Zimbalist, A., *Comparative Economic Systems: Recent Views*
Darity, W., *Labor Economics: Modern Views*
Jarsulic, M., *Money and Macro Policy*
Samuelson, L., *Microeconomic Theory*
Bromley, D., *Natural Resource Economics: Policy Problems and Contemporary Analysis*
Mirowski, P., *The Reconstruction of Economic Theory*
Field, A., *The Future of Economic History*
Lowry, S., *Pre-Classical Economic Thought*
Officer, L., *International Economics*
Asimakopulos, A., *Theories of Income Distribution*
Earl, P., *Psychological Economics: Development, Tensions, Prospects*
Peterson, W., *Market Power and the Economy*
Mercuro, N., *Law and Economics*

This series is devoted to works that present divergent views on the development, prospects, and tensions within some important research areas of international economic thought. Among the fields covered are macromonetary policy, public finance, labor and political economy. The emphasis of the series is on providing a critical, constructive view of each of these fields, as well as a forum through which leading scholars of international reputation may voice their perspectives on important related issues. Each volume in the series will be self-contained; together these volumes will provide dramatic evidence of the variety of economic thought within the scholarly community.

Public Utility Regulation

The Economic and Social Control of Industry

edited by
Kenneth Nowotny
New Mexico State University

David B. Smith
New Mexico State University

Harry M. Trebing
Michigan State University

Kluwer Academic Publishers
Boston / Dordrecht / London

Distributors

for North America: Kluwer Academic Publishers, 101 Philip Drive,
Assinippi Park, Norwell, Massachusetts, 02061, USA

for all other countries: Kluwer Academic Publishers Group, Distribution
Centre, Post Office Box 322, 3300 AH Dordrecht, The Netherlands

Library of Congress Cataloging-in-Publication Data

Public utility regulation: the economic and social control of industry/
    edited by Kenneth Nowotny, David B. Smith, Harry M. Trebing.
        p.   cm. — (Recent economic thought series)
    Includes index.
    ISBN 0–7923–9019–9
    1. Public utilities — Government policy — United States.
I. Nowotny, Kenneth.   II. Smith, David Brian.   III. Trebing, Harry
Martin, 1926–   .   IV. Series.
HD2766.P84   1989
363.6′9073 — dc20   89–8062
                                                                          CIP

Contents

Contributing Authors   vii

Acknowledgments   ix

1
Introduction   1
David B. Smith

2
The Economics of Public Utility Regulation: An Overview   9
Kenneth Nowotny

Commentary by William M. Dugger   28

3
Pricing and the Electric Utility Industry   35
J. Robert Malko and Philip R. Swensen

Commentary by John Wenders   78

4
Telecommunications Regulation — The Continuing Dilemma   93
Harry M. Trebing

Commentary by Basil L. Copeland, Jr.   131

5
Natural Gas Pipelines and Monopoly   137
Curtis Cramer

Commentary by W. W. Sharkey   155

6
Urban Water Supply: The Divergence Between Theory and Practice   163
Patrick C. Mann

Commentary by Alfred L. Parker   179

7
Natural Monopoly Measures and Regulatory Policy   185
Douglas Gegax

Commentary by Ronald R. Braeutigam   217

8
The Contribution of Economic Theory to the Regulatory Process:
Strengths, Weaknesses, and Future Directions   223
Marilyn C. O'Leary and David B. Smith

Index   239

Contributing Authors

Ronald R. Braeutigam
Department of Economics
College of Arts & Sciences
Northwestern University
Evanston, IL 60201

Basil L. Copeland, Jr.
123 Corvallis Drive
No. Little Rock, AR 72118

Curtis Cramer, Chairman
Department of Economics
University of Wyoming
Laramie, WY 82071

William M. Dugger
Department of Economics
DePaul University
25 E. Jackson
Chicago, IL 60604

Douglas Gegax
Department of Economics/30001
New Mexico State University
Las Cruces, NM 88003-0001

J. Robert Malko
Department of Business Administration
College of Business
UMC-35
Utah State University
Logan, UT 84322

Patrick C. Mann
Department of Economics
West Virginia University
Morgantown, WV 26506-6025

Kenneth Nowotny
Center for Public Utilities
New Mexico State University
Box 3MPD
Las Cruces, NM 88003

Marilyn O'Leary
8 Tumbleweed, N.W.
Albuquerque, NM 87120

Alfred L. Parker, Chairman
Department of Economics
University of New Mexico
Albuquerque, NM 87131

W. W. Sharkey
Bellcore
435 South Street
Morristown, NJ 07960

David B. Smith, Director
Center for Public Utilities
New Mexico State University
Box 3MPD
Las Cruces, NM 88003

Philip Swensen, Chairman
Department of Business Administration
College of Business
UMC-35
Utah State University
Logan, UT 84322

Harry M. Trebing, Director
Institute for Public Utilities
113 Olds Hall
Michigan State University
East Lansing, MI 48824

John Wenders
Department of Economics
University of Idaho
Moscow, ID 83843

Acknowledgments

The editors wish to thank our contributors who have shown infinite patience and goodwill during the preparation of this collection. The three of us excepted, the work our contributors have produced is of the first rank. We would also like to acknowledge the enthusiasm of Warren Samuels, Series Editor, who urged this work on us from the start, and Zachary Rolnik who accepted all of our excuses.

Public Utility Regulation

1 INTRODUCTION

David B. Smith

This is a book about the application of economic theory to a unique form of social control — public utility regulation. A central theme of this work is to examine the role that economics has played in shaping the rationale and direction of regulatory practices. While economic theory has played an important role in the shaping of regulatory policy in the past, it has an even greater potential role to play in the future as the regulatory community grapples with the many challenges of a changing economic environment. This is a very timely and much needed piece of work that can serve as a reference for decision makers who are facing the challenging problems of deregulation and competition.

This work is comprised of 13 selected articles that guide the reader from an initial discussion of why we decided to regulate certain industries in the first place to a specific analysis of what role economic theory has played in the electric, natural gas, telecommunications, and water industries, and whether it should be allowed to play an even more dominant role in the future. The reader is then provided with a more modern version of what economists mean by the concept of natural monopoly and a menu of policy options that will allow society to derive any benefits from such a market structure. Finally, the role that economics can and will play in the regulatory process is discussed by two former commissioners from a state regulatory commission.

The first two essays are intended to provide an overall framework within which the 11 following articles may be placed and analyzed. Professor Nowotny provides the reader with a 100-year overview of the study of public utility economics and the main issues that economists have struggled with over this time period. He stresses that in the study of this field, economists have grappled with the questions of what is meant by a public utility, why control needs to be exercised over such an entity, and what the "optimal" form of social control should be. He believes that if control of profits is viewed as the primary goal of regulation rather than optimal or efficient prices, then economics still has a role to play in the regulatory process: analyzing the consequences of the regulatory effort. He concludes by reminding the reader that regulation is constantly evolving and that it cannot be placed into a simple static framework of economic optimization.

Dugger supports Nowotny's position for the social control of the market by defining what he views as the proper role for the regulator: "a substitute for the social control of the market." Dugger is concerned, however, as to what extent, certainly over a period of time, regulators abandon this charge and turn, instead, to other objectives. While the regulator may still claim to exercise social control over regulation, the question is in whose interest? The consumer? The firm? The stockholder? Dugger discusses the capture theory of regulation, which postulates that regulators come to identify more with the needs of the industry than with the consumer. He argues that industry-specific regulators (e.g., those who regulate electric, natural gas, telecommunications, trucking, and airlines) are more vulnerable to industry capture than the function-specific regulator (e.g., the Environmental Protection Agency and the Occupational Safety and Health Administration). These regulators are less prone to industry capture because of the many diversified industries they regulate. Dugger supports the "process" approach advocated by Nowotny by pointing out the new challenges that diversification by public utilities will bring to regulators. This appears to be an increasing trend by utilities, and such a movement will be subjected to careful scrutiny by regulators in an effort to determine what the effect will be upon the utility's customers.

A very thorough discussion of how one moves from abstract microeconomic theory to its application, modification, and adoption within a rate case scenario is provided by the Malko and Swensen chapter. Malko and Swensen provide a discussion of marginal cost pricing as a methodology for pricing electricity in the 1970s. They take the established regulatory process as a given and proceed to discuss how to use the economist's tools to make regulation as effective as possible. Their chapter provides an in-depth overview of the need to set pricing objectives that serve as a policy guideline around which to design rates. They next provide an analysis of some theoretical and quantitative issues relating to the application of marginal cost pricing as an alternative to traditional rate designs. Finally, the authors provide an actual "case experience," which points out the challenges involved when attempting to implement marginal cost pricing.

Has the traditional approach to regulation allowed society to capture all of the benefits of economies of scale and scope? Has regulation even achieved the goal of simulating imperfect competition? Professor Wenders addresses these and other questions in his paper, which argues that we must adopt a more market-oriented approach to extract the benefits of natural monopoly. Wenders's paper, in contrast to the Malko-Swensen paper, discusses why he feels a market-oriented approach to the regulation of natural monopoly may be more effective than the traditional approach. While the presence of natural monopoly has brought with it the need for regulation, the costs and inefficiencies of regulation have outweighed the perceived benefits of economies of scale and scope. The political regulation of the electric industry has produced its own set of economic distortions that prevent regulation from even approximating an imperfectly competitive outcome. Wenders contends that it is a mistake to assume that the political process that governs the behavior of regulation will give both the regulators and the regulated the incentive to produce and price in the most efficient way. Wenders argues that as we move from a regulated natural monopoly to one more market oriented and competitive, the most challenging policy task confronting the electric industry will be to encourage politically viable, competitive institutions that limit the market power created by past regulation.

Is it time to abandon regulation in favor of the competitive market in the telecommunications industry? Professor Trebing cautions the reader to evaluate such a proposal very carefully before charting a course of action that we may regret later. Trebing first places the telecommunications industry in historical perspective and then introduces the many forces that are both encouraging and subduing competition in telecommunications at the present time. He believes that if competition is to prevail in telecommunications, it is essential for freedom of entry to exist; for this will allow new sellers to compete with established firms. Trebing feels that unlimited entry is not present in most markets and believes that the contestable markets theory has very limited applications to imperfect

markets. He offers a revised theory of the regulated firm, which postulates that because of the presence of both monopoly and competition,
the firm will choose to engage in the practices of price discrimination and
cross subsidization. These practices will occur *not* because of rate-base
regulation but because of the presence of imperfect markets. Hence,
deregulation will introduce a new type of behavior that Trebing feels has
not been adequately dealt with by deregulation proponents. Trebing
rejects the notion of price caps as a substantive solution for dealing with
the cost allocation problem caused by imperfect markets. He believes
instead that regulatory reform can provide society with the most effective
means to deal with the cost allocation problem. He offers a proposal
advanced by Martin Glaeser as a starting point for how costs might be
allocated in today's telecommunications industry. This methodology,
along with other elements of Trebing's reform model, combines the best
features of rate-base/rate-of-return regulation while still accommodating
the growth of competition.

Basil Copeland agrees with the Trebing Chapter and urges that
emphasis be placed not on deregulation but upon enlightened regulation
instead. Copeland, like Trebing, is concerned over the presence of the
current telecommunications environment, which consists of firms operating in both monopolistic and competitive markets. He has little confi-
dence that the contestable markets theory will resolve the problems of
price discrimination and cross subsidization. Copeland argues that a firm
that operates in both types of market structures will not only cause the
average cost of capital to increase for utility rate payers but will also
contribute to a resource misallocation problem. This will occur as capital
is shifted from low-risk markets to high-risk markets *not* by the marketplace but by utility managers' decisions, which may not reflect the desires
of society. Copeland concludes by suggesting that if the cost allocation
problem between monopolistic and competitive markets is viewed as
insurmountable, then perhaps the optimal solution is to forbid the regulated firm to operate in competitive unregulated markets.

While the natural gas industry has experienced both deregulation and
competition, are all of the pieces now in place to insure that resources
will be efficiently allocated in this industry? Professor Curtis Cramer
warns that there are still certain characteristics of this industry that must
be resolved before all of the perceived benefits of competition may be
realized by all parties. Professor Cramer points out that while we are
observing increased competition from the end users and the production
phase of the natural gas industry, we must not yet conclude that the
market will lead to the most efficient allocation of resources in this

industry. Cramer is concerned that certain ties that bind buyers and sellers are in conflict with a competitive segmented industry. He points out that the pipeline's bottleneck facility is the crux of the problem and has not been adequately addressed. Cramer emphasizes that the pipeline bottleneck problem must be subjected to continuous social control to prevent distortions, which may occur due to deregulation and competition. Specific forms of social control must include the following: adoption of contract carriage, removal of obligation to serve, unbundling of services, adoption of open network architecture, and restrictions of pipeline mergers and acquisitions that substantially lessen competition. He stresses that unless we move quickly to resolve these issues, which act to block end users from low-cost producers, any alleged benefits predicted to occur through deregulation will be short lived.

As one moves from a condition of monopoly to competition, will a stable or unstable equilibrium state exist? How much research has been devoted to this topic to enable us to predict what the outcome will be? Sharkey points out that while economists have analyzed both the behavior of firms within a regulatory environment and the forms of regulation that appear to be the most effective, little work if any has been devoted to the transition from monopoly to competition. He discusses two characteristics of the natural gas industry that may make competition potentially unstable. These characteristics are an indivisibility in the short-run production function and the network characteristics of this industry. In both cases, he describes how it might not be possible to rely upon market prices alone to create a stable equilibrium. Because of this, he points out that some minimal degree of coordination or cooperation may be required. Sharkey cautions that until we have a better understanding of equilibrium behavior of competing firms in decreasing cost or networking industries, any deregulatory polices should be implemented with caution.

What is the status of marginal cost pricing in the water utility industry? How can this industry benefit from implementing marginal cost pricing into more of its traditional rate designs? Professor Patrick Mann discusses the current pricing practices utilized in pricing water. He points out that there have been important research developments in water demand and costing that generally have not been translated into pricing reform. The industry has been very slow in converting research developments into practice. The result of this is that the water service industry continues to be characterized by inefficient rate designs. This neglect of pricing and costing research has produced the general underpricing of urban water service in the United States. Mann believes that costing and pricing practices in the water industry must be adapted to a changing environment. The use of the marginal cost standard in the implementation of peak demand and spatial pricing would make a substantial contribution toward the more efficient utilization of such a precious resource.

While there may be a gap between costing and pricing research and the implementation of this knowledge in the pricing of water, Professor Parker is not surprised by these results. He urges the economist to be patient in the desire to implement certain costing methodologies and to take advantage of parallel situations currently being experienced in electricity and natural gas. Professor Parker, like Mann, discusses the existing gap between economic pricing theory and the actual implementation of that theory. While he acknowledges that such a gap does exist in the water industry, he points out that economists have experienced similar frustrations in the electricity and telecommunications industries as well. However, he is optimistic that the theory-application gap can be closed more quickly if we all learn from the pricing experience currently occurring in electricity, natural gas, and telecommunications. If we have a better understanding of both the *types* of constraints that act to resist marginal cost pricing and the *rationale* for these constraints, perhaps it will be possible to speed up the rate at which more innovative, cost-based rate designs are implemented in the water industry.

What do economists mean by the term *natural monopoly*? If all economies of scale have been exhausted, does a natural monopoly no longer exist? What is the relevance of subadditivity to the concept of a natural monopoly? Professor Gegax provides the reader with an intensive and exhaustive discussion of the concept of natural monopoly, its definition at the present time, and implications for regulatory policy. A large amount of the Gegax paper is devoted to expanding the traditional notion of a natural monopoly to a more extensive definition by including the presence of subadditivity in addition to the more restrictive requirement of economies of scale. It is subadditivity, not economies of scale, that determines whether it is less costly for a single firm or for two or more firms to produce a given set of outputs at the lowest cost. Gegax then discusses how one might regulate an industry if it is a natural monopoly that includes external subsidies and Ramsey pricing, both of which could be achieved through regulation. His reinspection of production and cost functions leads to a more general definition of natural monopoly.

If a natural monopoly does exist, does this imply that the only choice to society is regulation? What policy options become available if one shifts attention from competition *within* a market to competition *for* a market? Professor Braeutigam provides not only a thorough review of the Gegax paper but addresses additional issues as well. He agrees with

Gegax that it is subadditivity, not economies of scale, that determines the presence of natural monopoly. He expands the Gegax analysis of natural monopoly into the next question: If an industry is determined to be a natural monopoly, does this mean that regulation is the only logical choice? Braeutigam contends that not only has the concept of natural monopoly been revised in recent years but that economists are shifting their emphasis to competition *for* a market instead of competition *within* a market. This represents a movement away from the notion that if a natural monopoly exists, then regulation is the only alternative form of control. Braeutigam discusses three ways (bidding, contestability, and intermodal competition) in which one might introduce competition for a market even if a natural monopoly exists within a market. All three of these methods could be viewed as alternatives to traditional regulation. Braeutigams expands the Gegax discussion of how to regulate by including additional types of regulation such as peak-load pricing and nonlinear tariff practices. He concludes his paper with a discussion of the social contract that is gaining support in some state jurisdictions as an alternative to traditional rate-of-return regulation.

What role has economic theory played in the decision-making process? What are some of the constraints (of which economists must be aware) that may preclude the adoption of efficient pricing in all instances? Can economic theory play a significant role in the future? The O'Leary and Smith chapter concludes this volume by analyzing the role that economics has and can play in the regulatory process. They state that the economist must gain a better understanding of the nature of the decision-making process undertaken by commissioners. The goal of economic efficiency may or may not be attained because of the many inputs that are received by commissioners in their deliberation. The economist must not be discouraged about this process but must learn to work effectively within it, as economics can play an invaluable role in assisting commissions as they grapple with the changing economic environments in electricity, natural gas, telecommunications, and water supply.

2 THE ECONOMICS OF PUBLIC UTILITY REGULATION: AN OVERVIEW

Kenneth Nowotny

One might hope that a student of the economics of public utility regulation could be more positive today in assessing the literature than was Schumpeter three decades ago. In his *History of Economic Analysis*, Schumpeter observed, with respect to public utility analysis, "The historian of economic analysis has little to report beyond a rich crop of historical and 'descriptive' work, some of which has retained its interest to this day" [1]. He went on to say " . . . public utilities should have proved both an important field of application and an important source of particular patterns for the theorist. Very little was accomplished, however, that will bear comparison with Dupuit's earlier contributions" [1]. Finally, to show his view of the field, Schumpeter summed up,

> . . . The various "theories" of valuation for indemnity, taxation, and rate regulation purposes that the legal mind produced offer curious examples of logical muddle. Many economists did useful work in trying to clear it up and seem, for example, after efforts extending over more than half a century to have convinced lawyers that the attempt to define a "reasonable" rate of return with reference to the value of a property that is itself derived from expected returns, involves circular reasoning. But this suffices to characterize the level of this branch of economic analysis [1].

9

It is apparent that Schumpeter was uncomfortable with hiding his disdain for the field of study up to that time.

Schumpeter's comments do, however, raise an interesting series of questions: Was Schumpeter's assessment of the field a fair one; if so, why, if not, why not; what is the status of the economics of public utility regulation since Schumpeter's *History*; how has it changed and why? Finally, a useful question, what can we expect from this field of study in the future?

The Nature of the Economics of Public Utility Regulation

Ideally, the study of public utilities and their regulation would identify 1) precisely what is and is not a public utility, 2) the fundamental reason or reasons for which society would wish to exercise particular control over such enterprise, and 3) the best way of exercising such control. The history of the study of public utility regulation lies upon a winding path, more or less from one to three above.

Has the question of what characterizes a public utility been answered? In 1925, L. R. Nash of Stone and Webster wrote in *The Economics of Public Utilities* [2],

> while it is thus generally true that public utilities are subject to competition in at least a part of their service, freedom from competition from other public service of the same kind is of substantial advantage both to the utilities and their customers. . . . The reason for this lies primarily in the high capital costs and fixed charges constituting at least one-third of the total cost of service.

He said, in effect, public utilities are natural monopolies. The reference here must, of course, be to falling *short-run* average cost and, thus, not to economies of scale. This is clear since on the very next page he observed,

> A typical public utility serving a large community has a capitalization not less than four times its annual revenues. In very large cities where extensive transmission and substation systems, paving and other costs incident to congestion are encountered, the ratio may be materially higher than that stated [2].

That is, implicitly, utilities may have faced diseconomies of scale, but still have been considered natural monopolies. This should be kept in mind upon reading the last chapters of this book. Nash is cited here not for his reputation as a scholar, but rather because he was a utility analyst for a well-known consulting firm writing a textbook published in 1925. His understanding of the situation must have been the accepted wisdom of most analysts in the field. He was certainly in no position to plow new ground.

Alfred Marshall had, after all, just noted in *Industry and Trade* [3] that, "The supply of water, gas, or electricity to any locality cannot be distributed over several rivals: for to say nothing of its wastefulness, . . . " He then pointed out that though such monopolies may not be "absolute," there are obstacles to setting up competition: 1) huge capital requirements, and 2) human inertia [3]. Marshall was keenly aware of the difference between short- and long-term analysis. A major subhead in his chapter on "Competition and Monopoly in Transport" is

> In regard to short periods most of the costs of a railway are "fixed"; but large problems of railway policy relate chiefly to long periods, in regard to which much fewer costs are fixed [3].

This is why H. H. Liebhafsky wrote in his *American Government and Business* that "Probably no *satisfactory operational* definition of the concept of a 'public utility' can be given. None exists in the literature" [4]. The problem revolves around the relationship between questions one and two above: Should a public utility per se be regulated because it *is* a public utility, or are there public utilities that need no regulation, or does the fact of regulation make a firm a public utility?

What is "natural" about a natural monopoly? Is the relevant set of attributes connected with cost or demand considerations? To say that a firm can supply an entire market more cheaply than two begs the question; one might say, simply, that demand is insufficient, as with a good restaurant in a very small town. It is a short-run problem that can be remedied by population growth. If economies of scale are required for a firm to be a public utility, fine, but that excludes fixed costs as the origin of the natural monopoly attribute.

Fortunately, and as usual, James C. Bonbright rescued economic analysis of public utilities, as a field, in his *Principles of Public Utility Rates*. Discussing the issue of declining average costs as a requirement of natural monopoly, or public utility status Bonbright observed,

> This assumption is quite unwarranted. It ignores the point that, even if the unit cost of supplying a given area with a given type of public utility service must increase with an enhanced rate of output, *any specified* required rate of output can be supplied most economically by a single plant or single system [5].

Thus, Bonbright pointed out the nature of economies of scope several years before it was given an identity and theoretical legitimacy by microeconomic theorists. The fundamental attribute that makes a firm a public utility is that for *any* given level of output, one firm can produce that output more cheaply than two or more. Of course, this could not be said of a restaurant and removes inadequate demand as a determining factor.

If it can be, at least provisionally, accepted that the term *natural monopoly* has an explicable definition, and that the determining attribute of a public utility is natural monopoly, one can then proceed to the question of Why control the enterprise? What compelling reason or reasons leads the society to desire to exercise social control over some or many aspects of the operation of a public utility? J. M. Clark answered the question, just asked, very simply:

> We may fairly start, then, with the assumption that cost of production under monopoly is less than it would be under competition which duplicates the service. The task of regulation is to give the consumer as much of the saving as justice and expediency permit [6].

Now this is hardly an answer likely to receive the approval of a neoclassical economist such as Schumpeter, but it certainly sets the issue. The monopolist left to his/her own devices will extract as much consumers' surplus as possible. Clark's notion was a fairly old one, even when he wrote that consumers should be protected from monopoly exploitation. This is what, after all, at least initially, inspired much "Granger" legislation following the Civil War for regulating utilities in the first place.

To the more strictly neoclassical point of view, however, was added *optimum rationing*, noted by Bonbright in 1940, on the heels of Harold Hotelling's classic article in 1938 [7, 8]. In effect, the monopolist's price is likely to diverge from marginal cost to such a degree as to reduce the maximum welfare of the economy. Now the interesting thing is that if consumer protection is to be the justification for regulation, one must then seek an answer to the question "What is the best way to implement social control?" If, on the other hand, optimum rationing is the rationale for regulation, the answer to the question of what to do is axiomatic, or at least, appeared so to Hotelling. But as Bonbright noted at the time, "A system of public utility rates no less than a system of prices in general performs not one great economic function but many" [7].

Schumpeter to the contrary notwithstanding, Clark had arrived at the "right" conclusion to appropriate utility rates in 1923 in *Studies in the Economics of Overhead Costs* [9]. To demonstrate the truth of the previous assertion requires, unfortunately, the quotation of a paragraph.

Clark said,

> The critical features of this method of rate-making are: the arranging of the
> rate so that the charge for additional use covers only the output costs, the
> covering of capacity and consumer costs in a way which does not fall as a
> burden on additional use, and fixing of differential costs as a minimum, with
> liberty to apportion residual costs on principles of justice and expediency.
> The first principles are definitely recognized in modern electrical rate systems,
> while the third makes itself felt with quite sufficient force, whether it is
> recognized as a part of the system or not. Manufacturers who could generate
> their own current are in a position to secure the lowest rate the utility can
> make, above differential cost, while smaller consumers have no such bargain-
> ing advantage.

There, in one paragraph, in 1923, Clark enunciated the principles of a
two- or three-part tariff with a marginal cost tail rate *and* Ramsey pricing
— a feat neoclassical economists required another fifty years to accomplish. Given Clark's heritage, it is doubtful that he was unaware of
welfare implications of his discussion. If there was ever any doubt about
the essence of the implications, there should not have been after about
eight years of debate in economic journals between 1942 and 1949. Nancy
Ruggles summarized and documented this debate in two articles in the
Review of Economic Studies [10, 11]. Fundamentally, the issues in the
marginal cost controversy (Ronald Coase so entitled a 1946 article) revol-
ved around the optimality of marginal cost pricing for investor-owned
utilities. If such utilities had to cover all costs in a decreasing-cost situation, then marginal cost pricing, per se, would be unattractive. Would a
simple proportional mark-up from marginal cost (MC) be the least
suboptimal or should some other scheme, (e.g., multi-part tariffs) be
applied? Many, at the time, argued for pure marginal cost pricing (in
the event one could agree on measurement problems) while W. Arthur
Lewis, Coase, and others, argued for a multi-part tariff. Apparently, for
the time being, the multi-part tariff pricers have won the day [12–23].

One can say then that, prior to 1949, discussions in the field of public
utility economics led, more or less, to the conclusion that 1) natural
monopolies are public utilities that 2) need to be regulated for the
protection of consumers, or which is the same thing, as the fact that
demand will be repressed below some "optimal" level of consumption,
and that 3) prices should be set so as to mimic, more or less, those that
would result if the industry followed the dictates of competition. Such
rates, in an arena of investor-owned utilities, will of necessity be comprised of two or three parts, including a marginal cost consumption
charge and the possibility of price discrimination in the first block(s),

where jointness of production allows and own-price elasticity requires. Either Schumpeter missed some of this along the way, misdesignates public utility economists, or holds the above conclusions in unsupportively low esteem. The fact of the matter is that by the time Schumpeter was finishing his *History*, most of the outline of modern public utility economics had been drawn.

The Economics of Public Utility Regulation Since 1950

Fortunately for the vita of more modern public utility economists, not all the issues of public utility regulation had been settled by 1950, and some were still open to a good bit of debate. While the marginal cost controversy of the 1940s explored many of the implications of marginal cost pricing, still open was the issue of how best would an investor-owned utility collect income with which to pay its stockholders and bondholders. This argument, of course, led to the advocacy of Ramsey pricing.

Although the issue of what to charge during peak and off-peak periods had been discussed earlier, it was yet to be formalized to the degree that occurred following the early 1950s. Whether or not, and under what conditions rate regulation *of the nature then practiced* did more harm than good became an issue in the 1960s. And, along the same lines, contestable market theory raised the issue in the 1970s as to whether or not regulation was needed at all, and if so, under what conditions. Finally, a reinspection of production and cost functions has led to a more general definition of *natural monopoly*, which includes economies of scope, and thus precludes economies of scale as the only necessary if sufficient condition.

The following discussion will proceed in more or less the same direction as the preceding one: issues of what to regulate, first, and how to regulate, second. Two of the strongest attacks on the institution of regulation have come from the Chicago School of economists or economists associated with similar modes of thought. Stigler and others sought to demonstrate that utility regulation did not, in fact, change anything, and thus, while costs were incurred in the act of regulation, there was no offsetting benefit.

Others have attempted to show that regulation's primary beneficiaries are the regulated, due to the state's ability to coerce the absence of competition. Still others argue that the prime beneficiaries of regulation are the regulators, by virtue of income and authority.

One of the first to formally recognize the nature of an unwholesome alliance between regulators and regulated was C. Wright Mills when he noted that perhaps the relationship between a particular Wall Street law firm and the Securities and Exchange Commission (SEC) was a bit too cozy [24, p. 290]. Mills's notion of a power elite was picked up by G. W. Domhoff who briefly examined the extent to which regulatory agencies are dominated by regulated firms [24]. Along similar lines Morton Mintz and Jerry S. Cohen spent an entire chapter in their *America, Inc.* indicting the influence regulated firms had on regulators, and of course, virtually the entire book *The Monopoly Makers* from the Nader study group was devoted to examining the hypothesis that regulation primarily serves business, not the consumer [25, 26].

> Mark Green made this previous point quite emphatically in 1974: In the area of economic regulation, the verdict is in. Academics and advocates of varying persuasion nearly all have pronounced the ICC, FCC, FMC, CAB and FPC "guilty" of favoring their regulated clientele over consumer interests [26].

The group of authors challenging the benevolence of existing regulatory institutions just cited came at the problem, in one degree or another, from more or less the left of the political spectrum. Regulation was not serving the consumer particularly well. Coming from a more mainstream or, perhaps, rightist perspective was another group of analysts: by and large, mainstream economists who, nonetheless, were also suspicious of the advantages of economic regulation.

George J. Stigler noted, "The *central* tasks of the theory of economic regulation are to explain who will receive the benefits or burdens of regulation, what form of regulation will take, and the effects of regulation upon the allocation of resources" [27] (emphasis added).

Stigler made, as the prime alternative candidate to Stigler's approach, the notion that regulation is instituted in the public interest. Stigler then went on to cite examples of the way in which much regulation did *not* serve the public. He concluded that regulation exists, in its various forms precisely because of the ability of business firms to manipulate political process on their own behalf. It is a simple matter of supply (the coercive powers of the state) and demand (the need of firms to restrict entry and price competition).

Richard Posner, in the same issue of the *Bell Journal* as Stigler's article, took to task both Stigler and the public interest types (e.g., Bonbright) for failing to explain the existence of internal subsidies in regulated firms [28]. Posner viewed economic regulation as a method of organizing excise taxes (prices above cost) with which to subsidize the consumption of some group (prices below cost). Posner, unlike Stigler, however, directed himself primarily at public utility regulation. Stigler discussed only nonpublic utility regulation. Posner summarized by saying, "Perhaps few subsidies are in the public interest; there may still be cases where, given a decision to subsidize, regulation is the cheapest means of doing so" [28].

Posner went on to suggest some institutional reforms including making the size and nature of such subsidies as explicit as possible to "eliminate some of the more captious instances of the phenomenon" [28]. Posner also suggested giving regulatory agencies taxing power so as to levy an excise tax on the subsidizing service and thus preclude the requirement to restrict entry into those activities [28].

A couple of points should be emphasized at this juncture: 1) in his original article, Stigler cited no evidence from public utility firms, and 2) Posner's notion of entry into the subsidizing service was quite apt, given the history of the telephone, gas pipeline, and electric generating industries since 1971.

Later, Posner reviewed the literature on economic regulation, directly evaluating the "public interest" theories [29] and economic theories. Posner found the public interest theories particularly wanting. He said,

> Were this theory of regulation correct, we would find regulation imposed mainly in highly concentrated industries (where the danger of monopoly is greatest) and in industries that generate substantial costs or benefits [29].

It would seem that Judge Posner forwarded a most promising reason to adopt the public interest theory as a *theory of public utility regulation*! If, on the other hand, one is looking for a general theory that explains the differential licensing of beauticians and barbers *and* the regulation of airline common carriers, it should not be surprising to learn that we will have to look elsewhere. Needless to say, Posner did.

Once again, in evaluating the economic theory of regulation as posed by Stigler and others, Posner was forced to conclude, the theory "is still so spongy that virtually any observations can be reconciled with it" [29].

It is interesting that Stigler, Posner, and others who admit to being of the Chicago School of economists have intellectual legitimacy, at least by heritage, in finding fault with regulation. It is interesting because, one of the founding fathers of the Chicago School, Henry Simons, hated, so dearly, the institution of regulation. One should, however, be reminded of Simons' conclusions:

> In general, however, the state should face the necessity of actually taking over, owning and managing directly, both the railroads and the utilities, and all

other industries in which it is impossible to maintain effectively competitive results [30].

Simons mistrusted the private monopolist more than the public bureaucrat. Given the same essential facts available to his protégés (Stigler, Posner, and Harold Demsetz), Simons's distrust of the interaction of regulator and regulated led to broadly different conclusions.

In fact, in Posner's discussion of cable television franchises, he asserted, "No problem of monopoly need arise" [31]. Posner envisioned a process of competitive bids for a particular franchise, the winner being the bidder of the lowest price, as for example, in the U.S. defense industry.

Following that line of argument, Harold Demsetz expanded on the point:

> In the case of utility industries, resorting to the rivalry of the marketplace would relieve companies of the discomforts of commission regulation. But it would also relieve them of the comfort of legally protected market areas. It is my *belief* that the rivalry of the open market place disciplines more effectively than do regulatory processes of the commission [32] (emphasis added).

Harry M. Trebing has pointed out the numerous deficiences of the competitive bidding process elsewhere [33]. It should be noted here, however, that Stigler, Posner, Demsetz, et al., are able to arrive at their conclusions by achieving a level of abstraction that blinds them to the real world impediments to effectuating such proposals [33]. On the other hand, time, technology, and politics have tended to lend some credence to the views of those scholars attacking institutions of regulation.

Alfred Kahn and President Carter managed, with the assistance of Congress to administer the coup de grace to the Civil Aeronautics Board (CAB). Much of the Interstate Commerce Commission's (ICC) authority over transportation common carriers has been diminished. The Federal Communications Commission (FCC) and Judge Harold H. Greene have seen fit to introduce a good deal of competition into long-distance communications, and cable TV companies have been substantially deregulated [34]. The wellhead price of natural gas has been given to the marketplace; particularly is this so with the Federal Energy Regulatory Commission's (FERC) Order 451. The long-run consequences of all of this activity is yet to be seen. Kahn has already expressed some doubts about the wisdom of abolishing the CAB [35]. Producers of oil and natural gas are currently looking for protection from competition. Consumers are evidently not thrilled by telephone competition and quasi-deregulation, nor is it clear that the average consumer of telephone services has been entirely well served by the decrees of the FCC or Judge Greene.

Much of this, of course, begs the point in a discussion of the formal analysis of public utility regulation. It is a rare analyst who has claimed that airlines, trucking firms, or gas wells were natural monopolies. It is quite possible that market growth has exhausted many of the telephone company's economies of scale and certainly technology may have eliminated all telecommunications economies of scope. There may still be reasons to exercise social control over some or all of these industries, but to call such control public utility regulation is likely to be a misnomer. Edythe Miller has made the point that economic efficiency is only one of many goals a society may adopt in implementing economic regulation [36].

But the economic regulation of electric utilities, pipelines, local telephone, and water distribution systems has continued. There have been proposals to deregulate bulk power generation and sales, but to date, these notions haven't gone very far.[1] In the midst of the clamor to deregulate in the last decade, why do these bastions of regulation remain so strong? The sensible answer was given by Bonbright in 1961:

> By a generally, though not universally, accepted linguistic convention, there is further requirement that the primary purpose of the regulation must be, ostensibly at least, the protection of the public in the role of consumers [5].

In other words, the buyer requires protection from the monopolist, or to maximize social welfare, consumption of the monopolist's service must be extended beyond that which monopoly would willingly supply. Nothing has changed except, perhaps, the industries classified as natural monopolies: where the classification endures, so does public utility regulation.

Discussions as to the origin of the classification *natural monopoly* have become, at once, more rigorous, but no more definitive. William Baumol and Robert Willig have sought to distinguish between those monopolists who have a sustainable set of prices (i.e., natural monopolists) and those who do not have a sustainable set of monopoly prices and who therefore, can be controlled by the *threat* of market entry (i.e., who exist in a contestable market) [37]. Baumol and Willig noted that "fixed costs of sufficient magnitude generally guarantee the existence of sustainable prices for a monopolist" [37]. They then proceeded to define *sufficient magnitude* in mathematically rigorous prose. However, such sustainable prices yield only zero profits if there are no entry barriers (i.e., the market is potentially contestable). However, sunk costs can be an entry barrier. Now sunk costs are those "that can only be diminished, even in the long run, by closing down the enterprise altogether" [37]. Because

> The need to sink money into a new enterprise ... imposes a difference
> between the incremental cost and the *incremental risk* that are faced by an
> entrant and an incumbent [37].

In setting prices, the incumbent incurs no opportunity cost from sunk
cost, the entrant does. One should probably conclude that the refinement
in the definition of fixed and sunk costs usefully resolves some of the
questions implicit in, say, Marshall's discussions noted earlier. On the
other hand, that the Baumol-Willig discussion contributes to an a priori
empirical evaluation of the existence of natural monopoly is doubtful.
One can, however, conclude, that the natural monopoly from which
efficiency (or the consumer) needs protection is that which has sunk costs
sufficient to constitute an entry barrier. Certainly, one could conclude
that, if nothing else, the nature of the distribution system of electric, gas,
telephone, and water utilities constitutes such a sunk cost. In the presence
of changing technology (cellular systems, cable TV), it is not clear how
much longer the local telephone monopoly will hold up.

If, in fact, natural monopolies of an irksome nature exist, and if they
should be regulated, then how best ought we go about it? Bonbright
observed,

> Regulation, then, as I conceive it, is indeed a substitute for competition; and
> it is even a partly imitative substitute. But so is a Diesel locomotive a partly
> imitative substitute for a steam locomotive, ... What I am trying to empha-
> size ... is that the very nature of a monopolistic public utility is such as to
> preclude an attempt to make the emulation of competition very close [5].

In other words, to say that regulation should imitate competition is to
engage in three kinds of counter-factual fallacy. The first should be
obvious: If the firm is a natural monopoly, then competition cannot exist.
Then how can one imagine what *would* happen when it cannot. An
example of this is the whole marginal cost pricing controversy. If marginal
cost is less than average cost, then the simple price equals marginal cost
rule will generate losses and the need for social subsidy of the firm.
Virtually the whole spectrum of incentives and efficient signals disappears
and such a result would hardly be imitative of competition.

The second fallacy is that the public utility sector should do what the
rest of the economy is doing, when, of course, the rest of the economy is
characterized by oligopoly, oligopsony, uncertainty, government subsidies, cost-plus contracts, externalities, maldistributed income, and ten-
ured university faculty. Such a situation hardly recommends itself as 1)

something to be replicated by public utility regulation or 2) as a place to measure the success or failure of replicating hypothetical competition in public utilities.

The third fallacy derives from theoretical welfare economics, the theory of the second-best [38]. Lipsey and Lancaster later summarized,

> Our intent in writing the original article was to indicate that piecemeal application of single Paretian welfare conditions in a situation in which *not all* such conditions could be satisfied might well decrease, rather than increase, welfare [39].

In an economy with thoroughgoing resource misallocations, at least by Paretian efficiency definitions, having public utilities meet those conditions may not only *not* improve welfare, but could make everyone worse off. That is, replicating competition in public utility regulation may not be such a great idea and at most, should be taken as a kind of rough and ready guide.

Now such a notion hardly leads to determinacy of results. The analyst must first decide on the appropriate rule, and then decide whether following the rule will make society better or worse off. There are a variety of problems when confronting the issue of regulating an enterprise such as a public utility. Does one restrict profits and thereby let prices be a residual quantity, or set prices and let profits be the residual? If profits are to be the focus, what will be the measure, and likewise, how shall one price?

If consumer protection is to be the prime motive, then one must restrict profits, with a sharp eye on price. If efficiency is to be the prime consideration, then one must price efficiently, period. In terms of welfare considerations, utility analysts were introduced several times to the notion of peak-load pricing and welfare maxima.[2] Boiteaux and Houthakker were in the arena early, with Steiner and Williamson entering later. The issue of peak-load pricing arises because of the question of the optimality of marginal cost pricing. Is peak-load pricing to ration capacity merely a special case of marginal cost pricing, or is it a particular means of price discrimination? Williamson and his predecessors resolve the question by begging it: At the capacity constraint, marginal cost becomes undefined (infinite, or a vertical line). This, of course, means marginal cost can be anything one wants it to be, and a peak-load price is *not* inconsistent with marginal cost pricing. The dodge is convenient, but not altogether convincing. At capacity, cost becomes undifferentiable and a first derivative is nonsense.

Williamson does point out, in effect, that optimal pricing leaves profits as a residual:

If there are indivisibilities, if increasing or decreasing returns to scale exist, or if capacity is given rather than subject to determination, optimal pricing will yield the zero net revenue result only accidently if at all [40].

It should be pointed out that the peak-load pricing issue, while perhaps of general interest, bears with particular force on public utilities. The telephone company is the only public utility with a busy signal; all the others must serve every customer the moment they knock on the door. Public utilities may not, like a restaurant, queue people outside the door, nor like a movie theater, put up a "sold out" sign. While one might say this is due to the legal requirement to serve, it is more so due to the nature of the technology: When a customer is linked to the system, the customer has access to capacity, whether or not it is sufficient. In this sense, capacity is like a public good; it is nonexclusive. But unlike a public good, capacity is *not* nonrival. At capacity, my attempt to water my yard leads to an unsatisfactory shower for my neighbor. Thus, when demand approaches the limits to capacity, there is an absolute need to ration.

If, however, against the advice of neoclassical economists, not optimal-pricing but control of profits is the regulatory effort, economics still has a role: analyzing the consequences of the regulatory effort.

Legislatures and administrative agencies have, by and large, chosen to regulate profits in the effort to assure reasonable prices. This has been done primarily through rate-of-return regulation, specifying an allowable *rate* of profit to be applied to a utility firm's equity capital. This potentially leads to distortions in the firm's incentives and gives rise to the Averch-Johnson-Wellisz hypothesis [41]. This hypothesis, in effect, demonstrates the theoretical conditions under which rate-of-return regulation will lead to an input ratio in which the capital input is inefficiently over-represented. This does *not* imply rate-base padding, (i.e., fraudulent misrepresentation), but rather a choice of techniques that are more capital intensive than the unregulated firm would adopt.

Akira Takayama made some corrections in Averch and Johnson's mathematics, but, in a discussion of the proposition that the ratio of marginal products of inputs must equal the ratio of their respective marginal costs, concluded that

It is the present contention of the author that this criterion does not have convincing support as a measure of efficiency, for such an allocative principle would be valid under the competitive situation only, and it will not be generally valid under other situations according to second best Theorems [42].

A host of articles, particularly in the *Bell Journal*, have sought to test the empirical validity of the A-J-W effect, with mixed results [43–52]. What Takayama was pointing out is, if the A-J-W effect exists, what can economists say about its impact on economic welfare? Apparently Takayama thought the answer was very little.

A. A. Alchian and R. A. Kessel focusing on regulated firms, and then Williamson in a more general context [53, 54] pointed out that a regulatory constraint on profits could lead to *expense* expansion, rather than, or in addition to, capital expansion. This was generalized later by Liebenstein in his theory of X-inefficiency [55]. This set of notions has recently had some institutional implications as public utility commissions have begun to look at the notion of incentive regulation or have made a variety of attempts at measuring efficiency [56].

The specific mechanism, the theoretical approach, the empirical validation notwithstanding, an attempt to focus on the control of profits is likely to lead to distortions elsewhere in the firm. Baumol and Klevorick pointed out that A-J-W distortions, under certain conditions, could be good in the sense that they may offset the monopoly distortions inherent in the situation [57].

Of course the issue of pricing did not die with the peak-load discussion. Baumol and others resurrected an article by an otherwise long-forgotten economist — Frank Ramsey. The issue is comparatively simple. If the object is to maximize social welfare, the firm is subject to scale economies, but since it must at least break even, an additional constraint has been added to the optimization problem. The result is Ramsey pricing (i.e., charging each customer according to demand elasticities, subject to the firm making just enough money to pay its expenses and meet the mortgage) [58].

Ramsey pricing is simply price discrimination where the purpose is to break even rather than to maximize the profits of the monopolist. One ought to point out that Ramsey pricing is subject to all of the restrictions placed on the advocacy of optimality rules that derive from second-best considerations. Moreover, as E. G. Furobotn and T. R. Saving have observed,

> Efficiency can be defined only relative to a particular distribution of income; if a specific value judgment is not made, no point on the transformation function can be regarded as unambiguously superior to any other [59].

Furobotn and Saving's remarks are particularly interesting in the face of Ramsey pricing. The effect of such price discrimination is to differentially require income contributions above cost from different customers. Those customers with the most options (highest elasticity) will contribute the least, perhaps nothing. Although one would hesitate to offer a hard-and-fast rule, the likelihood is that those with the greatest income are likely to be those with the most options (of course, not always). Thus, we must not only approve of the income distribution prior to a round of Ramsey pricing, but also after. If the first distribution is optimal, can the second also be optimal?

The institutional realities, however, of Ramsey pricing are that telephone and gas utilities are particularly interested in its application due to intermodal competition. For some parts of some utilities' markets, utilities have lost their monopoly power. In general, rather than recognizing the need to, in effect, devalue their currency (take write-offs), utilities are seeking to maintain antiquated revenue requirements through price discrimination. Ramsey pricing lends intellectual currency to the utilities' efforts; that the currency is bogus is not widely recognized. The problem arises from the notion that pricing all of the various outputs at their interpretable marginal cost will not yield sufficient revenues to cover total costs.

But if a market can be served by a profit-maximizing enterprise at a price that yields at least a normal profit, then the property devoted to the market by the utility must be, in a market sense, overvalued. If a grocery store cannot sell kiwi fruit at a price that yields a profit, it cannot then raise the price of bread to cover the losses: Customers will go elsewhere to buy bread. But the inelastic customer can't go elsewhere! This is one reason utility regulation was instituted in the first place: to protect consumers (farmers) from undue discrimination by utilities (railroads) [60].

It was noted previously that by 1950, not all of the issues in the analysis of public utility regulation had been finally settled. It is just as true in 1989, and likely to be no more settled ten years from now.

The Search for Certainty

A good deal of the reason that issues remain unresolved is the latter-day neoclassical economist's search for certainty rather than for reason. It would probably be more helpful if analysts would recognize regulation as a *process* rather than attempt to fit it into static efficiency considerations. Public utility regulation in particular and economic regulation in general have been in a state of evolution since the creation of the first state regulatory agencies and the Interstate Commerce Commission (ICC).

From the very beginning, consumers of railroad services sought protection from monopoly exploitation, and railroads sought protection from competition. These are not mutually exclusive goals. The competition from which protection was sought was long-haul; the monopoly from which protection was sought was short-haul. Although the railroads certainly benefited from control over market entry, would society have been better off if the railroad wars of the 1870s and 1880s had continued unabated?

Instruments of control were refined by amending legislation throughout the life of the ICC. The railroads were confronted with serious intermodal competition by the 1930s. The options confronting Congress were deregulation or more comprehensive regulation; it took the latter course. Forty-five years later Congress began the process of reversing the decision. Economists have questioned the wisdom of the Motor Carrier Act of 1935 since it was introduced. The bill certainly had the full support of railroads and the ICC.

It is rather fruitless to speculate on whether or not forty-five years is a long time in market adjustment terms. In comparison to the steel industry (perhaps comparably capital intensive), the adjustments made by Congress to ICC regulation may not be very long at all. In comparison to the needs of *that particular marketplace*, the history of transportation regulation is instructive for current problems. Long-haul communications appear to be open to entry, and markets may very well be contestable. Short-haul communications (local and rural telephone service) are yet, evidently, subject to natural monopoly control (subadditive costs).

If, by some criterion of joint cost allocation, it can be said that, historically, the long-haul has subsidized the short-haul, then competition in long-haul can only mean an end to such subsidies and a rise in short-haul rates. This is, in fact, what has happened. It may very well be that some short-haul markets may be so unremunerative as to invite abandonment (viz., the railroad and airline experience). A devaluation of current property put to public use will be a stop-gap solution only: Eventually the property must be retired and replaced. Is there a genuine replacement cost that will yield a remunerative investment in such markets?

The point here is that if there is not such a remunerative scheme, does society wish to see such markets abandoned by telecommunications service? The answer is, probably not. If not, then society must struggle, experiment, and try various and sundry highly imperfect instruments to achieve social goals that have little to do with economic optimization. It may very well be, as Vickrey has pointed out, that economic analysis can make the nature of those social choices more clear [61]. What economic analysis *cannot* do however is to gainsay those choices on the basis of efficiency criteria.

Notes

1. See, for example, FERC, No. I in RM85-17.
2. Oliver Williamson observed that the problem of peak-load pricing has been "solved" at least four times. In the *Bell J.* 7:1 (Spring 1976) "Symposium on Peak Load Pricing," it appears to have been "resolved" three more times with more complex specifications by M. Crew and, Kleindorfer, John Wenders, and D. T. Nguyen.

References

1. Schumpeter, Joseph A. *History of Economic Analysis*. New York: Oxford University Press, (1954) 1968.
2. Nash, L. R. *The Economics of Public Utilities*. New York: McGraw-Hill, 1925.
3. Marshall, Alfred. *Industry and Trade*. 4th ed. London: Macmillan, 1923. Reprint. New York: August M. Kelley, 1970.
4. Liebhafsky, H. H. *American Business and Government*. New York: John Wiley and Sons, Inc., 1971.
5. Bonbright, James C. *Principles of Public Utility Regulation*. New York: Columbia University Press, 1961.
6. Clark, John M. *The Social Control of Business*. 2nd ed. New York: Augustus M. Kelley, 1928. Reprint, 1969.
7. Bonbright, James C. "Major Controversies as to the Criteria of Reasonable Utility Rates." *Amer. Econ. Rev.* 30:5 (February, 1941): 378–389.
8. Hotelling, Harold. "The General Welfare in Relation to the Problems of Taxation and of Railway and Utility Rates." *Econometrica* 6 (July 1938): 242–269.
9. Clark, John M. *Studies in the Economics of Overhead Costs*. Chicago: University of Chicago Press, 1923. Reprint, 1981.
10. Ruggles, Nancy. "The Welfare Basis of the Marginal Cost Pricing Principle." *Rev. Econ. Stud.* 17:2 (1949–1950): 29–46.
11. ———. "Recent Developments in the Theory of Marginal Cost Pricing." *Rev. Econ. Stud.* 17:2 (1949–1950): 107–26.
12. Kahn, A. E. *The Economics of Regulation*. New York: John Wiley and Sons, 1970.
13. Coase, R. H. "Price and Output Policy of State Enterprise: A Comment." *Econ. J,* 55:217 (April 1945): 112–113.
14. Frisch, Ragnar. "The Dupuit Taxation Theorem." *Econometrica*. 7 (July 1939): 145–53.
15. Houthakker, H. S. "Electricity Tariffs in Theory and Practice." *Econ. J.* 61 (March 1951): 1–25.
16. Lewis, W. A. "The Two Part Tariff." *Economica* 8:31 (August 1941): 249–270.
17. ———. "Fixed Costs." *Economica*. 8:42 (1946): 231–258.
18. Meade, J. E. "Price and Output Policy of State Enterprise." *Econ. J.* 54 (December 1944): 321–328.
19. Montgomery, R. H. "Government Ownership and Operation of Railroads." *Ann. Amer. Acad. Pol. Sci.* 201 (January 1939): 137–145.
20. Wilson, T. "Price and Output Policy of State Enterprise: A Comment." *Econ. J.* 55 (December 1945): 454–461.
21. Henderson, A. M. "The Pricing of Public Utility Undertakings." *The Manchester School*. 15:3 (September 1947): 223–250.

22. ———. "Prices and Profits in State Enterprise." *Rev. Econ. Stud.* 17:1 (1948–1949): 13–24.

23. McKenzie, Lionel W. "Ideal Output and Interdependence of Firms." *Econ. J.* 61:244 (December 1951): 785–803.

24. Mills, C. Wright. *The Power Elite*. London: Oxford University Press, (1956) 1959.

25. Mintz, Morton and Jerry S. Cohen. *America, Inc.* New York: Dell Publishing Co., 1971.

26. Green, Mark, ed. *The Monopoly Makers*. New York: Grossman Publishers, 1973.

27. Stigler, George. "The Theory of Economic Regulation." *Bell J. Econ.* 2:1 (Spring 1971): 3–21.

28. Posner, Richard A. "Taxation by Regulation." *Bell J. Econ.* 2:1 (Spring 1971): 22–49.

29. ———. "Theories of Economic Regulation." *Bell J. Econ.* 5:2 (Autumn 1974): 335–358.

30. Simons, Henry C. "Introduction: A Political Credo." In *Economic Policy for a Free Society*, edited by Henry C. Simons. Chicago: University of Chicago Press, 1948.

31. Posner, Richard A. "The Appropriate Scope of Regulation in the Cable Television Industry." *Bell J.* Econ. 3 (Spring 1972): 98–129.

32. Demsetz, Harold. "Why Regulate Utilities?" In *Regulation in Further Pespective*, edited by W. G. Shepherd and Thomas G. Gies. Cambridge, Mass.: Ballinger Publishing Co., 1974, pp. 125–136.

33. Trebing, Harry M. "The Chicago School Versus Public Utility Regulation." *J. Econ. Issues.* 10 (March 1976): 97–126.

34. Bolter, Walter G., et al. *Telecommunications Policy for the 1980's: The Transition of Competition*. Englewood Cliffs, N.J.: Prentice Hall, 1984.

35. Kahn, A. E. "Airlines Gain from Tough Competition." Albuquerque Journal, August 28, 1986, A5.

36. Miller, Edythe S. "Controlling Power in the Social Economy." *Rev. Soc. Econ.* 43:2 (October 1985): 129–139.

37. Baumol, W. J., and Robert D. Willig. "Fixed Costs, Sunk Costs, Entry Barriers, and Sustainability of Monopoly." *Quart. J. Econ.* 96:3 (August 1981): 405–431.

38. Lipsey, R. G., and K. Lancaster. "The General Theory of the Second Best." *Rev. Econ. Stud.* 24 (1956–1957): 11–32.

39. ———. "McManus on Second Best." *Rev. Econ. Stud.* 26:3 (June 1979): 225–226.

40. Williamson, O. E. "Peak Load Pricing and Optimal Capacity." *Amer. Econ. Rev.* 56 (September 1966): 810–827.

41. Averch, Harvey, and Leland L. Johnson. "Behavior of the Firm Under Regulatory Constraint." *Amer. Econ. Rev.* 52 (December 1962): 1052–1069.

42. Takayama, Akira. "Behavior of the Firm Under Regulatory Constraint." *Amer. Econ. Rev.* 59 (June 1969): 255–260.

43. Bailey, E. E., and John C. Malone. "Resource Allocation and the Regulated Firm." *Bell J. Econ.* 1 (Spring 1970): 129–142.

44. Callen, J. G., F. Mathewson, and H. Mohring. "The Benefits and Costs of Rate of Return Regulation." *Amer. Econ. Rev.* 66 (June 1976): 290–297.

45. Cory, G. R. "The Averch-Johnson Proposition: A Critical Analysis." *Bell J. Econ.* 2 (Spring 1971): 358–373.

46. Courville, Leon. "Regulation and Efficiency in the Electric Utility Industry." *Bell J. Econ.* 5 (Spring 1974): 53–74.

47. Edelson, Noel M. "Resource Allocation and the Regulated Firm: A Reply to Bailey and Malone." *Bell J. Econ.* 2 (Spring 1971): 374–378.

48. Kafoglis, Milton Z. "Output of the Restrained Firm." *Amer. Econ. Rev.* 59 (September 1969): 583–589.

49. Peterson, H. Craig. "An Empirical Test of Regulatory Effects." *Bell J. Econ.* 6 (Spring 1975): 111–26.

50. Spann, Robert M. "Rate of Return Regulation and Efficiency in Production: A Test of the Averch-Johnson Thesis." *Bell J. Econ.* 5 (Spring 1974): 38–52.

51. Sudit, E. F. "Additive Nonhomogeneous Production Functions in Telecommunications." *Bell J. Econ.* 4 (Autumn 1973): 499–514.

52. Vinod, H. D. "Nonhomogeneous Production Functions and Applications to Telecommunications." *Bell J. Econ.* 3 (Autumn 1972): 531–543.

53. Alchian, A. A., and R. A. Kessel. "Competition, Monopoly, and the Pursuit of Pecuniary Gain." In *Aspects of Labor Economics*. Princeton: Princeton University Press, 1962.

54. Williamson, O. E. "Managerial Discretion and Business Behavior." *Amer. Econ. Rev.* 53:5 (December 1963): 1032–1057.

55. Liebenstein, Harvey. "Allocative Efficiency vs. 'X-Efficiency.'" *Amer. Econ. Rev.* 56 (June 1966): 392–415.

56. Joskow, Paul R., and Richard Schmalansee. "Incentive Regulation for Electric Utilities." *Yale J. Reg.* 4:1 (Fall 1986): 1–50.

57. Baumol, W. J., and A. K. Klevorick. "Input Choices and Rate-of-Return Regulation: An Overview of the Discussion." *Bell J. Econ.* 1 (Autumn 1970): 162–190.

58. Baumol, W. J., and David Bradford. "Optimal Departures from Marginal Cost Pricing." *Amer. Econ. Rev.* 60:3 (June, 1970): 265–283.

59. Furobotn, E. G., and T. R. Saving. "The Theory of the 'Second Best' and the Efficiency of Marginal Cost Pricing." In *Essays in Economic Regulation,* edited by Harry M. Trebing, 49–61. East Lansing: Michigan State University Public Utility Studies, 1970.

60. Gegax, Douglas, and Kenneth Nowotny. "A Critique of Ramsey Pricing." Presented at Annual NARUC Georgetown Conference, December 1985. To be published in *Proceedings*. E. Lansing: Michigan State University, Institute for Public Utilities.

61. Vickrey, William. "Utility, Strategy and Social Decision Rules." *Quart. J. Econ.* 74:4 (November 1960): 507–534.

Commentary by William M. Dugger

Kenneth Nowotny has written a thoughtful overview of the economics of public utility regulation in the United States. His overview shows considerable insight into the major trends and the technical nuances of public utility regulation theory. He treats the different strands of thought even-handedly, describing developments in both the reactionary "Chicago School" and in the liberal circles of "Nader's Raiders." Although he emphasizes developments since 1950, his overview goes back to the 1920s. Pricing issues are explained carefully. He includes discussions of marginal cost pricing, peak-load pricing, and Ramsey pricing. (Ramsey pricing charges customers according to their demand elasticities in order to garner enough revenue to cover production costs.) He also discusses the characteristics of public utility companies and of public utility regulation. He emphasizes economic theory more than administrative practice or regulatory law. He includes a helpful bibliography.

Professor Nowotny raises many interesting questions in his overview of the subject. Three are of particular interest: 1) What is a public utility? 2) Why regulate them? 3) What is the best method of social control? Nowotny does a fine job of selecting the central questions, but as in any overview of this kind, the questions cannot be developed in sufficient detail. Why regulate public utilities? Indeed, why not nationalize them, as suggested by that old Chicago Schooler Henry C. Simons? And then, why not run them along the lines of the Tennessee Valley Authority (TVA)? What lessons, if any, are there to be learned from the experience of the TVA? What possibilities exist for small-scale, community-owned public utility companies? Is small-scale community-generated electrical power a viable option? How about consumers serving on the board of directors of public utility companies? How about changes in the state regulatory boards and in consumer action groups? In short, what kind of new, progressive experiments in public ownership and public management are going on out there? Nowotny's brief overview does not explore these and like questions in much detail. But his overview is quite good nonetheless.

What is a Public Utility?

Nowotny does develop this question in more detail, for in the United States it is a very important one. The conservative and powerful system of state and federal courts in the United States resisted government regulation of business for many years by strictly limiting government regulation to specific areas of business. Generally, the courts limited regulation to public utilities only. Although Nowotny did not have the space to explore it, this legal conservatism has strongly colored regulation and social control in the United States. U.S. courts, exercising their judicial review of legislative acts, frequently disallowed regulation of activities that, in Europe, were regulated as a matter of course. Until the Great Depression of the 1930s shook the economic system to its very foundations, the conservative courts in the United States would generally allow government regulation only if two conditions were met: First, the good or service being regulated had to be a necessity. Second, either an extortionate price or a harmfully inferior standard of service had to be imposed upon the consumer. If these conditions were met, even conservative U.S. courts would uphold the governmental right to regulate the provision of the goods or service, because it was possessed of the "public interest." A company providing such a good or service was a "public utility." Of course, considerable discretion was applied in deciding what was a necessity. Also, considerable disagreement arose over whether a price was too high or a standard of service too low. The issues did not necessarily revolve around the question of monopoly, either. Nevertheless, for the years before the sea change of the Great Depression, these were the legal characteristics of a public utility. And, generally speaking, the conservative courts in the United States interpreted the characteristics narrowly, disallowing many legislative initiatives to regulate business [1, 2].

Nowotny's excellent survey of the issues suggests a direct observation approach to the contemporary definition of a public utility. Direct observation of what people in the United States now call public utilities yields a short list: electric power, gas, water, telephone, and maybe cable television. These are public utilities to the man in the street. All the companies on this exclusive list share an important characteristic. They all incur a large sunk cost in order to deliver their goods or services directly to the consumer's home. So the man in the street has no difficulty in identifying such companies as "public utilities." But the public utility concept is far more extensive than commonly understood. Public utilities include such diverse entities as railroads, natural gas pipelines, airlines, trucking lines, and insurance companies. These companies do not all incur large sunk costs in order to deliver to consumers' homes. But companies on this more inclusive list, with the possible exception of trucking lines serving metropolitan areas, share two characteristics: 1) A significant portion of the public cannot avoid dealing with the firm. They must buy its goods or services, or suffer harm. In economic terms,

Nowotny explains that such a buyer is an "inelastic customer." They cannot go elsewhere for the good or service and they cannot do without it. At the close of the nineteenth century, for example, this was the case for the farmers who had to ship their grain to market on the railroads or not ship at all. No wonder they pushed for railroad regulation. 2) The supplier is far more powerful than those with whom it deals. This second characteristic gives the company an unfair advantage. For example, the wellhead price that gas pipelines could pay used to be tightly regulated. Independent oilmen, owning producing gas wells, were no match for the integrated oil companies who often owned or controlled the major gas pipelines that gathered gas from the gas fields and then moved it to the major urban markets. So, like the farmers facing the railroads, the independents as producers sought protective regulation of the pipelines as public utilities. Of course, with the price and production revolutions in petroleum brought on by the Oil and Petroleum Exporting Countries (OPEC), the independents changed their minds about regulating wellhead prices. With high OPEC energy prices, the regulated wellhead price was below the unregulated price. So the independents clamored for and won deregulation.

To greater or lesser degree, all large companies possess these last two characteristics. That is, all large companies are more powerful than those with whom they deal, particularly more powerful than the independent consumer. Also, all large companies have at least some portion of the public that must deal with them, or suffer some degree of harm. This means that all large companies are endowed with a strong public interest. So essentially all large companies are public utilities. The public, however, has brought only a few of them under proper social control. Particularly in the United States, most large companies have been able to avoid effective social control. The modicum of social control that has been exercised in the U.S. is under constant threat of being eliminated through deregulation or through adverse court decisions.

The most significant question raised by this exercise in defining a public utility is, why are most large companies *not* regulated? Why has social control been extended to them only in times of crisis or war? Furthermore, why has the trend in recent years been toward deregulation? Will the issue of the 1990s be that of reregulation? A public interest continuum could be constructed to describe the issue. At one end of the continuum would be the traditional public utilities — water, gas, electricity. These companies are endowed with the public interest to such an extent, that even the befuddled public in the United States has enough sense to regulate them. At the other end of the continuum would be the independent small businessmen. These businessmen lack both power and public significance. They can be left to their own devices, trusting that commercial rivalry will control them. Even if it does not, little harm is done to the public. They may harm themselves, but the harm is not a matter of pressing social concern. In the vast middle of the continuum, running from high public interest to low public interest would be all the other companies. The zero public interest extreme of the continuum should be unregulated. The 100% public interest extreme of the continuum should be regulated, even nationalized. But exactly where the line should be drawn between the two extremes is the interesting and important question. It is also the crux of social control.

Economists as well as businesses can be placed along this public interest continuum. Those who see great need for the social control of nationalization or regulation draw the line very close to the 100% public interest extreme. Rexford G. Tugwell, progressive supporter of Roosevelt's New Deal, is representative of those economists who are close to the 100% public interest extreme. This position has fallen from grace in recent years. Kenneth Nowotny is a moderate. He draws his line roughly in the middle, wisely so. But this middle position is not representative of current fashion. Those who see little need for the social control of nationalization or regulation draw the line very close to the 0% extreme. Richard Posner is such an extremist, now quite fashionable with the deregulators. He draws his line as close as he can to the 0% extreme, minimizing the need for social control.

The Posner position has been elevated recently to a tenet of the faith among many U.S. economists. Most economists at the 0% extreme believe that whatever social control of business is needed is already exercised by "the market." The extremists like Posner believe that even oligopolies and monopolies are in no need of regulation. Such companies, according to the current fashion, are selling in "contestable markets." The so-called contestable market is in no need of the social control of regulation or nationalization because the possibility of a new business rival entering the market keeps even the monopolist from exercising their monopoly power. Which is to say that even when a mugger holds a knife to his victim's throat, the victim does not need an actual policeman at her side — the mere possibility that a policeman might come to her rescue is enough to save her from harm. Power is weakness. War is peace. Black is white. Fashion is truth. Fortunately for this volume, Nowotny believes none of that.

Nowotny's even-handed approach in his overview is laudatory, compared to the shrillness and bias of current fashion. But he has been far too easy on the current fashion designers, who pass off apology as theory. The contestable market concept is particularly suspect. Contrary to the fashion designers in economics who push the contestable market apology, market structure, like any other major feature of reality, does matter.

Capture and Different Types of Regulators

Related to the question of what is a public utility is the question, what is a regulator? This much is beyond dispute: A regulator is supposed to be a substitute for the social control of the market. A regulator is supposed to protect the public interest because the market cannot. But hotly disputed is the issue of capture: To what extent are public regulators captured by the companies they regulate, allowing the companies to use the regulators for their own private interest at the expense of the public interest? Is a regulator a sham? Nowotny spends far too little time in his overview on this question.

A regulator exercises social control over the regulated, but in whose interest? This is the question of capture. In recent years the capture view has been very influential in the United States, and many industries have been deregulated as a result. Such deregulation should have reduced industry prices and should have improved industry standards of safety and product quality. The airlines, trucking lines, railroads, pipelines, long-distance telephones, and others have been deregulated in the past decade. Some prices have gone down, some have gone up. Some services have been cut back. Some services have been expanded. In the airlines, serious safety questions have emerged since deregulation. In telephones, service deterioration has become a concern. So, to a large extent, the promise of deregulation has not been realized, at least not yet.

The deregulation of the airlines, trucking lines, railroads, pipelines, and long-distance telephones has involved the dismantling of industry-specific regulators. An industry-specific regulator is a regulatory agency that regulates one specific industry. The Civil Aeronautics Board was a prime example of an industry-specific regulator in the United States. It regulated the airline industry before being phased out in 1985 under the provisions of the Airline Deregulation Act of 1978. Such industry-specific regulators are generally believed to be the most prone to industry capture [3].

But a second type of regulator has become prominent in recent years: the function-specific regulator. In contrast with the industry-specific regulator, the function-specific regulator does not regulate one particular industry. Instead it exercises social control over a particular function performed by different industries. The prime example of such a function-specific regulator in the United States is the Environmental Protection Agency, charged with the regulation of dangerous substances in all industries. Another such regulator is the Occupational Safety and Health Administration. These function-specific regulators are generally believed to be less prone to capture than the industry-specific regulators because of the more diffused impact of the former. The deregulation push has barely touched most function-specific regulators. They seem to have strong public support, probably because they are directed at improving the perceived quality of individual and community life. Their public support in the United States continues strong, even in the face of the Reagan Administration's claims that their regulations were imposing a heavy burden on the U.S. economy [4, 5]. Industry-specific regulators are usually heavily involved in rate setting or price fixing in the industry they regulate. They also frequently set the requirements that must be met by new entrants to the industry. Both their price setting and their entry restricting activities have direct profit implications for the regulated industry. High prices coupled with restricted entry can generate monopoly profits, so the incentive to capture the industry-specific regulator is very strong. On the other hand, function-specific regulators do not fix prices and they do not restrict entry into an industry. So the incentive to capture the function-specific regulator is less strong, even though such a regulator can drive up the costs of production. All this boils down to the fact that the function-specific regulator is a far more independent type than the industry-specific regulator.

Further Questions

A major new question to be addressed in the area of public utility regulation is the impact of diversification on public utilities and their customers. The telephone industry is diversifying into a number of activities only loosely related to telephones. Both the regional telephone companies and AT&T are leading the way into diversification that other utilities are sure to follow. Diversification will raise difficult issues in determining the rate base for the utility part of a diversified enterprise. How much of the diversified enterprise's administrative investment should go into the rate base of the regulated part of the enterprise and how much into the unregulated part? Similar issues will arise in allocating joint costs to the regulated and unregulated parts of the enterprise. Will the movement of regulated utilities into unregulated areas of the economy have adverse impacts on competitive industries? Will regulated utilities abandon their marginal customers in the regulated branch of their diversified enterprise for greener pastures in the unregulated branch?

In sum, the field of public utility regulation continues to be a controversial and stimulating one. And Professor Nowotny has provided a fine overview of it.

References

1. Tugwell, Rexford G. *The Economic Basis of Public Interest*. New York: Augustus M. Kelley, 1968.
2. Solo, Robert A. *The Political Authority and the Market System*. Cincinnati: South-Western Publishing, 1974.
3. Reynolds, Larry. "Foundations of an Institutional Theory of Regulation." *J. Econ. Issues*. 15 (September 1981):641–656.
4. Council of Economic Advisers. *Economic Report to the President*. Washington, D.C.: Government Printing Office, 1982.
5. Tolchin, Susan J., and Martin Tolchin. *Dismantling America: The Rush to Deregulate*. Boston: Houghton Mifflin, 1983.
6. Crandall, Robert W., and Lester B. Lave, eds. *The Scientific Basis of Health and Safety Regulation*. Washington, D.C.: The Brookings Institution, 1981.
7. Lave, Lester B. *The Strategy of Social Regulation*. Washington, D.C.: The Brookings Institution, 1981.

3 PRICING AND THE ELECTRIC UTILITY INDUSTRY

J. Robert Malko and
Philip R. Swensen

Since the early 1970s, the costs of providing electricity have increased significantly due to such factors as general inflation, the energy dilemma, increases in system peak demand, rising fuel costs, and difficulties in obtaining financial capital [1]. Table 3–1 presents electricity prices and usage information for residential customers in the United States during the time period 1955–1984. As indicated by the information presented in Table 3–1, the average revenue per kilowatt-hours used by residential customers increased by approximately 3.5 times between 1970 and 1984. In response to the rising costs of providing electricity and related environmental and consumer concerns, the process of designing electricity rates emerged from the closet of regulatory neglect to a new prominence by the late 1970s [2].

During the 1970s, professional economists became very active in providing significant analysis and input to regulatory commissions and energy utilities concerning the process of designing electricity rates [3]. The focus of this paper is to discuss and examine the importance of using marginal cost pricing principles, such as time-of-use pricing, forward-looking costs, and the objective of economic efficiency, in the process of designing electricity rates.

Table 3–1. Residential Electricity Prices 1955–1984.

	Residential Class — Total Electric Utility Industry				
	Average Kilowatt-hour Used Per Customer (Kilowatt-hour)	Average Revenue per Kilowatt-hour Used (Dollars)	Average Annual Bill Per Customer (Dollars)	Price Indexes	
				Electricity (Index: 1967 = 100)	Consumer (Index: 1967 = 100)
Year	(1)	(2)	(3)	(4)	(5)
1955*	2,773	$0.0265	$ 73.48	95.2	80.2
1960	3,854	0.0247	95.19	99.8	88.7
1965	4,933	0.0225	110.99	99.1	94.5
1970	7,066	0.0210	148.39	106.2	116.3
1971	7,380	0.0219	161.62	113.2	121.3
1972	7,691	0.0229	176.12	118.9	125.3
1973	8,079	0.0238	192.28	124.9	133.1
1974	7,907	0.0283	223.77	147.5	147.7
1975	8,176	0.0321	262.45	167.0	161.2
1976	8,360	0.0345	288.42	177.6	170.5
1977	8,693	0.0378	328.99	189.3	181.5
1978	8,849	0.0403	356.74	203.4	195.3
1979	8,843	0.0443	391.30	219.1	217.7
1980	9,025	0.0512	461.81	253.4	246.8
1981	8,825	0.0580	512.30	291.5	272.4
1982	8,743	0.0644	563.09	320.3	289.1
1983	8,814	0.0683	601.77	330.6	298.4
1984	8,993	0.0714	642.23	351.8	311.1

* Does not include data for Alaska and Hawaii.

Source: Edison Electric Institute, "Statistical Year Book of the Electric Utility Industry," 1971 and 1977, Tables 44S and 61S, 1978–1984 data received by telephone and mail from staff members of the Edison Electric Institute in Washington, D.C.

This paper is organized into the following three major sections. First, a framework for the electricity costing and rate-making process is presented. Second, some important theoretical and quantitative issues relating to the application of marginal cost pricing to electricity rate design are analyzed. Third, significant activities of the Public Service Commission of Wisconsin and electric utilities in Wisconsin relating to the use of marginal costs in the design of electricity rates and the implementation of time-of-use rates are examined.

Framework for the Electricity Costing and Rate-making Process

During the 1970s and early 1980s, the "Great Rate Debate" concerning the electricity costing and rate design process focused on some central issues including 1) economic efficiency as a primary price objective, 2) marginal cost versus accounting cost as the primary basis for designing rates, and 3) time-of-use rate form versus the traditional declining-block rate form as the basic rate structure [4]. In order to provide a road map for addressing and analyzing a hierarchy of electricity costing and rate-making issues and problems, a framework consisting of the following important components is presented: 1) select and rank pricing objectives, 2) costs as the basis for rates to meet pricing objectives, 3) alternative cost measures, 4) alternative cost-of-service methods, 5) rate design, and 6) related activities [5]. This proposed framework is a practical outcome resulting from the Great Rate Debate.

Select and Rank Pricing Objectives

Establishing pricing objectives is the *primary* component of a framework for the electricity costing and rate-making process. Carefully defined and clearly specified objectives are needed so that subsequent public and private decisions can be made in light of their impact on the achievement of the overall goals. According to Professor James Bonbright, "while the ultimate purpose of rate theory is that of suggesting feasible *measures* of reasonable rates and rate relationships, an intelligent choice of these measures depends primarily on the accepted objectives of rate-making policy. . . ." [6] In other words, pricing objectives provide guidelines for selecting among alternative measures of cost of service versus value of service. Rate-making is a strategic decision because the results affect the long-run course or direction of the electric utility and its customers [7].

Professor Bonbright proposes that the three primary pricing objectives for a desirable rate design include: 1) the revenue requirement or financial need objective, which takes the form of a fair-return standard for regulated utilities, 2) the fair-cost apportionment objective, based on the principle that the burden of meeting total revenue requirements must be distributed fairly among the beneficiaries of the service, and 3) the optimal-use, or consumer-rationing objective, under which rates are designed to discourage the waste of public utility services while promoting all use that is economically justified by its benefits and costs [8]. Many professional economists accept these three objectives or criteria because of their consistency with the proper functions of prices.

In order to help cope with the serious problem of rising costs of providing electricity services, the United States Congress passed the Public Utility Regulatory Policies Act (PURPA) of 1978 [9]. This legislation establishes a set of three purposes or objectives for the pricing of electricity: 1) conservation of energy by users of electricity, 2) efficient use of facilities and resources by utilities, and 3) equitable rates to consumers.

There are important similarities between Bonbright's primary purposes and PURPA's purposes [10]. Both PURPA's conservation objective and Bonbright's consumer-rationing objective appear to mean the elimination of wasteful use of electricity. PURPA's equity objective is consistent with Bonbright's fair-cost apportionment objective with respect to the principle of fairness among customers. PURPA's equity objective is also consistent with Bonbright's revenue requirement objective with respect to the principle of fairness between the utility and its customer. PURPA's objective of utility efficiency is compatible with Bonbright's objective of optimal-use or allocative efficiency. These concepts of efficiency incorporate demand elements and supply elements in an economic context.

The following goals should be established as the primary objectives for the pricing of electricity: 1) the revenue requirement or utility financial need objective, 2) the equity objective, which includes the fair-cost apportionment of revenue requirement among customer classes, and 3) the optimal-use or consumer rationing objective, which includes considerations of efficiency and conservation [11]. In the process of ranking these primary objectives, considering trade-offs among these primary objectives, and including additional primary objectives for specific rate cases (such as industrial development), regulatory commissions and electric utilities need to address the circumstances of each electric utility (or homogeneous group of utilities), socio-economic conditions of utility customers, and other important factors relating to the public interest. In the process of applying these primary pricing objectives, regulatory commissions and electric utilities must consider that rate-making is a strategic decision because the results affect the long-run course of the utility business and its customers.

Costs as the Basis for Rates

After selecting and ranking pricing objectives, a standard is needed for designing electricity rates to meet the selected pricing objectives. The practical alternatives for what that standard should be include costs and noncosts. Noncost standards include value of service and ability to pay. Costs should be used by regulatory commissions and utilities as the *primary basis* for establishing electricity rates because cost-based rates satisfy the previously discussed primary pricing objectives, which are complex, relatively comprehensive, and sometimes conflicting, better than noncost-based rates.

Many researchers have concluded that electricity rates should be based on costs [12]. According to Professor James Bonbright:

> Nevertheless, one standard of reasonable rates can fairly be said to outrank all others in the importance attached to it by experts and by public opinion alike — the standard of cost of services, often qualified by the stipulation that the relevant cost is necessary or cost reasonably or prudently incurred. True, other factors of rate making are potent and are sometimes controlling — especially the so-called value-of-service factor in the determination of the individual rate schedules. But the cost standard has the widest range of application. Rates found to be far in excess of costs are at least highly vulnerable to a charge of "unreasonableness." Rates found well below cost are likely to be tolerated, if at all, only as a necessary and temporary evil [13].

Professor Bonbright additionally indicates that a cost-price or cost-of-service standard meets three primary objectives for electricity rates. With respect to the objective of fairness among the different customers, Bonbright states that "cost-price standard probably enjoys more widespread acceptance than any other standard except for the even more popular tendency to identify whatever is fair with whatever is in one's self-interest" [14]. Concerning the objectives of revenue requirement and optimum utilization, Professor Bonbright states that "consumers should be encouraged to take whatever amounts they wish to take, as long as

they are made to identify the utility enterprise for the costs of rendition"
[15]. PURPA also requires that measures of costs be considered in struc-
turing electricity rates in order to meet the pricing objectives of conservation, efficiency, and fairness [16].

Electricity rates should be *based* primarily on an acceptable measure
of costs, but should not be slavishly set equal to costs [17]. According
to Dr. John Hopkinson in a paper presented in 1892, "Surely it is the
interest of those who supply electricity to secure such customers by
charging them a rate having some sort of relation to the cost of supplying
them" [18]. The extent to which rates should be based on costs depends
on how well such rates meet specified pricing objectives. The following
summary finding made by the Nevada Public Service Commission in
Docket No. 2357 on August 17, 1981, agrees with this approach or point
of view:

> In summary, the Commission finds that the costs of service standard is an
> appropriate means for pursuing the PURPA goals of conservation and effici-
> ency; and, that the cost of service standard should be utilized in designing
> electric rates insofar as the resulting rate design will serve those goals. But,
> that cost of service should not be considered an end in-and-of itself; there are
> other substantial considerations that must be taken into account in order to
> maintain equity.

Regulatory commissions and electric utilities during the 1980s generally use an acceptable measure of costs as the *primary basis* for establishing
electricity rates in order to meet pricing objectives. However, regulatory
commissions and electric utilities need to have the flexibility to give
secondary consideration to noncost standards, such as value of service,
for establishing electricity rates in order to meet pricing objectives.

Alternative Cost Measures

Assuming costs are selected as the basis for designing rates to meet
pricing objectives, then a specific measure of costs needs to be selected.
The two fundamentally different *measures* or approaches for measuring
the costs of providing electricity are accounting cost and marginal cost
[19]. Synonyms or practical variants of accounting costs include embedded costs, fully allocated costs, and fully distributed costs. Synonyms
or practical variants of marginal costs include differential costs and
incremental costs [20].

Accounting or embedded costs refer to average accounting costs or sunk costs. When determining the embedded costs of generating a kilowatt of electricity, the costs of providing capacity that were incurred, for example, ten years ago are averaged with the costs of providing the most recent capacity additions *and* the known operating costs are considered. A projected embedded cost study considers a forward test year and reflects projected operating (fuel) costs for that year, but a projected embedded cost study still reflects sunk or historical capacity valued in historical dollars.

Marginal cost is the additional cost incurred by producing one more unit of output. In mathematical terms, marginal cost is the first derivative of the total cost function with respect to quantity. For electricity, marginal cost is the cost of producing and selling a single additional unit (a kilowatt and/or a kilowatt-hour) of product. Short-run marginal cost refers to the additional cost incurred by producing one more unit of output when some inputs or factors of production are variable (for example, fuel) and some inputs are fixed (for example, size of plant or capacity). Long-run marginal cost refers to the additional cost incurred by producing one more unit of output when all inputs are variable. Since the concept of the cost of one additional unit is not feasible to apply, in a perfect manner, to an electric utility that adds, in discrete or lump blocks, to generation facilities, transmission facilities, and distribution facilities capable of producing or transporting more than a single unit of quantity or output, economists generally view marginal cost as the theoretical norm.

Underlying the Great Rate Debate of the 1970s is the issue of the superiority of accounting cost versus the superiority of marginal cost as the primary basis for designing electricity rates. According to a topic (summary) paper published by the comprehensive Electric Utility Rate Design Study (1975–1982):

> Many factors affect the decision to select accounting or marginal costs as the basis for electric rates. The Study does not provide a simple answer for making this important choice. Rather, the issues which the decision maker should consider in weighing alternatives have been highlighted. Moreover, because the choice rests in part on judgment, it is recommended that the pricing objectives of the utility and its regulators guide that choice. [21].

In order to focus on the desirability of selecting accounting cost versus selecting marginal cost as the primary basis for designing electricity rates, some important comparative advantages and disadvantages associated with using accounting cost versus using marginal cost are presented in the next major section of this paper.

Alternative Cost of Service Methods

After selecting a specific cost measure for the basis for electricity rates, there is a need to select and apply a specific cost-of-service method. There are a menu of alternative costing methods associated with *both* accounting cost and marginal cost [22].

Traditional accounting cost-of-service studies categorize accounting costs in the following three steps: 1) functionalization (e.g., generation, transmission, distribution), 2) classification (e.g., demand, energy, customer), and 3) allocation to customer classes (e.g., residential, commercial, industrial). Decisions in each step are a function of generally accepted accounting principles, a knowledge of utility operations, and judgment. The third step, allocating demand-related costs to customer classes, necessitates the development of "allocation factors." Although numerous ways of computing such factors have been developed and proposed, the choice of a particular allocation factor, such as "average and excess," rests on judgment. There does not exist a scientific basis for ranking one specific way of allocating joint costs higher or better than the others. Time-differentiated accounting costs creates the complexity of allocating joint costs to time periods relative to the traditional three steps of a cost-of-service study. The selection of time period allocation factors also rests on judgment. Important criteria for selecting among alternative accounting costing methods include consistency with pricing objectives, conceptual validity, and ease of implementation.

Marginal costing methods that focus on short-run marginal costs acknowledge both the utility's limited ability to make large changes in capacity and the fact that capacity additions depend in part on the characteristics of the existing plant. These methods typically calculate short-run marginal costs over a period of future years to reflect the utility's evolving cost situation. Using an alternative view, the long-run method typically calculates a "pure" long-run marginal cost to the utility of providing an increment of electricity, given all new, optimal capacity. Important criteria for selecting among alternative marginal costing methods include consistency with pricing objectives, conceptual validity, and ease of implementation. In the next major section of this paper, some alternative marginal costing methods are compared and examined.

Rate Design

Translating results from a specific cost-of-service study into defined rate schedules requires the consideration of pricing objectives and the exercise

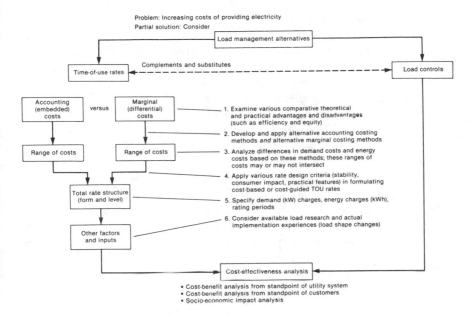

Figure 3–1. Some activities for considering load-management alternatives. *Source:* J. Robert Malko and Ahmad Faruqui, "Implementing Time-of-Day Pricing of Electricity: Some Current Challenges and Activities," presented at Public Utility Conference, Graduate School of Business Administration, Rutgers University, Newark, New Jersey, October 1979; appears in *Issues in Public Utility Pricing and Regulation*, edited by M. Crew, Lexington Books, 1980.

of judgment. Alternative basic rate forms for electricity include time-of-use rates, declining-block rates, flat rates, and inverted rates [23]. Prior to the mid-1970s, the primary rate form used by most electric utilities in the United States was the declining-block rate form. However, the primary limitation, based on cost considerations, associated with the application of a declining-block rate structure is its failure to provide consumers with price signals that clearly indicate that the cost of providing electricity typically varies between peak and off-peak time periods. Since the late 1970s, several electric utilities have developed and implemented time-of-use or peak-load pricing structures for industrial, commercial, and, to a lesser extent, residential customers [24]. Figure 3–1 presents a framework for considering time-of-use pricing as part of a load management program. In a later section of this paper, activities of the Public Service Commission of Wisconsin and electric utilities in Wisconsin concerning the implementation of time-of-use rates are discussed.

Important Related Activities

Important related activities to electricity rate design include 1) load research, 2) cost-benefit analysis, 3) information flow with customers, 4) actual application/implementation of rates, and 5) reporting and analysis of results [25]. Figure 3–2 provides a diagram of these activities and their interrelationships relating to the consideration and implementation of time-of-use rates. Thoughtful attention to and consideration of these related activities are essential for an effective and successful electricity pricing program.

In this section of the paper, a framework has been developed for addressing and analyzing a hierarchy of electricity costing and rate-making issues and problems. In the next section of the paper, some theoretical and quantitative issues relating to the application of marginal cost pricing to electricity rate design are analyzed. It is important to consider these issues within the context or perspective of the proposed costing and rate-making framework.

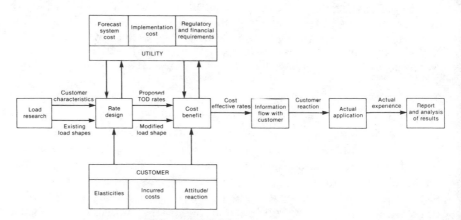

Figure 3–2. Activities for consideration and implementation of time-of-day pricing. *Source:* J. Robert Malko, Dennis J. Ray, and Nancy L. Hassig, "Time-of-Day Pricing of Electricity Activities in Some Midwestern States," presented at the Midwest Economics Association Annual Meeting, Chicago, Illinois, April 1979; appears in *Journal of Business Administration*, Volume 12, Spring 1981, and also appears in *Energy Crisis: Policy Response*, edited by Peter Nemetz, The Institute for Research of Public Policy, Montreal, Canada, 1981.

Marginal Cost Pricing: Some Theoretical and Quantitative Issues

In this section of the paper, the following four important issues concerning the use of marginal costs in the design of electricity rates during the past fifteen years are defined and discussed: 1) comparative advantages and disadvantages of marginal costs versus accounting costs, 2) the second-best problem, 3) the revenue reconciliation problem, and 4) estimation of the marginal costs of generation.

Marginal Costs Versus Accounting Costs

As discussed previously, the two fundamentally different *measures* of costs are accounting costs and marginal costs [26]. There are various methods of computing costs using either accounting cost or marginal cost. For the purposes of rate-making, there exists a long-standing dispute as to which of these costs best suits the frequently conflicting objectives of the producers and consumers of electricity. According to Professor James Bonbright:

> Unfortunately, however, the harmony attainable under a cost-price system of utility rates is far from complete. On the contrary, the functions are in partial conflict, sometimes seriously so. The major source of the conflict lies in the fact that a cost-price standard is subject of many different interpretations and that the interpretation which would best comport with any single objective of rate-making is almost sure to be ill-adapted to the attainment of some of the other objectives [27].

In order to focus on the desirability of selecting accounting cost versus selecting marginal cost as the primary basis for designing electricity rates, a listing of some of the important comparative advantages and disadvantages associated with using accounting cost versus using marginal cost is presented [28].

The following are important advantages associated with the use of accounting cost as the primary basis for designing electricity rates:

1. Revenues based on accounting (or historical embedded) cost pricing will equal the utility's revenue requirement.
2. Since accounting costs are known costs, the allocation or apportionment of revenues to customer classes by using accounting costs is viewed as being fair and equitable.

3. Accounting costs have been the traditional measure of cost used for designing electricity rates.

The following are important disadvantages associated with using accounting cost as the primary basis for designing electricity rates:

1. Accounting costs are historical and, as such, do not anticipate and reflect forward-looking or future costs.
2. Accounting costs do not have any relationship with the utility's system planning horizon.
3. Accounting costs do not address the pricing objective of economic efficiency.

The following are important advantages associated with the use of marginal costs as the primary basis for designing electricity rates:

1. Marginal costs indicate that the appropriate cost-based rate form or structure for the pricing of electricity is a peak-load or time-of-use structure.
2. Marginal costs are forward-looking costs, expressed in real terms or current dollars, associated with resources that are expected to be used in the planned production process (system plans) of providing additional quantities of electricity.
3. Marginal costs address problems associated with moving in the direction of an efficient allocation of limited resources used in the production of electricity.

The following are important disadvantages associated with using marginal costs as the primary basis for designing electricity rates:

1. Revenues derived from rates based on marginal costs generally do not equal the revenue requirement, which is based on accounting costs; hence, the revenue reconciliation problem.
2. Marginal costs are less familiar and more complex than accounting costs for application in the electricity rate design process.
3. Theoretical issues and problems associated with second-best pricing rules have not been completely resolved for the pricing of electricity.

The selection of accounting cost or marginal cost as the basis for designing electricity rates is primarily a function of the selection and ranking of *pricing objectives* by a regulatory commission or electric utility [29]. However, if a regulatory agency selects marginal costs as a primary basis for designing electricity rates, then this selection does not rule out or prohibit the consideration and use of accounting costs in the rate design process (or vice-versa) [30]. The practical design and implementation of marginal cost-based electric utility rates is by no means a simple task. Prior to a discussion of current models available for the estimation of marginal costs, it is useful to briefly address two of the more persistent criticisms of marginal cost pricing. The first is more theoretical in nature, namely the second-best problem. The second criticism has major practical implications and comes under the heading of the revenue reconciliation problem.

The Second-Best Problem

The theory of second best is a proposition concerning the efficiency of the market when some products are not priced at their respective marginal costs [31]. In the absence of strict marginal cost pricing, economic efficiency cannot be assured and, in fact, there may be gains in the simultaneous deviation from marginal cost prices of other products. Unfortunately, the practicality of implementing second-best pricing rules in the designing of electricity rates presents some significant problems. In order to be certain that second best pricing adjustments actually improve overall economic efficiency, prices, marginal costs, and demand functions for at least all related goods and services to electricity, such as factors of production, substitutes, and complements, must be known. Moreover, the electricity supply industry has input-output ties with other sectors (which may have distortions in their pricing practices), in addition to supplying consumers in competition with a mix of competitively and monopolistically determined prices. It is, therefore, unlikely that even the *direction* that prices should diverge from marginal cost to insure a contribution to a second-best solution can be determined.

The conclusion seems quite clear and is best summarized by Professor Kevin Lancaster.

> The second best solution requires simultaneous, fully coordinated, pricing directives for all industries in the regulated sector — not just coordinated *principles* of pricing policy, but *actual prices* computed on a simultaneous basis from a single model. If this cannot be done a true second best solution cannot be achieved and it would be ludicrous for a local regulatory authority to try

and correct the distortions of the American economy by manipulating a minute fraction of it.

Unless a simultaneous second best solution is determined for the complete regulated sector, therefore, it would seem that the next best thing (the "third best"?) is to ignore second best elements in pricing policy at the decentralized level [32].

Parenthetically, it seems strange that the proponents of the accounting cost as the primary basis for rates have repeatedly used the second-best argument to discard marginal cost pricing, when in fact their own approach ignores the issue of economic efficiency altogether [33].

The Revenue Reconciliation Problem

The primary justification for the marginal cost pricing of electricity is the furthering and emphasizing of the economic efficiency objective. It is also true that electric utilities, as natural monopolies, are constrained by regulation to certain prescribed levels of allowable revenue (revenue requirement) based on accounting costs. There is no reason, other than coincidence, for the revenues generated from rates set at marginal costs to match those revenues based on accounting cost so prescribed by the regulatory authorities. Such revenue differences can be large or small, deficiencies or excesses, and can be a function of the utility's construction cycle. Accommodation of this "revenue reconciliation" problem presents one of the most challenging issues in the implementation of marginal cost based electricity rates [34].

There are two distinct, but related, problems concerning revenue reconciliation. The first refers to how the overall revenue difference between revenues based on marginal cost and the revenue requirement based on accounting cost is spread across customer classes. The second relates to how marginal costs are used to design rates that match the revenue target for (within) each customer class. As might be expected, there are two sets of broadly defined procedures for implementing between-class and within-class revenue reconciliations.

Determining Class Revenue Targets. When deviations from marginal cost prices must occur to insure overall or between-class revenue reconciliation, the following methods are employed to construct those deviations.

1. **Inverse Elasticity Rule:** Basically this rule requires that deviations in price from marginal costs should be inversely proportional to the price elasticity of demand.

2. **Customer Cost Giveback:** This procedure is an attempt to set class revenue targets by adjustments to customer costs. The underlying assumption is that the class demand curve is fundamentally inelastic, and therefore the demand will be basically unresponsive to changes in customer charges.

3. **Equiproportional Adjustment:** This adjustment calls for uniform, across-the-board rebates or surcharges to all customers within a given class and between classes.

4. **Embedded Cost-Based Revenue Targets:** This method calls for the use of the same *relative* distribution of marginal cost-based revenues among the classes as would result from an accounting, or embedded, cost study.

Table 3–2 presents, in brief form, the basic advantages and disadvantages of these alternative revenue reconciliation methods.

Designing Rates Within a Customer Class. The following are methods employed to adjust marginal costs for the purpose of designing time-of-use rates, or block rates, *within classes* to achieve the desired level of revenue.

1. **Lump Sum Transfer Adjustment:** This method requires that marginal cost-based rates be used, and then any revenue surpluses or deficiencies would be transferred in a lump sum on a per customer basis.

2. **Inverse Elasticity Rule:** With this method, customer classes are segregated based on their characteristic use of electricity and the availability of alternate energy sources. The rule then requires that deviations from marginal cost-based rates be inversely proportional to the price elasticity of demand in each market segment.

3. **Practical Applications of the Inverse Elasticity Rule:** The direct application of the inverse elasticity rule is difficult due to the lack of required data. As a result, the application of the rule for rate design is based on practical approximations. Consumption that is assumed to have the highest elasticity will be priced closest to marginal cost. These price adjustments necessarily reflect judgments as to the relative demand elasticities of various components (customer, demand, energy) of electricity consumption.

4. **Customer Cost Adjustment:** This adjustment is simply a rebate or surcharge based on the customer charge to reconcile the revenue requirements of each class. This rule is based on the assumption

Table 3–2. Revenue Reconciliation Procedures for Setting Class
Revenue Targets.

	Advantages	Disadvantages
Inverse Elasticity Rule	Economic: based concept. Will result in economic efficiency if properly applied.	Required data unavailable. Heterogeneous intra-class elasticities. Practical applications require judgmental class elasticity estimates.
Customer Cost Giveback	Will result in economically efficient rates *if* customers unresponsive to customer charge.	May be insufficient to reconcile marginal cost-based revenues to company revenue target. Has largest effect on residential customers raising questions of equity and fairness.
Equi-Proportional Adjustment	Objective, fair and equitable. Simple to administer.	Probably will not result in most economically efficient rates.
Embedded Cost-Based Revenue Targets	May be consistent with existing methods.	Probably will not result in economically efficient rates.

Source: *An Evaluation of Reconciliation Procedures for the Design of Marginal Cost-Based Time-of-Use Rates*, prepared by Gordian Associates, Electric Utility Rate Design Study, Report Number 69, Electric Power Research Institute, Palo Alto, California, November 1979.

that the customer charge is characterized as less elastic than are the demand or energy usage charges.

5. **Equi-Proportional Adjustment:** This method calls for the uniform adjustment from marginal cost-based rates for all customers within a given class. Thus, all customers are faced with the same *relative* adjustment to their energy bill.

Table 3–3 summarizes the essential advantages and disadvantages encountered in the application of these adjustment methods required to design rates (time-of-use tariffs) based on marginal cost for a given customer class.

Table 3–3. Revenue Reconciliation Procedures for Designing
Time-Of-Use Rates.

	Advantages	*Disadvantages*
Lump Sum Transfer Adjustment	Will result in economically efficient rate structure.	Probably not comport with traditional views of fairness and equity. In theory, multiple transfer mechanisms feasible that affect individuals differently. In real world, nondistortive transfer probably not feasible.
Theoretical Inverse Elasticity Rule	Promotes an economically efficient rate structure.	Detailed data on customer demand functions and elasticities unavailable. Can result in complex rate structures. Probably not comport with traditional notions of fairness and equity.
Practical Applications of the Inverse Elasticity Rule	Does not require detailed elasticity data. May result in economically efficient rate structure.	Highly subjective. May not comport with traditional notions of fairness and equity.
Large User Pricing Rule	May yield an economically efficient rate structure. Relatively objective.	May be discriminatory. Could result in complex rate structure.
Equi-Proportional Adjustment	Objective, straight-forward approach. Satisfies traditional notions of fairness and equity.	May not yield economically efficient rate structure.

Source: *An Evaluation of Reconciliation Procedures for the Design of Marginal Cost-Based Time-of-Use Rates*, prepared by Gordian Associates, Electric Utility Rate Design Study, Report Number 69, Electric Power Research Institute, Palo Alto, California, November 1979.

Although the task of revenue reconciliation is not insignificant, there exist workable solutions that enable the pricing of electricity to more closely adhere to the marginal cost of supply. Such pricing assuredly contributes to an increase in overall production efficiency in that the appropriate (forward-looking) price signals are given to the consuming public.

Estimating the Marginal Costs of Generation

The theoretical value of marginal costs as a basis for the design of electricity rates is now being widely recognized. Most would agree, however, that the implementation of time differentiated marginal costs to real-world rates is more difficult. As might be expected, one of the major difficulties lies in the acquisition and analysis of the appropriate data required to come to a reasonable evaluation of marginal costs. Conceptually the definition of marginal cost is simple, but the application of that concept to the task of data analysis and modeling presents the practitioner with some significant challenges indeed. Although there are a number of models designed to accomplish the task of estimating reasonable time differentiated marginal costs of generation, significant attention has been afforded the following four models: 1) Cicchetti, Gillen, and Smolensky (CGS), 2) Ernst and Whinney (E&W), 3) Gordian, and 4) the National Economic Research Associates (NERA). We shall *briefly summarize* the major elements of these models [35].

Cicchetti, Gillen, & Smolensky: The CGS model estimates both capacity and the energy-related components of the marginal costs of generation. First, concerning capacity, CGS calculates the present value of the difference between the stream of costs from two plans — one normal and one assuming a one-year advancement in the construction of a generating planned unit. The incremental cost of the second alternative is higher due to the earlier capital expenditure and to the earlier ultimate replacement to maintain capacity. Second, cost estimates will be affected by anticipated changes in operating costs. Finally, CGS recognizes that short-term changes in demand might be accommodated with term purchases from other utilities. When increased capacity is thus purchased, the marginal costs simply become the prices paid for the power purchased.

Ernst & Whinney: The E&W method for calculating marginal costs of generation depend on the development of a mathematical production function. If the functional form of the production function is known, it can be mathematically optimized for the least-cost solution for any target level of output. Depending on the assumptions of the production function, the calculated costs can be either short-run or long-run. Obviously, the form of the production function will in part be determined by the technology of the generating unit. The E&W model accommodates several existing technologies with estimated production functions. Several constraints are imposed in the solution process to insure that the results are feasible and consistent with real-world conditions.

Gordian Electric Utility System Model: The Gordian model for estimating marginal costs of generation is based on a proprietary computer simulation model which estimates both the short-run operating costs of existing generating units and the long-run planning for future additions to capacity. Essentially the model consists of three submodels: 1) a nonlinear simulation program that models utility operating and reliability characteristics, 2) a linear programming algorithm for capacity optimization, and 3) a submodel that develops proforma financial statements and ratios. These submodels work together interactively such that the estimated results are internally coherent and consistent.

National Economic Research Associates Model: This estimation tool has divided the marginal generation costs into two components — namely, capacity and operating costs. The model begins with the assumption that optimization requires the cost minimization of meeting a predetermined load curve. The optimization employs the use of a linear programming technique that optimizes an objective function while simultaneously satisfying a number of imposed constraints. NERA assumes that a number of types of units, each characterized by different capacity and operating expenses, can meet a given demand for electricity. It is also assumed that those units with higher initial costs have lower operating costs, and vice versa. While recognizing that this model makes no attempt to incorporate all of the complexities of real-world utilities, it is widely considered a useful vehicle for estimating marginal generating costs.

Table 3–4 summarizes the basic differences in the four models discussed. It briefly outlines the basic costing methodologies employed by the alternative models according to functional analysis of cost, including generation capacity costs and generation energy cost.

Since the mid-1970s significant progress has been made in the design and implementation of empirical models for the estimation of marginal energy costs as well as marginal generation capacity costs. If, however, an electric utility faces an excess of generating capacity into the foreseeable future, which is the case for many electric utilities currently, then the estimation of marginal distribution costs becomes an increasingly important component of a marginal cost study. Additional research is needed in the important areas of estimating marginal distribution costs and marginal customer costs.

To summarize, several models have been developed and applied for

Table 3–4.   Summary of Four Marginal Costing Methodologies by Functional Analysis of Cost.[1]

	CGS	Ernst & Whinney	Gordian	NERA
		GENERATION CAPACITY COSTS		
Calculation	Cost of moving next plant forward one year in the construction schedule net of fuel savings from displacing less efficient plants in dispatch. Alternatively, the cost of additional capacity purchased from other utilities. ($/kW)	Capacity and energy costs not differentiated. Production functions estimated for each generation technology. Total and marginal cost functions derived for each technology. Nonlinear, neuristic program used to determine minimum cost system and marginal system cost to meet additional unit of output. ($/kWh)	Shadow price from linear program model. Annualized capital cost of next plant in optimal expansion plan net of fuel savings associated with displacing less efficient plants in dispatch. ($/kW)	Annualized capital cost of unit used to meet an increase in system peak. ($/kW)
Allocation	Distributed equally among all hours of peak period designated by LOLP. ($/kWh)	Not necessary.	Graduated peak responsibility based on LOLP. ($/kW)	Graduated peak responsibility based on LOLP. ($/kW)

GENERATION ENERGY COSTS

Treatment of Losses	Percentage of peak demand at each voltage level.	No information.	No information.	Percentage of peak demand at each voltage level.
Calculation	System lambda.	See Generation Capacity Cost Section.	Running cost of unit which picks up next increment of load in economic dispatch of system using simulation program.	Running cost of next unit online to meet load according to economic dispatch. In practice, system lambda.
Allocation	Weighted average of all values within the rating period in which they occur. ($/kWh)	See Generaticn Capacity Cost Section.	Available directly from the simulation program for each rating period in which they occur. ($/kWh)	Weighted average of all values within the rating period in which they occur. ($/kWh)
Treatment of Losses	Marginal energy loss on peak or at any other time derived from the average loss of load factor.	No information.	No information.	Percentage of sales based on average losses as percentage of peak losses.

[1] Capacity-related and energy-related generation costs are presented separately to aid in the comparison of the methodologies.
Source: J. Robert Malko, Darrell Smith, and Robert G. Uhler, *Topic Paper #2, Costing for Ratemaking*, Electric Utility Rate Design Study, Report Number 85, Electric Power Research Institute, Palo Alto, California, August 1981.

estimating the marginal cost of electricity generation. Methods are also available to address the revenue reconciliation problem. During the past ten years, these tools have been used more frequently by regulatory commissions and electric utilities in the design of rates. In the next major section of the paper, the utilization of these marginal cost tools, including estimation models and revenue reconciliation procedures, by a state regulatory commission and some major electric utilities are discussed.

Implementation Activities: A Wisconsin Experience

In this section of the paper, significant activities of the Public Service Commission of Wisconsin (PSCW) and electric utilities in Wisconsin concerning the use of marginal costs in the design of electricity rates and the implementation of time-of-use rates are examined [36]. Other states, such as California and New York, have also made substantial progress concerning the use of marginal costing and the implementation of time-of-use electricity rates during the past ten years [37]. However, the experience in Wisconsin is emphasized in order to focus on significant electricity rate design reform activities in one regulatory jurisdiction since the early 1970s. Approximately 50% of all retail electricity sales in Wisconsin are currently priced under mandatory time-of-day rate structures based on marginal costs.

This section of the paper discusses important activities by the PSCW and Wisconsin electric utilities relating to 1) the use of marginal cost in the design of electricity rates, 2) the use of both marginal and accounting costs as guides for class revenue allocation, and 3) the adoption and implementation of time-of-use pricing by day and by season.

During the early 1970s the Wisconsin electric utilities, like many electric utilities in the United States, were experiencing significantly increasing costs due the rising cost of fuel for electricity generation, the need to finance a doubling of generating capacity every ten years, and the leveling-off of the benefits of economies of scale of generating plants. The PSCW, like most state regulatory commissions, was before this time period primarily concerned with the level of total revenue that the utility should be permitted to collect from its customers. The PSCW typically was not concerned about the allocation of costs to the various customer classes or the electricity rate design, but deferred the decisions concerning these activities to the electric utility.

On March 3, 1972, the Madison Gas & Electric Company (MG&E) filed with the PSCW a request to increase its electric and natural gas rates. "What began as a rather routine proceeding involving a medium-sized utility became, with the intervention of the Capital Community Citizens and the Environmental Defense Fund (EDF), a 'national' test case on electric rate design" [38]. This landmark case spanned a period of more than two years before completion. The environmental intervenors argued the need for a revised rate design in order to encourage efficient use and conservation of electricity in order to avoid the need for the projected new power plants and resultant environmental degradation. Many thought that the environmental intervenors were arguing for inverted rates. However, the environmental intervenors later de-emphasized their assumed interest in inverted and even flat rates and shifted their pricing emphasis to peak-load pricing [39].

In its significant August 8, 1974 order, the PSCW determined that the primary objective of electric utility rates is that price should track costs. In a more formal sense, utility prices should be based on the marginal cost of providing additional kilowatts of power and/or additional kilowatt-hours of energy. The PSCW specifically found:

> The principle of marginal cost pricing is an appropriate guide for the purpose of the design of rates of Madison Gas & Electric Company and other Wisconsin energy utilities. Such a principle has been shown to be the most effective way to obtain an efficient allocation of resources and to prevent wasteful use of electric energy [40].

The PSCW additionally indicated that long-run incremental cost (LRIC), as defined and estimated in this proceeding, provides a reasonable approximation to marginal cost, and that implementation of pricing on the basis of LRIC requires peak-load pricing (time-of-use rates) and that peak-load pricing must be implemented for large customers without delay. The order also indicated the importance of flattening rates, decreasing discounts in circumstances of diminishing economies of scale, and implementing seasonal rates.

The PSCW expressed its concerns of how to appropriately charge electric utility customers for the costs to society of producing and distributing electric energy that are not reflected in the electric utility rate costs (external costs). However, the PSCW disposed of this problem as one more appropriately handled by the state legislature through its taxation powers. Although there were serious concerns about addressing or reconciling how to adjust from marginal cost to equal the approved revenue requirement based on accounting cost, this problem was addressed somewhat lightly in this case because the costs based on the LRIC study were approximately equal to the approved revenue requirement based on accounting cost. The PSCW ordered Madison Gas & Electric Company and other large Wisconsin electric utilities to study the feasibility of various forms of time-differentiated rates and time-of-day metering. The PSCW also determined that more precise time-differentiated pricing to reflect more fully for costs of capacity is essential to modern cost conditions and to give effective recognition to marginal cost pricing. The PSCW believed this could be accomplished through prompt and energetic experimentation.

In this major rate case, the PSCW established its modern-day rate design objectives. These objectives include 1) the fair apportionment of costs, 2) cost justification for the rate design (especially marginal cost justification), and 3) efficient allocation of resources through rate design to encourage conservation and the efficient use of electricity. The PSCW believed that marginal cost analysis and time-of-use (by day and season) rates most appropriately met these rate design objectives. The PSCW also set into motion a forum for Wisconsin utilities, regulators, intervenors, and customers through meetings, seminars, and hearings to discuss and improve the marginal cost analysis and application of time-of-day rates.

During the early to mid-1970s, there was substantial concern by the Wisconsin legislature and citizens relating to environmental issues. In 1971, the Wisconsin Legislature enacted into law the Wisconsin Environmental Protection Act. The Wisconsin Environmental Protection Act is similar to the National Environmental Protection Act but went into greater depth in requiring environmental impact statements on all state agency actions affecting the environment, including the PSCW. Wisconsin's governor and many state legislators were also concerned about the environmental and monetary consequences of the utilities' need to double their generation capacity every ten years. These individuals were supportive of the PSCW's decision to adopt marginal cost pricing and time-of-use pricing in this significant MG&E case.

While the marginal cost issues were being examined in the MG&E case, Wisconsin Power & Light Company on August 2, 1973, filed for a rate increase in docket 2-U-7778. On March 8, 1974, the PSCW issued its final order in this case and ". . . approved the rate design based, in large part, on the LRIC study submitted by applicant" [41], the Wisconsin Power & Light Company. This utility was supportive of rate designs based on long-run incremental cost and requested that rates be designed to track incremental costs. These rates would ". . . produce increased revenues commensurate with increased growth so as to minimize revenue erosion" [42].

The Wisconsin Public Service Corporation in May, 1974, filed for an electric rate increase in docket 2-U-8016. In this proceeding, Wisconsin Public Service Corporation and the industrial customer intervenors vigorously opposed LRIC and marginal cost pricing. The PSCW in its order issued in February, 1975, conceded that it had greater difficulty in devising long-run incremental cost based rates than those rates based on accounting cost, but felt that 1) cooperation between engineers, accountants, and economists should solve problems that arise, 2) the inverse elasticity rule does, in fact, offer a solution to demonstrating how rates should deviate from LRIC in order to obtain the most efficient allocation of resources while generating only the approved amount of revenue, and 3) it is conceivable that the LRIC concept and the accounting cost concept could serve as complementary inputs in designing rates based on the cost of service standard [43].

In the subsequent rate increase application of Wisconsin Power & Light in docket 2-U-8085, PSCW staff performed comparative analyses of the five different LRIC and marginal cost studies presented in this proceeding. Staff found that a proportional reduction to all customer classes in these LRIC and marginal cost studies produced surprising uniformity in the cost responsibility for the primary customer classes. The PSCW noted this result in its December 9, 1975 order when it used the accounting cost studies and the long-run incremental or marginal cost studies as guidelines to determine revenue requirement targets for customer classes.

During mid-1975, the PSCW wanted to expedite the progress that the utilities were making concerning the improvement of the long-run incremental and marginal cost methods and the implementation of time-of-use pricing. On August 15, 1975, the PSCW issued a proposed administrative rule in docket 01-ER-1. The primary emphasis of this docket centered on time-of-day rates. Concerning marginal cost pricing, the proposed rule read as follows:

> 11.03 *Marginal and Incremental Cost.* All utilities making application for a change in their electric tariff schedules should, in their application or evidence in support thereof, supply as much information relating to marginal and long-run incremental costs and the reflection in the rate structure as is feasible.

In 1975, the Wisconsin Power Plant Siting Act was enacted [44]. This law requires electric utilities to file every two years their long-range demand forecasts and generation and transmission plans to meet the projected increased demands. This law added to the PSCW's oversight power relative to generation plants by supplementing the preconstruction certification requirements that had existed since 1931. The PSCW is required to approve the utility's plan or an alternate plan after public hearing and after consideration of environmental factors, energy conservation, and alternate methods of generation in addition to the traditional economic and engineering factors. This utility filing requirement added to the PSCW's knowledge and information relative to future expected cost and demand for electricity. This information has been very useful in the development of marginal cost studies and the design of time-of-use rates.

In the next Madison Gas & Electric Company case, docket 3270-UR-1, the PSCW in its order issued on November 9, 1976, again found that a proportional adjustment to the LRIC and marginal cost-based customer revenue allocations produced substantially uniform results in the cost responsibility of the primary customer categories. Thus, the PSCW again used both the accounting and marginal cost studies as guides to determine revenue allocation to the customer categories.

In an April, 1976 paper prepared and presented by PSCW staff, an analysis of embedded versus marginal cost methods and an approach to reduce proportionately the marginal cost based class revenue allocations to produce the authorized revenue requirement was presented [45]. PSCW staff members concluded, "In summary, rate design should not be based on a single absolute measure of cost. All cost studies should state the cost results in terms of reliability. The rate analyst needs measures of both average accounting costs and differential costs to determine the proper rate design" [46].

The PSCW had moved from its concerns in 1974 of how to reconcile long-run incremental cost or marginal cost to equal the approved revenue requirement based on accounting costs by use of the inverse elasticity rule or other means *to* a position that a proportional reduction of customer class marginal costs to equal the approved revenue requirement adequately dealt with the problem. Since 1976, the PSCW has essentially used both the embedded cost studies and the marginal cost studies as guidelines to determine the customer class revenue requirements. It should be further clarified that the PSCW typically has placed more emphasis on the embedded cost studies to determine the class revenue allocations than the marginal cost studies.

On January 5, 1978, the PSCW issued an interim order in the Wisconsin Electric Power Company cases docket 6630-ER-2/5. Due to the complexity of and the number of issues in these cases, the PSCW combined certain aspects of these cases and on various occasions approved rate increases to Wisconsin Electric Power Company (WEPCO) under various docket numbers. The January 5, 1978, order was an interim order due to the need to prepare an environmental impact statement on the revised rate design alternatives being considered in this case. This order resulted in, by far, the most significant implementation of time-of-day rates based on marginal cost for any one Wisconsin utility. Again, the revenue allocation to each customer class was based on all the cost-of-service studies presented. In designing the time-of-day rates for WEPCO customers, the PSCW first established the off-peak energy rate, which was based essentially on the marginal off-peak energy costs. The on-peak energy rate was established by applying the ratio of the marginal on-peak and the marginal off-peak energy costs to the already established off-peak energy rate. The on-peak demand charge was developed utilizing the residual of the revenue requirement for the particular customer class. No demand charge was to be applied to demands incurred during the off-peak hours. In July, 1978, the PSCW issued its final order in docket 6630-ER-2/5. This order finalized its earlier interim order and made relatively minor changes to the rate designs authorized in the interim order. This order also discussed the basis and objectives of marginal cost pricing and the time-of-day rate design.

On August 4, 1978, the PSCW issued a letter order to the Wisconsin electric utilities requiring them to include both embedded and marginal cost studies in their rate applications. The letter stipulated that unless such information was presented at the time of a rate increase request, the application would not be processed. This requirement was initiated recognizing the very heavy case load on the PSCW and its staff *and* the desire to expedite rate case decisions. The three commissioners at the PSCW also expressed their desire to encourage the electric utilities to continue their efforts to implement time-of-day and flat rates.

By an order dated May 22, 1979, the PSCW closed docket 01-ER-1, which began on August 15, 1975. The PSCW concluded that the proposed administrative rule was no longer necessary because of the progress made by the electric utilities on the submission of marginal cost studies and the implementation of time-of-day rates. The ruling went on to say, "The commission expects that the electric utilities will continue to support the implementation of marginal cost pricing and tariff reform" [47].

By the end of the 1970s, implementation of time-of-day pricing of electricity had reached a significant level in Wisconsin. Table 3–5 summarizes the scope of time-of-day pricing actually implemented in Wisconsin by 1979. Table 3–6 presents time-of-day rate structures that were being used by electric utilities in Wisconsin during the late 1970s. The PSCW and electric utilities in Wisconsin continued to expand time-of-day pricing activities during the early 1980s, and by the mid-1980s, approximately 50% of all retail electricity sales in Wisconsin were being priced under mandatory time-of-day rates for industrial, commercial, and large

Table 3–5. Status of Time-Of-Day Pricing in Wisconsin — 1979.

Utility	Customer Class	Affected Customers	Number	Sales	Revenue	Peak Demand	PSC Docket and Order Date	Implementation
Wisconsin Power & Light Company	Large Industrial and Commercial (Cp-1 and Cp-3)	Demand Greater than 500 kW	144	31	22	20	2-U-8085 November 12, 1976	February 1977
	Large Industrial and Commercial (Cp-1 and Cp-3)	Demand Between 200 and 500 kW	275	8	6	6	6680-UR-5 (Interim) December 22, 1978	December 1978
Madison Gas & Electric	Large Industrial	Largest Demand	2	13	10	10	3270-UR-1 November 9, 1976	January 1977
	Large Industrial and Commercial (Cg-2)	Demand Greater than 300 kW	109	20	17	17	3270-ER-5 January 22, 1979	June 1979
	Industrial Commercial Residential (Cg-3 and Cg-4)	Optional Demand Less than 300 kW	300 Max.	Unavbl.	Unavbl.	Unavbl.	3270-ER-5 January 22, 1979	June 1979

Company	Customer Class	Criteria					Case Number / Filing Date	Status
Wisconsin Public Service Corporation	Large Industrial (Cp-1)	Demand Greater than 1,000 kW	85	32	24	27	6690-ER-7 Pending	Pending
	Residential (Experimental)	Randomly Selected	501	Less than 1	Less than 1	Less than 1	6690-ER-5 February 18, 1977	May 1977 Until May 1980
Northern States Power Company	Large Industrial and Commercial	Demand Greater than 1,500 kW	34	22	16	13	4220-ER-8 March 12, 1979	April 1979
	Large Industrial and Commercial	Demand Between 500 and 1,500 kW	61	Unavbl.	Unavbl.	Unavbl.	4220-ER-10 Pending	Pending
Superior Water and Power Company	Large Industrial and Commercial	Demand Greater than 1,000 kW	13	60	53	41	5820-UR-3 Pending	Pending
Wisconsin Electric Power Company	Large Industrial (Cp-1, Rate Area 1)	Demand Generally Greater than 300 kW	452	31	23	24	6630-ER-2/5 January 5, 1978 (Interim) July 20, 1978 (Final)	January 1978
	Small Industrial and Commercial (Cg-3, Rate Area 1)	All Above 30,000 kWh/Month	2,099	12	13	14	6630-ER-2/5 January 5, 1978 and July 20, 1978	All by July 1980

Table 3–5. (Cont.)

Utility	Customer Class	Affected Customers	Number	Sales	Revenue	Peak Demand	PSC Docket and Order Date	Implementation
	Residential (Rg-2, Rate Areas 2 and 3)	Largest Annual Consumption	577	Less than 1	Less than 1	Less than 1	6630-ER-2/5 Jan. 5, 1978, and July 20, 1978	July 1978
	Large Industrial (Cp-1, Rate Areas 2 and 3)	Demand Greater than 300 kW	39	6	4	3	6630-Er-8 March 6, 1979	March 1979
	Commercial (Cp-1, Rate Areas 2 and 3)	All Above 30,000 kWh/Month	209	2	2	2	6630-ER-8 March 6, 1979	July 1980
	Residential (Rg-1, Rate Areas 1 through 3)	Next Largest	3,000	Unavbl.	Unavbl.	Unavbl.	6630-ER-8 March 6, 1979	Schedule Pending

Source: J. Robert Malko, Dennis J. Ray, and Nancy L. Hassig, "Time-of-Day Pricing of Electricity Activities is Some Midwestern States," presented at the *Midwest Economics Association Annual Meeting*, Chicago, Illinois, April 1979; appears in *Journal of Business Administration*, Volume 12, Spring 1981; and also appears in *Energy Crisis: Policy Response*, edited by Peter Nemetz, The Institute for Research of Public Policy, Montreal, Canada, 1981.

residential customers [48]. Optional or voluntary time-of-day rates are available to a significant segment of the residential customer class in Wisconsin in order to consider and reflect the comparative advantages and disadvantages of mandatory versus voluntary time-of-day rates for residential customers [49]. Table 3–7 presents the status of residential time-of-day pricing in Wisconsin by the end of 1982.

The PSCW currently continues to follow the practical marginal cost policies and rate design objectives that it established in the period from 1973 through 1979. The PSCW uses both the embedded cost studies and the marginal cost studies submitted in each rate case as guidelines to determine the customer class revenue allocation. The embedded cost studies are used as the primary guides for customer class revenue allocations, but marginal costs are considered in this process. The marginal cost studies are used as the primary guides for the establishment of rate design and rate levels for each customer class. The PSCW establishes the time-of-day rates by setting the on-peak and off-peak energy costs equal to the marginal on-peak and off-peak energy charges and establishes the demand charges and customer charges from the residual revenue requirement of the class. The PSCW follows this procedure because the marginal energy costs are more accurately determined than the marginal demand costs during the current excess capacity conditions. In addition, energy consumption is considered to be more elastic than the customer's demand. The PSCW believes it is more important to track the marginal energy costs more closely than the marginal capacity costs because of the excess capacity currently existing in Wisconsin. This approach is a practical consideration of the demand-energy tilt issue. It is projected that no new (additional) power plants will be needed in Wisconsin until after the year 2000.

In summary, the PSCW and major electric utilities in Wisconsin during the past fifteen years have overcome many of the theoretical and practical problems associated with marginal cost pricing by implementing pragmatic approaches to cost of service analysis and rate design in order to meet electricity pricing objectives. Approximately 50% of all retail kilowatt-hours sold in Wisconsin are currently billed under mandatory time-of-use rates based on marginal cost principles. Virtually all other electricity consumption in Wisconsin is billed on flat rates that were developed utilizing marginal cost analysis. This substantial progress associated with electricity pricing reform is attributable to the following institutional and political factors:

1. the growing concern by state officials, utility executives, and the general public about the potential economic and environmental

Table 3–6. Time-Of-Day Electricity Prices in Wisconsin[a] — 1979.

Utility and PSC Order Number With Approved Rate	Customer Class	Summer Prices			Winter Prices			On-Peak Hours[b]	Fixed Charge $/Month
		On-Peak Energy $/kWh	Off-Peak Energy $/kWh	On-Peak Demand $/kW	On-Peak Energy $/kWh	Off-Peak Energy $/kWh	On-Peak Demand $/kW		
Wisconsin Power and Light Company 6680-UR-5 December 21, 1978	Large Industrial and Commercial (Cp-1 and Cp-3)	.0253	.0123	4.75[c]	.0253	.0123	4.75[c]	8 A.M.–10 P.M. Mon.–Sat.	12.50
Madison Gas and Electric Company Sp-3 and 4 by 3270-UR-1. November 9, 1976 Cg-2, 3 & 4 by 3270-ER-4/5. January 21, 1979	Largest Industrial (Sp-3 and Sp-4)	.0253	.0100	6.45[d]	.0200	.0100	5.10[d]	10 A.M.–9 P.M. Mon.–Fri.	—
	Large Industrial and Commercial (Cg-2)	.034	.0100	1.10+ 5.96[e]	.0268	.0100	.78+ 4.10[e]	10 A.M.–9 P.M. Mon.–Fri.	20.00
	Optional Industrial, Commercial and Residential (Cg-3)	.1125	.0150	—	.0782	.0150	—	10 A.M.–9 P.M. Mon.–Fri.	5.50 or 11.00
	Optional Industrial and Commercial (Cg-4)	.034	.0100	6.78	.0268	.0100	4.69	10 A.M.–9 P.M. Mon.–Fri.	7.50 or 15.00

Wisconsin Electric Power Company 6680-ER-8. March 6, 1979	Large Industrial (Cp-1 Rate Areas 1, 2 and 3)	.0280	.0140	3.96[f]	.0280	.0140	2.87[f]	8 A.M.–8 P.M. C.S.T. Mon.–Fri.	645.00
	Small Industrial and Commercial (Cg-3, Rate Area 1 and Cg-1. Rates Areas 2 and 3)	.0300	.0150	6.38	.0300	.0111	3.52	9 A.M.–9 P.M. C.S.T. Mon.–Fri.	200.00
	Residential (Re-2. Rate Area 1)	.0897	.0143	—	.0568	.0143	—	7 A.M.–7 P.M. C.S.T. Mon.–Fri.	5.00

[a] Specific rates may vary depending upon power factor, fuel adjustment, voltage level, or other factors. Refer to approved rate sheets for detailed occurring information.

[b] All hours are considered off-peak on holidays.

[c] Billed demand is the larger of the highest on-peak demand or 50 per cent of the highest off-peak demand. Interruptible customers pay a demand charge of $3.50 per kW of interruptible load prorated for hours of interruption to hours in the billing period.

[d] Demand charge slightly different between the two customers on this rate.

[e] Total demand charge equals the sum of the first price times the maximum fifteen-minute demand plus the second price times the maximum two-hour demand during on-peak hours. Interruptible customers pay no on-peak demand charge for their interruptible loads.

[f] Billed demand is the highest on-peak demand. The demand charge is reduced by 70 per cent for interruptible loads (Cp-2 rate).

Source: J. Robert Malko, Dennis J. Ray, and Nancy L. Hassig, "Time-of-Day Pricing of Electricity Activities in Some Midwestern States," presented at the *Midwest Economics Association Annual Meeting*, Chicago, Illinois, April 1979; appears in *Journal of Business Administration*, Volume 12, Spring 1981, and also appears in *Energy Crisis: Policy Response*, edited by Peter Nemetz, The Institute for Research of Public Policy, Montreal, Canada, 1981.

Table 3-7. Status of Residential Time-of-Day Rates in Wisconsin — 1982.

Utility	Mandatory		Voluntary	
	Number of Customers	Implementation	Number of Customers	Implementation
Wisconsin Electric Power Company	3,514	January, 1978	10,417	October, 1980
Wisconsin Power and Light Company	675	June, 1981	1,300	November, 1977
Wisconsin Public Service Corporation	500	Experiment May, 1977 to May, 1980	249	November, 1980
Northern States Power Company	0	April 1981	974	July, 1980
Madison Gas and Electric Company	185	February, 1980	170	July, 1979

Source: J. Robert Malko and Terrance B. Nicolai, "Implementating Residential Time-of-Day Pricing of Electricity in Wisconsin: Some Current Activities and Issues," presented at *Ninth Annual Symposium on Problems of Regulated Industries*, sponsored by the Institute for Study of Regulation and the University of Missouri-Columbia, held at Kansas City, Missouri, February 1983; appears in *Proceedings* of this conference; also appears in *Electric Ratemaking*, February/March 1983 issue.

problems associated with the continuing growth in demand for electricity and the corresponding need to construct new power plants;

2. the innovative, aggressive, and relatively uniform pursuit of marginal cost pricing by regulatory commissioners serving at different time periods;

3. the professional, well-trained, and committed commission staff;

4. the cooperative attitude and sharing of relevant information by the utilities, commission staff, and intervenors; and

5. the progressive implementation of pricing reform with sound understanding and knowledge of associated risks and uncertainties.

Summary and Conclusions

During the 1970s, the electricity costing and rate-making process emerged from the closet of regulatory neglect to a new prominence in the United States. Professional economists became very active in providing significant analysis and input to regulatory commissions and energy utilities concerning the process of designing electricity rates and the application of marginal cost pricing principles.

During the 1970s and early 1980s, the Great Rate Debate concerning electricity costing and rate-making focused on some central issues including 1) economic efficiency as a primary pricing objective, 2) marginal cost versus accounting cost as the primary basis for designing rates, and 3) time-of-use rate form versus the traditional declining-block rate form as the basic rate structure. In order to address these issues and other related electricity costing and rate-making issues, a framework consisting of the following important components has been developed and discussed: 1) select and ranking pricing objective, 2) costs as the basis for rates to meet pricing objectives, 3) alternative cost measures, 4) alternative costs methods, 5) rate design, and 6) related activities such as load research and customer information. Establishing a well-defined set of pricing goals or objectives is the essential component of a workable framework for the electricity costing and rate-making process. Electricity rates should be based on costs; however, the extent to which rates should be based on costs is a function of how effectively such rates meet pricing objectives.

The following four issues concerning the application of marginal cost pricing principles to electricity rate design have been defined and examined: 1) comparative advantages and disadvantages of marginal costs versus accounting costs, 2) the second-best problem, 3) the revenue reconciliation problem, and 4) the estimation of marginal generation costs. The selection of accounting cost or marginal cost as the primary basis for designing electricity rates is principally a function of the selection and ranking of pricing objectives by a regulatory commission or a utility *and* consideration of comparative advantages and disadvantages of these cost measures. The second-best problem and the revenue reconciliation problem relating to the use of marginal costs in the design of electricity rates are effectively resolvable in a practical sense. A menu of methods for estimating marginal generation costs have been developed and applied.

During the past fifteen years, the Public Service Commission of Wisconsin and electric utilities in Wisconsin have made significant progress concerning the use of marginal costs in the design of electricity rates and the implementation of time-of-use rates. The PSCW and Wisconsin utilities have effectively and pragmatically utilized *both* marginal costs and accounting costs in designing electricity rates and meeting pricing objectives. Marginal costs serve as the primary basis for designing rates within a customer class. Accounting costs provide the primary guidelines for establishing revenue levels or targets for customer classes, but marginal costs are considered in this process. Approximately 50% of all retail electricity sales in Wisconsin are priced under mandatory time-of-day rate structures for industrial, commercial, and large residential customers. Optional or voluntary time-of-day rates are available to a large segment of the residential customer class.

The implementation process of time-of-use pricing in Wisconsin started during periods of construction of major power plants during the 1970s. Even though the marginal cost structure changed significantly with the completion of such construction projects, the process of implementation of time-of-use pricing has continued during the 1980s.

It is hoped that the policy research and the implementation activities concerning the practical use of marginal cost pricing principles (including time-of-use rates) during the past fifteen years has significantly contributed to a workable foundation to meet the challenges of electricity rate design issues during the 1990s.

References

1. For a discussion concerning increasing costs of providing electricity, see Malko, J. Robert, and Robert G. Uhler. "The Rate Design Study: Helping Evaluate Load Management." *Public Utilities Fortnightly*. October 11, 1979, 11–17.

2. For a discussion of the importance of electricity rate design issues, see the following papers:

(i) Malko, J. Robert. "The Rate Design Study: Helping Regulators Evaluate Load Management." Presented at Ninety-Second Annual Convention and Regulatory Symposium. National Association of Regulatory Utility Commissioners, Houston, Texas, November 1980. Appears in *Proceedings: Ninety-Second NARUC Annual Convention*, NARUC, Washington, D.C., 1981.

(ii) Cudahy, Richard D., and J. Robert Malko. "Electric Peak-Load Pricing: Madison Gas and Beyond." *Wisconsin Law Review*. 1976:1, 47–78.

3. For an indication of the active role of professional economists in the electricity rate design process, see the following:

(i) Cicchetti, Charles J., William J. Gillen, and Paul Smolensky. *The Marginal Cost and Pricing of Electricity*. Cambridge, Mass.: Ballinger Publishing Company, 1977.

(ii) Kahn, Alfred E. "Recent Developments in Cost Analysis and Rate Design." Presented at the 1977 Symposium on Problems of Regulated Industries. Sponsored by Foster Associates, Inc., the Missouri Public Service Commission, and the University of Missouri-Columbia. Appears in *Proceedings* of this conference.

(iii) Turvey, Ralph, and Dennis Anderson. *Electricity Economics: Essays and Case Studies*. Baltimore: The Johns Hopkins University Press, 1977.

4. For a discussion concerning these issues, see the following:

(i) Malko, J. Robert, Darrell Smith, and Robert G. Uhler. *Topic Paper #2, Costing for Ratemaking*. Electric Utility Rate Design Study, Report Number 85. Palo Alto: Electric Power Research Institute, August 1981, chapter 9.

(ii) Parmesano, Hethie S., and Catherine S. Martin. "The Evolution in U.S. Electric Utility Rate Design." In *Annual Review of Energy*, edited by J. Hollander and H. Brooks, Annual Reviews, Inc., Volume 8, 1983.

5. For a comprehensive discussion of a framework for the electricity costing and rate-making process, see the following:

(i) Malko, J. Robert, Darrell Smith, and Robert G. Uhler. *Topic Paper #2, Costing for Ratemaking*. Electric Utility Rate Design Study, Report Number 85. Palo Alto: Electric Power Research Institute, August 1981.

(ii) Malko, J. Robert, and Ahmad Faruqui. "Implementing Time-of-Day Pricing of Electricity: Some Current Challenges and Activities." Presented at Public Utility Conference, Graduate School of Business Administration, Rutgers University, Newark, New Jersey, October 1979. Appears in *Issues in Public Utility Pricing and Regulation*, edited by M. Crew, Lexington Books, 1980.

6. James C. Bonbright, *Principles of Public Utility Rates*, New York: Columbia University Press, 1961, p. 290.

7. Malko, J. Robert, Darrell Smith, and Robert G. Uhler. *Costing for Ratemaking Topic Paper*. Electric Utility Rate Design Study, Report Number 85. Palo Alto: Electric Power Research Institute, 1981, chapter 3.

8. Bonbright, James C. *Principles of Public Utility Rates*. New York: Columbia University Press, 1961, 291–292.

9. Malko, J. Robert, and Ahmad Faruqui. "Implementing Time-of-Day Pricing of Electricity: Some Current Challenges and Activities." Presented at Public Utility Confer-

ence, Graduate School of Business Administration, Rutgers University, Newark, New Jersey, October 1979. Appears in *Issues in Public Utility Pricing and Regulation*, edited by M. Crew, Lexington Books, 1980.

10. Malko, J. Robert, Darrell Smith, and Robert G. Uhler. *Costing for Ratemaking Topic Paper*. Electric Utility Rate Design Study, Report Number 85, Palo Alto: Electric Power Research Institute, 1981, chapter 3.

11. For a comprehensive discussion of pricing objectives for electricity, see Koger, Robert Keith. "Decision Analysis Applied to Electric Utility Rate Design." Ph.D. thesis, North Carolina Stae University, 1984.

12. Malko, J. Robert, Darrell Smith, and Robert G. Uhler. *Costing for Ratemaking Topic Paper*. Electric Utility Rate Design Study, Report Number 85. Palo Alto: Electric Power Research Institute, 1981, chapter 4.

13. Bonbright, James C. *Principles of Public Utility Rates*. New York: Columbia University Press, 1961, 67.

14. Bonbright, James C. *Principles of Public Utility Rates*. New York: Columbia University Press, 1961, 295.

15. Bonbright, James C. *Principles of Public Utility Rates*. New York: Columbia University Press, 1961, 295.

16. Public Utility Regulatory Policies Act, Title I, Section III (d)(1).

17. Caywood, Russell. *Electric Utility Rate Economics*. McGraw-Hill, 1972, 37.

18. Hopkinson, John. "On the Cost of Electric Supply." Presidential Address to the Junior Engineering Society, November 1892. Appears in *Transactions of the Junior Engineering Society*, 3:1, 1–14.

19. For a discussion of various terms relating to regulated utility costing and pricing, see Malko, J. Robert, and Gary Couillard. "Cost-Based Pricing in Wisconsin: A Process in Flux." Presented at Wisconsin Telephone Seminar, Madison, Wisconsin, April 1976.

20. Bonbright, James C. *Principles of Public Utility Rates*. New York: Columbia University Press, 1961, 298–299.

21. Malko, J. Robert, Darrell Smith, and Robert G. Uhler. *Costing for Ratemaking Topic Paper*. Electric Utility Rate Design Study, Report Number 85. Palo Alto: Electric Power Research Institute, 1981, p. 21.

22. Malko, J. Robert, Darrell Smith, and Robert G. Uhler. *Costing for Ratemaking Topic Paper*. Electric Utility Rate Design Study, Report Number 85. Palo Alto: Electric Power Research Institute, 1981, chapters 5 and 6.

23. An informative primer on various electricity rate structures is a Public Service Commission of Wisconsin Report, *Generic Preliminary Environmental Report on Electric Utility Tariffs*, Docket No. 1-AC-10 (November 1, 1976).

24. For a discussion of these implementation activities, see the following papers:

(i) Uhler, Robert G., and J. Robert Malko. "Electricity Pricing for Conservation and Solar Energy Systems." In *Economics of Energy Conservation and Use of Solar Energy*, edited by F. Keith and R. West. CRC Press, Vol. 1, 1980.

(ii) Malko, J. Robert, and Ahmad Faruqui. "Implementing Time-of-Day Pricing of Electricity: Some Current Challenges and Activities." Presented at Public Utility Conference, Graduate School of Business Administration, Rutgers University, Newark, New Jersey, October 1979. Appears in *Issues in Public Utility Pricing and Regulation*, edited by M. Crew, Lexington Books, 1980.

(iii) Malko, J. Robert, and James D. Simpson. "Considering and Implementing Time-of-Day Pricing of Electricity: Activities in Some Eastern States." Presented at Eastern Economics Association Annual Meeting, Montreal, Canada, May 1980.

(iv) Malko, J. Robert, Dennis J. Ray, and Nancy L. Hassig. "Time-of-Day Pricing of Electricity Activities in Some Midwestern States." Presented at the Midwest Economics Association Annual Meeting, Chicago, Illinois, April 1979. Appears in *Journal of Business Administration*, 12:2 (Spring 1981) pp. 143–170. Also in *Energy Crisis: Policy Response*, edited by Peter Nemetz. The Institute for Research for Public Policy, Montreal, Canada, 1981; pp. 143–170.

(v) Malko, J. Robert, and James Simpson. "Time-of-Use Pricing in Practice: An Analysis of Some Recent Regulatory Actions." Presented at the Ninth Annual Conference, Institute of Public Utilities, Williamsburg, Virginia, December 1977. Appears in *Assessing New Pricing Concepts in Public Utilities*, edited by H. M. Trebing. Michigan State University Public Utilities Papers, 1978.

25. For a discussion of these related activities, see Malés, René, H., and Robert G. Uhler. *Load Management: Issues, Objectives, and Options.* Electric Utility Rate Design Study, Report Number 100. Palo Alto: Electric Power Research Institute, February 1982.

26. For a discussion on the rationale for using accounting costs or marginal cost in the ratemaking process, see Malko, J. Robert, Darrel Smith, and Robert G. Uhler. *Topic Paper #2, Costing for Ratemaking.* Electric Utility Rate Design Study. Report Number 85. Palo Alto: Electric Power Research Institute, August 1981.

27. Bonbright, James C. *Principles of Public Utility Rates.* New York: Columbia University Press, 1961, 71.

28. For a discussion on the advantages and disadvantages of accounting versus marginal costs, see

(i) Parmesano, Hethie, and Catherine S. Martin. "The Evolution in U.S. Electric Utility Rate Design." *Annual Review of Energy*, edited by J. Hollander and H. Brooks. Annual Reviews, Inc., Volume 8, 1983, 51–56.

(ii) Malko, J. Robert, and Terrance B. Nicolai. "Using Accounting Cost and Marginal Cost in Electricity Rate Design." Presented at the Eleventh Annual Rate Symposium on Problems of Regulated Industries. Sponsored by the Institute for the Study of Regulation, the American University and the University of Missouri-Columbia, Washington, D.C., February 1985. Appears in the *Proceedings* of this conference.

29. For a discussion of pricing objectives and their importance in the ratemaking process, see

(i) Malko, J. Robert, Darrel Smith, and Robert G. Uhler. *Topic Paper #2, Costing for Ratemaking.* Electric Utility Rate Design Study, Report Number 85. Palo Alto: Electric Power Research Institute, August 1981.

(ii) Parmesano, Hethie, and Catherine S. Martin. "The Evolution in U.S. Electric Utility Rate Design." *Annual Review of Energy*, edited by J. Hollander and H. Brooks. Annual Reviews, Inc., Volume 8, 1983, 51–56.

(iii) Koger, Robert Keith. "Decision Analysis Applied to Electric Utility Rate Design." Ph.D. thesis, North Carolina State University, 1984.

30. Malko, J. Robert, and Terrance B. Nicolai. "Using Accounting Cost and Marginal Cost in Electricity Rate Design." Presented at Eleventh Annual Rate Symposium on Problems of Regulated Industries. Sponsored by the Institute for the Study of Regulation,

the American University and the University of Missouri-Columbia, Washington, D.C., February 1985. Appears in the *Proceedings* of this conference.

31. For a discussion of the theoretical development of the second-best problem, refer to the following:

   (i)   Baumol, W. J. "Optimal Departures From Marginal Cost Prices." *Amer. Econ. Rev.* 60 (1970): 265–283.

   (ii)   Bertrand, T. J. "Second-Best Congestion Taxes in Transport Systems." *Econometrica.* 45 (1977): 1703–1716.

   (iii) Bohm, P. "On the Theory of Second Best." *Rev. Econ.* Stud. 34 (1967): 310–314.

   (iv)   Furubotn, E., and T. Saving. "The Theory of Second Best and the Efficiency of Marginal Cost Pricing." In *Essays on Public Utility Pricing and Regulation*, edited by H. M. Trebing. MSU Public Utilities Studies, Michigan State University, 1971.

   (v)   Hotelling, H. "The Relation of Prices to Marginal Costs in an Optimum System." *Econometrica.* 7 (1939): 151–160.

   (vi)   Lancaster, K. J., and R. G. Lipsey. "McManus on Second Best." *Review of Economic Studies.* 26 (1958): 225–226.

   (vii) Lipsey, R. G. "Comment." In *Essays on Public Utility Pricing and Regulation*, edited by H. M. Trebing. MSU Public Utilities Studies, Michigan State University, 1971.

   (viii) Lipsey, R. G. and K. J. Lancaster. "The General Theory of Second Best." *Rev. Econ. Stud.* 24 (1956): 11–32.

   (ix)   Rees, R. "Second Best Rules for Public Enterprise Pricing." *Rev. Econ. Stud.* 34 (1968): 261.

32. *The Problem of the Second Best and the Efficient Pricing of Electrical Power.* Prepared by Gordian Associates and Kevin J. Lancaster, Electric Utility Rate Design Study, Report No. 70, Palo Alto: Electric Power Research Institute, August 1979, 92–93.

33. See also Kahn, Alfred E. In *Rate Design and Load Control: Issues and Directions.* by Robert G. Uhler, Electric Utility Rate Design Study, Report No. 61, Appendix H, Palo Alto: Electric Power Research Institute, November 1977.

34. It is not our intent to present a comprehensive summary of actual implementation procedures for revenue reconciliation methods. The reader is encouraged to follow the activities of regulatory commissions and major electric utilities in such states as California, New York, Nevada and Wisconsin. For further discussion of the revenue reconciliation problem, see the following:

   (i)   *An Evaluation of Reconciliation Procedures for the Design of Marginal Cost-Based Time-of-Use Rates.* Prepared by Gordian Associates, Electric Utility Rate Design Study, Report Number 69, Palo Alto: Electric Power Research Institute, November 1979.

   (ii)   Baumol, J. W., and D. Bradford. "Optimal Departures from Marginal Cost Pricing." *American Economic Review.* June 1970.

   (iii) Kahn, A. E. *The Economics of Regulation: Principles and Institutions.* New York: John Wiley and Sons. 1970, 145.

   (iv)   Ramsey, F. "A Contribution to the Theory of Taxation." *Econ. J.* March 1927.

   (v)   Wenders, John T. "Peak Load Pricing in the Electric Utility Industry." *Bell J. Econ.* 7:1 (Spring 1976).

35. It is not our intent to present an exhaustive summary of the capability of models for the estimation of the marginal costs of electricity generation. It can be expected that the capability of such models are constantly changed and upgraded. The interested reader might profitably contact the individual developers and relevant consulting firms for a more detailed explanation of model capabilities. For a more comprehensive discussion of these models, and their use for estimating marginal generation costs, see:

   (i)   Malko, J. Robert, Darrell Smith, and Robert G. Uhler. *Topic Paper #2, Costing for Ratemaking*. Electric Utility Rate Design Study, Report Number 85. Palo Alto: Electric Power Research Institute, August 1981, chapter 8.

   (ii)   *An Evaluation of Four Marginal Costing Methodologies*. Prepared by Temple, Barker, & Sloane, Inc. Electric Utility Rate Design Study, Report Number 66. Palo Alto: Electric Power Research Institute, July 1979.

   (iii)   *Comments on Temple, Barker & Sloane's "Evaluation of Four Marginal Costing Methodologies"*. Prepared by Advisory Group I and Consultants, Electric Utility Rate Design Study, Report Number 67, Palo Alto: Electric Power Research Institute, June 1980.

36. For a discussion of these Wisconsin activities, see the following papers:

   (i)   Nicolai, Terrance B., and J. Robert Malko. "Electricity Costing and Rate-making: Some Current Issues." Presented at Twelfth Annual Rate Symposium on Problems of Regulated Industries. Sponsored by the Institute for Study of Regulation and the University of Missouri-Columbia, Arlington, Virginia, February 1986. Appears in *Proceedings* of this conference.

   (ii)   Malko, J. Robert, and Terrance B. Nicolai. "Using Accounting Cost and Marginal Cost in Electricity Rate Design." Presented at Eleventh Annual Rate Symposium on Problems of Regulated Industries. Sponsored by the Institute for the Study of Regulation, the American University and the University of Missouri-Columbia, Washington, D.C., February 1985. Appears in *Proceedings* of this conference.

   (iii)   Malko, J. Robert, and Terrance B. Nicolai. "Implementating Residential Time-of-Day Pricing of Electricity in Wisconsin: Some Current Activities and Issues." Presented at Ninth Annual Symposium on Problems of Regulated Industries. Sponsored by the Institute for Study of Regulation and the University of Missouri-Columbia, Kansas City, Missouri, February 1983. Appears in *Proceedings* of this conference; (also appears in *Electric Ratemaking*, February/March 1983).

   (iv)   Kaul, James, Dennis Ray, and J. Robert Malko. "Estimating Usage Response of Wisconsin Industrial Customers to Time-of-Day Electricity Rates: A Preliminary Analysis." Presented at Midwest Economics Association Annual Meeting. Chicago, Illinois, March 1980.

   (v)   Simpson, James, and J. Robert Malko. "Environmental Impact Analysis of Electricity Tariffs: A Wisconsin Framework," presented at the NARUC Biennial Regulatory Information Conference. Ohio State University, Columbus, Ohio, October 1978. Appears in *Proceedings* of this conference.

   (vi)   Ray, Dennis J., J. Stanley Black, and J. Robert Malko. "Developing and Implementing a Peak-Load Pricing Experiment for Residential Electricity Customers: A Wisconsin Experience." Presented at the Midwest Economics Association Annual Meeting, Chicago, Illinois, April 1978.

(vii)   Malko, J. Robert, and David Stipanuk. "Electric Peak-Load Pricing: A Wisconsin Framework." *Public Utilities Fortnightly*. July 1976.

37. For a discussion of activities in other states, such as California and New York, see the following papers:

(i)   Malko, J. Robert, and James D. Simpson. "Considering and Implementing Time-of-Day Pricing of Electricity: Activities in Some Eastern States." Presented at Eastern Economics Association Annual Meeting. Montreal, Canada, May 1980.

(ii)   Malko, J. Robert, and Ahmad Faruqui. "Implementing Time-of-Day Pricing of Electricity: Some Current Challenges and Activities." Presented at Public Utility Conference, Graduate School of Business Administration, Rutgers University, Newark, New Jersey, October 1979. Appears in *Issues in Public Utility Pricing and Regulation*, edited by M. Crew, Lexington Books, 1980.

(iii) Malko, J. Robert, Dennis J. Ray, and Nancy L. Hassig. "Time-of-Day Pricing of Electricity Activities in Some Midwestern States." Presented at the Midwest Economics Association Annual Meeting, Chicago, Illinois, April 1979. Appears in *Journal of Business Administration*, 12 (Spring 1981). (Also appears in *Energy Crisis: Policy Response*, edited by Peter Nemetz, The Institute for Research of Public Policy, Montreal, Canada, 1981.)

38. Public Service Commission of Wisconsin, *Findings of Fact and Order*, Docket 2-U-7423, August 8, 1974.

39. Cudahy, Richard D., and J. Robert Malko. "Electric Peak-Load Pricing: Madison Gas and Beyond." *Wisconsin Law Review*. 1976:1, 47–78.

40. Public Service Commission of Wisconsin, *Findings of Fact and Order*, Docket 2-U-7423, August 8, 1974.

41. Public Service Commission of Wisconsin, *Findings of Fact and Order*, Docket 2-U-7778, March 8, 1974.

42. Public Service Commission of Wisconsin, *Findings of Fact and Order*, Docket 2-U-7778, March 8, 1974.

43. Public Service Commission of Wisconsin, *Findings of Fact and Order*, Docket 2-U-8016, February 24, 1975.

44. For a discussion of capacity planning activities in Wisconsin, see Malko, J. Robert. "Regulatory Strategic Planning and Electric Utilities." Presented at Ninety-Seventh Annual Convention and Regulatory Symposium. National Association of Regulatory Utility Commissioners, New York City, New York, November 1985. Appears in *Proceedings* of this conference.

45. Malko, J. Robert, and Gary Couillard. "Cost-Based Pricing in Wisconsin: A Process in Flux." Presented at Wisconsin Telephone Seminar, Madison, Wisconsin, April 1976.

46. Malko, J. Robert, and Gary Couillard. "Cost-Based Pricing in Wisconsin: A Process in Flux." Presented at Wisconsin Telephone Seminar, Madison, Wisconsin, April 1976.

47. Public Service Commission of Wisconsin, *Findings of Fact and Order*, Docket 01-ER-1, May 22, 1979.

48. See the following papers:

(i)   Nicolai, Terrance B., and J. Robert Malko. "Electricity Costing and Ratemaking: Some Current Issues." Presented at Twelfth Annual Rate Symposium on Problems of Regulated Industries. Sponsored by the Institute for Study of Regulation and the University of Missouri-Columbia, Arlington, Virginia, February 1986. Appears in *Proceedings* of this conference.

(ii)   Malko, J. Robert, and Terrance B. Nicolai. "Using Accounting Cost and Marginal Cost in Electricity Rate Design." Presented at Eleventh Annual Rate Symposium on Problems of Regulated Industries. Sponsored by the Institute for the Study of Regulation, the American University and the University of Missouri-Columbia, Washington, D.C., February 1985. Appears in *Proceedings* of this conference.

49. See the following papers:

(i)   Malko, J. Robert. "Residential Time-of-Day Pricing of Electricity: Issues and Activities." Presented at Tenth Annual Symposium on Problems of Regulated Industries. Sponsored by the Institute for the Study of Regulation, the American University, and the University of Missouri-Columbia, Washington, D.C., February 1984. Appears in *Proceedings* of this conference.

(ii)   Malko, J. Robert, and Terrance B. Nicolai. "Implementing Residential Time-of-Day Pricing of Electricity in Wisconsin: Some Current Activities and Issues." Presented at Ninth Annual Symposium on Problems of Regulated Industries. Sponsored by the Institute for Study of Regulation and the University of Missouri-Columbia, Kansas City, Missouri, February 1983. Appears in *Proceedings* of this conference. (Also appears in *Electric Ratemaking*, February/March 1983.)

Commentary by John Wenders

Two views are emerging on how to deal with industries that are allegedly "naturally" monopolistic. The traditional view is that the market cannot be relied upon to adequately protect consumers against a wasteful duplication of facilities and monopoly power, and therefore detail regulation is needed. This is the view that has historically driven the regulatory process. A second view — and one that has only recently emerged and is not yet fully articulated — questions the assumptions behind the traditional natural monopoly argument and argues that even imperfect market discipline is likely to prove superior to the protective, politically oriented form of regulation that has actually emerged in the real world. For this view, the comparison is not between imperfect markets and perfect regulation, but between imperfect markets and imperfect regulation, a comparison that shows imperfect markets to be superior.

Economists play leading roles in both approaches. In the traditional approach, which takes regulation as a given, economists have used the conclusions of neoclassical welfare economics to argue that regulators should implement marginal cost pricing. Often the argument is used that this approach will produce the outcome that would emerge under effective competition. The Malko-Swensen paper is of this genre, as is much of my own work.

Economists who argue for a more market-oriented approach to traditional regulated industries bring an eclectic set of economic reasons and tools to bear on the question. Those economists concerned with an economic theory of regulation point out that the political mechanism works on a different set of incentives than the market mechanism and therefore will produce its own set of economic distortions. The politician's survival criterion is vote-getting, not the economic efficiency of marginal cost pricing. Thus, we cannot expect much success implementing marginal cost pricing because it has no political constituency. Only economists, such as Malko, Swensen, and I have much of an interest in its implementation, and we have little political clout. Further, the marginal cost pricing criterion simply assumes cost minimization by the regulated firm when, compared to the market mechanism, there is reduced incentive under regulation to do so. Finally, even though the marginal cost pricing approach at least tries to emulate the competitive outcome, it has certainly failed to do so. The strong winds of competition in all of the traditional natural monopolies — electricity, natural gas, and telecommunications — are ample testimony that regulation has not come anywhere near producing a competitive outcome.

The Malko-Swensen paper takes the traditional approach to regulation. It takes regulation as given and asks how the economist's tools can be used to make regulation as effective as possible, from the economist's viewpoint. The authors' viewpoint is by-and-large correct. With the exceptions noted below, I agree with most of it in its context. Its only major shortcoming is its failure to expose and judge the extent to which the good intentions or marginal cost pricing have been successful.

Given that Malko and Swensen have shown how economic analysis can be used to guide the given regulatory process, most of my remarks below are directed toward an exposition of why the alternative, market-oriented approach to the regulation of natural monopolies (such as the electric power industry) may be more effective than the traditional approach.

Politics and Economics

For the economist, there is an inconsistency between economic and political forces, and this is not recognized by the traditional approach. A typical view of the world is that markets are driven by greed and self-interest, and the political-regulatory constraints on such markets are driven by disinterested motives and good intentions — the public interest.

This public interest approach argues that the reason for regulation is to avoid market failure when an industry is naturally monopolistic [1]. This theory presumes that the goal of regulation is to stimulate competition where it is allegedly impossible because of economies of scale, *and* that this intention will in fact be carried out by the regulatory process. Few now believe that the regulatory process works in this way. Simply having good intentions in setting up a regulatory agency with real economic power does not assure that these intentions will be realized in the political marketplace. As Fred S. McChesney has recently observed: "The notion that government regulates in some disinterested, 'public interest' fashion to repair market failure has crumbled" [2].

A more realistic view is that the underlying motives of both economic and political actors are largely the same — self-interest, broadly interpreted — but the mechanism by which these motives are satisfied differs in the worlds of economics and politics. Simply put, resources are allocated according to expected profits in the economic marketplace and according to majority vote-getting in the political marketplace. The currency of the economic market is dollars, and the currency of the political market is votes. There is competition for votes in the political marketplace in exactly the same way there is competition for dollars of profit in the economic marketplace. If regulators do not compete for votes, they will be replaced by those who do. The same holds for entrepreneurs and profits.

Thus, the economic and political marketplaces both have competitive *mechanisms* by which resources are allocated, one driven by profits and the other by votes. The resource allocation outcome in either market at any point is the result of the balance reached between these two forms of competition. Changes can be effected only by changing the balance of either profit or vote incentives at the margin.

This approach to regulation, popularized by Sitgler [3], Peltzman [4], and Posner [5], is often called the *economic* theory of regulation. In its broadest interpretation, this approach emphasizes a balancing of interest group strengths and weaknesses at the margin, with the outcome determined by the stake of the various groups and the efficiency with which they can influence the regulatory process.

Capture

While the outcome in any specific instance depends on the relative interests and forces in question, the usual presumption is that the dominant group in the regulatory game is likely to be a small one that has a relatively large per capita stake in the outcome, and this leads to the conclusion that ". . . producer interest tends to prevail over the consumer interest" [4, p. 212]. Thus, in the scrap between producers and consumers over the gains from trade available, the capture form of the theory presumes that producers are able to capture the regulatory process at the margin to the detriment of consumers.

While the capture form of the economic theory of regulation has received the most attention, the general theory does not require it. This capture form presumes the empirical fact that it will be so costly for the large group, each with a small per capita stake, to determine its interest and make its political presence felt, that the payoff will not be worth it. If it is relatively cheap for members of a large group to know the impact of regulations on their well-being, and if the threat of the ballot box, either directly or indirectly, easily gets the attention of the regulators, then the outcome of the more general theory of regulation may be that the largest group will dominate the regulatory process. If a policy clearly and immediately benefits a lot of voters, even if only marginally, all of whom clearly know it, and if the regulatory process is sensitive to the political process, then the minority who will be hurt a lot by the policy will be outvoted by the majority. The fact that tenants greatly outnumber landlords, and rents make up a large and visible portion of tenants' expenditures, explains the political popularity of rent controls despite their universal condemnation by economists.

As Gary Becker has observed, the essence of an economic approach to regulation is that there be a balance at the margin, not capture.

> Although the "capture" theory is something attributed to Stigler, and he has made a few of these studies and encouraged others, he has also argued that rigid adherence to a "capture" theory is not consistent with the spirit of the economic approach. Analytically, economics is a theory of balance, not of all-or-nothing, as implied by the "capture" of legislation. Empirically, even small but vocal minorities have to be appeased: minority opposition is not automatically muted simply because the majority has 51 or 75 percent of the vote. In other words, the concept of a "minimum winning coalition" . . . conflicts with the economist's view of balance at the margin [6, p. 245].

Thus, a balance at the margin may indeed be struck where the minority few with a larger per capita stake are the net beneficiaries of regulation. But it may also be struck where they are not.

In most cases the theory has been used to explain how regulation has altered the distribution of gains between producers and customers, and the predominant capture form of the theory predicts that the former will prevail over the latter at the margin. Thus, in the electric power industry, where suppliers typically have been granted legal monopolies, the capture form of the theory predicts that regulation will favor producers over consumers.

The theory does not directly address the cross-subsidy question. However, it is clearly applicable and in its capture form suggests that regulation would underprice services to the few at the expense of the many. In the context of the electric power industry, the prediction is that the few large industrial users would be favored at the expense of the many residential users.

Capture in the Electric Power Industry

Neither of these predictions flowing from the capture version of the economic theory of regulation seems to hold for the electric power industry.[1] One of the reasons for the outcome where the few are able to gain advantage over the many is that voters simply find it costly to determine the relative costs and benefits of alternative courses of political action and to make their political power felt. However, traditional public utilities are unique among our regulated industries in the sense that *all* consumers have very good information about the direct effect to these industries on their well-being. Since they receive an explicit itemized bill for services every month, consumers are very aware of their utility bills.

Further, there is little organizational effort needed for utility consumers to affect the political process. Everyone knows that utility prices are regulated and by whom. Some local regulators are elected, and the rest are appointed by state governors [9, p. 26]. Thus, state regulators are close to the political process. The upshot is that little effort is needed to get state regulators' attention. The same is not true of most other regulated industries.

Thus, utility consumers are not only relatively well informed about the effect of utilities on their well-being, but they have a known, in-place, and well-defined political mechanism for complaint.

A second reason why consumers are sensitive to local electricity prices is because expenditure on electricity makes up a significant portion of their budgets, and their demand is rather inelastic in the short run. Thus, price increases have large, utility-reducing, income effects. Because all electricity is used via a relatively long-lived stock of appliances, consumers have little room in the short run to escape, or soften, a rate increase. In contrast, if the price of almost any other good rises, consumers can always substitute to some extent and thus avoid some of the bite of the price rise.

The sensitivity of consumers to electricity prices, the closeness of state regulators to the political process, and the fact that most electric power customers are in the residence class, explains why state regulators are very reluctant to raise rates, especially residential rates. As a general rule, the regulatory process has produced rates that are below marginal cost — especially during peak periods — and revenues that are well below those that would be produced by such marginal cost pricing. In addition, the residential class typically pays less than its share of revenue requirements and the industrial class pays more. For the electric power industry, and probably other public utilities as well, the capture form of the economic theory of regulation does not explain either the rate levels or cross-subsidies that prevail [7].

It is clear, then, that any discussion of regulation requires much more than the simple public-interest theory. Regulation, by its political nature, will produce economic distortions and inefficiencies. Might not the marketplace, even with its own distortions and inefficiencies, do better?[2]

Natural Monopoly

The traditional wisdom is that utilities are regulated because they are natural monopolies. I think it is useful to question this point of view.

By common usage, the natural monopoly argument for regulation is that because economies of scale and scope exist, regulation will improve economic welfare. This argument presumes that 1) there are such things as objective economies of scale and scope, and that they are discoverable independently of the market organization that produces them, and 2) the existence of these economies necessarily means that regulation will improve economic welfare. It is useful to deal with each of these.

Economies of Scale and Scope

Natural monopoly arguments implicitly presume that "true" costs, including objective economies of scale and scope, are independent of the market organization from which they emerge. This is questionable. Empirically, costs result from choices made by producers. Such choices are necessarily made in the context of the incentives provided by the existing institutional setting, so that the character of the market and its institutions will influence what kind of cost data we observe flowing from the choice process.

Thus, since objective costs can only emerge from the choices made in a market context, it is not correct to presume that the costs that have emerged under regulation are the same as those that would have emerged under competition. This would only be possible if we were able to set up these two forms of market organizations at the same time, under the same conditions, and then observe what kind of costs emerged under each. The natural monopoly argument presumes that the costs that have emerged under regulated monopoly are the same as the ones that would have emerged in an unregulated market.

Given that we cannot run two parallel experiments to discover the alternative character of costs that would emerge under competition and regulation, what do we know about these two alternative forms of market organization that might give us some hints as to what might emerge? My hypothesis is that the costs that would emerge under regulation would be both higher and more likely to display economies of scale than would costs under competition. There are three reasons for this. First, since public utility regulation presently has strong "cost-plus" elements, the incentive to minimize costs is weakened under this form of market organization. Thus, from an incentive standpoint, one would expect costs under regulation to be higher. Second, the higher costs of operation under regulation has been confirmed. There is now a good deal of evidence that once protection from competition is removed, formerly regulated firms almost always go through a period of painful cost reductions. Finally, with all output being supplied by a protected monopolist, the technology chosen and technological change are both likely to be directed toward the single firm monopolist's situation, resulting in production methods that display appropriate economies of scale. Technology and its rate of change are not exogenous. Conversely, I would expect that a flatter average cost curve would emerge under a competitive market organization merely because smaller firms would have a greater demand for this type of technology. In short, we might find that natural monopoly cost conditions are not a reason for regulation but result *because* the market was regulated as a monopoly.

Finally, even if continual economies of scale exist, so that duplication of facilities might be wasteful by comparison to some ideal, this, in itself, says nothing about what *prices* will result in either a regulated or unregulated environment. The natural monopoly argument for regulation presumes that only one thing — a move down the long-run costs curve — will result from the creation of a regulated monopoly. But, as Garrett Harden has taught us, you cannot do merely one thing. Creating a regulated monopoly might encourage a move down the cost curve, but it also sets in motion a lot of other changes (including an upward shift of the cost curve), most of which are antithetic to efficiency.

Connecting Costs and Prices

The natural monopoly argument for the regulation of markets is almost always stated like the following: "When economies of scale and scope are present, a single firm regulated monopoly *can* produce in a more efficient way than several competitive firms." (Alternatively, the argument states that in the presence of the economies of scale and scope, a regulated monopoly will avoid the wasteful duplication of facilities.) This is a non sequitur. These are purely supply-side arguments, and it is well-known that efficient production requires *both* that production be carried out in the most efficient way and that price also be set correctly. Yet, even if regulation resulted in reduced costs — something that is not true to begin with, this says nothing about how price will be set in either a regulated or unregulated monopoly environment. Further, the argument almost always says that economic efficiency *can* be improved by regulation, but almost never goes on to show how regulation *will* be more efficient either by ensuring that costs will be minimized or that the price will subsequently be set correctly. Even if competition produces, from a theoretical standpoint, an apparently wasteful duplication of plant, this apparent inefficiency is likely to be outweighed by the superior price and cost-minimizing discipline offered by an unregulated market.

This is the natural monopoly argument's fatal flaw: it presumes that the political process that governs the behavior of regulators will give *both* the regulators and the regulated the incentive to produce *and* price in the theoretically most efficient way. This is a classic and commonplace problem of using the unattainable as a guide to economic policy. At a general level, it is folly to use idealized states of the world as guides to economic policy in the absence of a real-world mechanism by which this idealized state can be reached.

The decision to regulate a market cannot be made by looking at idealized views of the world. One should not compare the state of a market with an idealized market and then conclude that since the idealized market has not been achieved that the market therefore should be regulated, since idealized regulation approximates idealized competition. Neither idealized competition nor idealized regulation are before us. The real alternatives are how both competition and regulation are likely to unfold. The question is whether or not leaving the market alone will result in performance superior to what is likely to result from regulation. As we have seen, the political regulation of an industry, including the electric power industry, necessarily produces its own set of economic distortions that are a far cry from the intentions of perfect regulation.

Thus, the most damning aspect of the natural monopoly argument is that it has no credible theory of regulation that connects regulatory practice with the idealized and unattainable state of the world held out as the goal of regulation. If regulation produced even an imperfectly competitive outcome, it would not be continually under attack by the competitive process. Yet this is what has happened in almost every regulated public utility market.

Not only does the natural monopoly argument presume a form of regulation much more efficient than our political system has been able to produce, but is also presumes that the market, if left alone under natural monopoly conditions, would produce both an unnecessary duplication of facilities and/or some kind of monopoly pricing. Neither of these presumptions has much of an empirical basis. Some duplication, from an idealized standpoint, exists in every industry. In a sense that is the price we pay for the efficiencies of a competitive market system. We gladly pay it in the unregulated sector of our economy, which is often held out as what regulation should emulate. Why should we not be willing, for the same reasons, to pay it in the electric power industry? Second, in every geographically oriented industry, such as the distribution part of the electric power industry, location confers situations where natural monopoly characteristics prevail. Such situations are not limited to the electric power or other utility industries. Small town and rural America is full of them. Yet we do not regulate these industries, and there is no evidence that they are excessively profitable or inefficient. They live under the threat of replacement if they become so.

In a sense then, the whole concept of natural monopoly may be a fictional product of neoclassical textbook cost curves. Entrepreneurs typically do not make decisions defined by the infinitesimal lumps of differential calculus. We are interested in cost because it presumably defines the supply price that is relevant for the exchange process. Exchanges may or may not be made in one-unit lumps. If the relevant marginal cost is a multi-unit lump, then the cost concept relevant for the determination of supply price is the average cost of the units in the lump, and cost curves defined by one-unit lumps are meaningless from either a decision-making or a welfare standpoint.

Competitive Institutions and Captives

Regulation has produced its own set of institutions and expectations. Lawyers, consultants, economists, and regulatory procedures have appeared to deal with the regulatory process. All have become accustomed to, if not happy with, the regulatory game. The converse is that regulation has thwarted the development of competitive institutions; those familiar with the regulatory game are not prepared to play the competitive game.

In particular, customers have allowed themselves to become "captives" of regulated monopolies under the expectation that regulation will protect them from market power. If the industry were organized in a more market-oriented and competitive way, customers would take steps to avoid becoming captives.

In short, in moving from a regulated, natural monopoly view of the electric power industry to one more market-oriented and competitive, care must be taken to encourage and foster the development of politically viable, competitive, institutions that limit the market power created by past regulation. This is the kernel of the policy task before the electric power industry.

Specific Comments on Malko-Swensen

1. The Malko-Swensen paper describes, from an economic perspective, a reasonable, practical approach to designing and implementing electricity rates in the context of today's regulatory procedures. However, it begs two questions: How typical is this procedure among the various regulatory commissions in the U.S.? And how do the results compare with ideal marginal cost pricing?

It is well known that regulatory commissions in Wisconsin, Illinois, and California are among the leaders in professing the use of marginal costs in rate setting. And to some extent every regulatory commission in the U.S. has at least been exposed to the marginal cost pricing rationale. Yet, I believe that the procedures of the leading states should not be taken as representative. Malko and Swensen provide no information on this point, but I suspect they would not disagree with my assertion that both the procedure outlined and Wisconsin's implementation of it are atypical among regulatory commissions in the U.S. and Canada.

2. One of the themes of my remarks is that good intentions are not enough. It would be useful to see how close the outcome of the procedure outlined by Malko and Swensen comes to some version of strict marginal cost pricing. Again, my own experience and research leads to the conclusion that generally speaking, during the 1970s, electricity has been under-priced relative to long-run marginal cost, especially during the summer peaks, and revenue requirements disproportionately shared by the indus--trial and large-user classes in favor of the residential class [7]. These conclusions are consistent with the modification of the economic theory of regulation exposed above.

I think recent market developments confirm this view, at least the part of it that argues the residential class has been favored at the expense of the industrial class. At the present time, there is general excess capacity in the U.S. and Canada. Putting aside why this excess capacity came about, theory suggests that such a situation would be accompanied by competitive price cutting in the industry. This is exactly what has occurred, and it has been the industrial class that has been able to benefit most from this price cutting.[3] This at least partially confirms my assertion that this class bore a disproportionate share of revenue requirements under the regulatory procedures in existence in the 1970s.

3. I think it is useful to discuss in more detail the logic behind time-of-use pricing.[4] Electricity demand is uneven over the day, week, and year. Generally speaking, annual peak demand occurs during the hot summer afternoons, although some utilities are still winter-evening peaking. Because of these demand variations, the marginal cost of serving peak-hour usage is greater than the cost of serving off-peak usage. The marginal costing methodologies outlined by Malko and Swensen are all designed to uncover these marginal cost variations. The failure of prices to follow costs results in a mispricing of electricity in both peak and off-peak periods, creating classic welfare loss triangles that measure such distortions.

A significant fraction of such distortions can be costlessly eliminated by seasonal pricing. That is, by simply having higher prices in the peak season (usually the summer). Seasonal pricing is costless to implement because it involves no metering changes to implement. Thus, for those small customers for whom time-of-day pricing cannot be justified on benefit/cost grounds, seasonal pricing is a costless alternative.

After seasonal pricing is implemented, the remaining distortions due to the failure of prices to follow costs over the day and week can be eliminated only by the installation of more expensive metering, capable of tracking usage over these periods. Benefit/cost tests usually show that it is of net benefit to implement time-of-day metering and pricing only for larger customers. Such pricing is probably not of net benefit for at least the smaller half of the residential and small commercial classes. However, as noted above, these smaller customers should be placed on cost-based seasonal rates as a cost-effective approximation to peak-load pricing. This alternative to full time-of-day pricing is especially important for summer peaking utilities.

4. I have some quibbles with Malko and Swensen's discussion of the determination of class revenue requirements and the use of the inverse elasticity rule.[5]

In a competitive world, there would be no such thing as exogenously determined class revenue requirements. Prices would gravitate to long-run marginal cost over time, and the revenues that would be collected from each class would fall out of this process. Class revenues per se are not an input into the pricing process but are an output of it.

Class revenue requirements appear in regulatory proceedings for two related reasons. First, the revenues that would flow from strict marginal cost pricing usually do not correspond very well to the revenue requirements determined by regulatory procedures. In the general inflationary period of the past twenty years, strict marginal cost pricing usually over-recovers regulatory revenue requirements. This is primarily due to the fact that regulatory procedures typically determine revenue requirements based on embedded, not marginal, production and debt capital costs. Because of the tendency of marginal cost pricing to over-recover revenue requirements some procedure must be devised to take account of this in pricing, the determination of class revenue requirements facilitates this process.

Second, as I have emphasized, regulatory proceedings are necessarily contentious and adversarial. Every participant wants to find a way to keep his own rates down at the expense of others. (I once heard an attorney define costs as "something to be allocated to others.") The determination of class revenue requirements facilitates the inevitable hearing-room squabble over whose ox will be gored most by any rate increase.

What should be the economist's position in this squabble? First of all, if the commission must — and it inevitably must — take account of political pressures in electric rate-making, it is in the determination of class revenue requirements that it should be done. Conversely, once class revenue requirements have been determined, political pressure should not be used to alter tail block rates from marginal cost. Second, if asked for a recommendation about the determination of class revenue requirements, the only logical response for the economist is to suggest that they should not alter the income distribution among the various customer classes. Clearly, if a competitive outcome is to be the goal of the regulatory process, then regulation should seek to produce the same income distribution as would prevail under competition. In the context of the electric power industry, this means that regulation should not seek to use electricity prices to redistribute income. We all know that commissions will typically not heed the economist's advice on this score, but this should not prevent us from giving it.

The upshot is that from the economist's standpoint, class revenue requirements should be set as an equal percentage of the revenues that would be raised under marginal cost pricing. If the residential class would pay 55% of the utility's revenues under strict marginal cost pricing, then it should pay that same percentage of the total revenue requirements determined by regulatory procedures.

Malko and Swensen, and others, have suggested that the inverse elasticity rule can be used to determine class revenue requirements. I disagree.

Such attempts have an intuitive appeal because of their reference to the preservation of economic efficiency, but they are an illegitimate application of that rule. The simplest rule is: if marginal cost-based prices result in an over- or under-recovery of revenue requirements, then revenues should be reconciled with revenue requirements by altering prices most where demand is the most inelastic. The problem is there is no unique price for any class of customers. The inverse elasticity rule is stated in terms of rate elements, not class revenues, and there is no unique elasticity of demand with respect to class revenues. How demand varies with respect to class revenues depends on which rate elements are used to change class revenues. Therefore, there is no way the rule can be applied to something for which no unique elasticity exists.

5. I also think it is important to understand that the inverse elasticity rule requires that all adjustments to rates be made in the customer charge. Any customer's demand for access to the electricity network, for which the customer charge is the relevant price, is of zero elasticity up to the point where it captures all of the consumer surplus from electricity usage. This is undoubtedly a very large number — ask yourself how much someone would have to pay you not to consume any electricity — and far exceeds the range necessary for the customer charge to meet any reasonable class revenue requirement. Thus, it is always economically feasible to meet class revenue requirements with adjustment in a perfectly inelastic market — the access market. When marginal cost prices over-recover revenue requirements, this means that the customer charge should be negative.

If, for political reasons, the commission cannot make complete revenue reconciliations using the customer charge, then adjustments should next be made in the early blocks of usage, which will be intramarginal for most customers and therefore have very low elasticity.

Notes

1. For a further discussion of the application of the economic theory of regulation to the electric power and telecommunications industries see [7] and [8]. Reference [7] presents some empirical evidence on the capture version of the theory as it relates to the electric power industry.

2. See [10] for an in-depth discussion of competitive aspects of the electric power industry and [11] for a discussion of more recent competitive developments in the industry.

3. Almost every issue of *Electric Week* [12] for the past decade contains references to competitive developments in the electric power industry. For reports in the press see [13–17].

4. For a more in-depth discussion of the benefits and costs of seasonal-time-of-day electricity rates see [18–20].

5. See [21] for a more detailed discussion of the inverse elasticity rule and its application to the determination of class revenue requirements.

References

1. Bonbright, J. C. *Principles of Public Utility Rates*. New York: Columbia University Press, 1961, pp. 121–134.

2. McChesney, F S. "Regulation, Taxes, and Political Extortion." Center for Policy Studies, College of Commerce and Industry, Clemson University, Working Paper No. 22, September 1986.

3. Stigler, G. J. "The Theory of Economic Regulation." *Bell J. Econ.* 2:1 (Spring 1971): 3–21.

4. Peltzman, S. "Toward a More General Theory of Regulation." *J. Law Econ.* 19:2 (August 1976): 211–240.

5. Posner, R. A. 'Taxation by Regulation." *Bell J. Econ.* 2:1 (Spring 1986): 22–50.

6. Becker, G. S. "Comment." *J. Law Econ.* 19:2 (August 1976): 245.

7. Wenders, J. T. "Economic Efficiency and Income Distribution in the Electric Utility Industry." *Southern Econ. J.* 52:4 (April 1986): 1056–1057.

8. Wenders, J. T. "The Economic Theory of Regulation and the U.S. Telecommunications Industry." *Telecommunications Policy.* 12:1 (March 1988): 16–26.

9. Gormley, W. T., Jr. *The Politics of Public Utility Regulation*. Pittsburgh: University of Pittsburgh Press, 1983, 26.

10. Joskow, P. L., and R. Schmalensee. *Markets for Power*. Cambridge, Mass.: The MIT Press, 1983.

11. Smith, V. L. "Currents of Competition in Electricity Markets." *Regulation.* 11:2 (1987): 23–29.

12. *Electric Utility Week*. New York: McGraw-Hill, various weekly issues.

13. Paul, B. "Electric Utilities Push New Marketing Plans to Meet Competition." *Wall Street Journal*. September 15, 1987, p. 1.

14. Weberman, B., and A. Snitzer. "Freewheeling." *Forbes*. August 10, 1987, 35–36.

15. Paul, B. "Electric Rates for Industry Are Being Cut." *Wall Street Journal*. April 4, 1986, p. 5.

16. Stelzer, I. M. "The Utilities of the 1990s." *Wall Street Journal*. January 7, 1987.

17. Sawhill, J. C., and L. P. Silverman. "Your Local Utility Will Never Be the Same." *Wall Street Journal*. January 2, 1986.

18. Wenders, J. T., and L. D. Taylor. "Experiments in Seasonal Time-of-Day Pricing of Electricity to Residential Users." *Bell J. Econ.* 7:2 (Autumn 1976): 531–552.

19. Wenders, J. T., and R. A. Lyman. "An Analysis of the Benefits and Costs of Seasonal-Time-of-Day Electricity Rates." In *Problems in Public Utility Economics and Regulation*, edited by Michael A. Crew. Lexington, Mass.: Lexington Books, 1979, 73–91.

20. Wenders, J. T., and R. A. Lyman. "Determining the Optimal Penetration of Time-of-Day Electricity Tariffs." *Electric Rate-making*. 1:5 (October/November 1982): 15–19.

21. Wenders, J. T. "The Marginal Cost Pricing of Electricity and the Determination of Class Revenue Requirements." *Electric Rate-making*, 2:1 (February/March 1983): 50–54.

4 TELECOMMUNICATIONS REGULATION — THE CONTINUING DILEMMA

Harry M. Trebing

It has become increasingly fashionable to describe telecommunications as an industry that has evolved from natural monopoly to competition with considerable assistance from the technological revolution in computers, satellites, microwave, and fiber optics. It is equally fashionable to point to regulation as the principal impediment to the successful completion of this transformation. Far from a force for good, critics charge that regulation acts to frustrate the workings of competitive markets, the attainment of efficiency goals, and the widespread diffusion of technological gains. Acceptance of this position calls for deregulation, or at least a serious reduction in the level of economic regulation.

The deregulation scenario is strongly supported by at least four major groups. Large volume users of telecommunications want access to new sources of supply and an opportunity to exploit their monopsonistic bargaining power but recognize that traditional regulation impedes such concessions. New entrants want unlimited access to all telecommunications markets and ask that regulation be confined to the dominant carriers to assure an opportunity to compete on a "level playing field." Incumbent carriers perceive that regulation will no longer protect them from market forces and that deregulation constitutes a significant step toward greater freedom to set prices, diversify, and offer new services. A number of politicians at the federal and state levels also support deregulation, perhaps reflecting a faith in competition, a desire to lower prices and expand services, or simply the results of intensive lobbying by special interest groups. Finally, the movement toward deregulation has received a stamp of credibility from neoclassical economists who have adopted a highly critical view of any form of price-earnings control.

There are two important reasons why this competition-deregulation scenario requires careful examination. First, it forecloses any question about the sustainability of competition in the telecommunications industry and the possibility that highly flawed markets may result in levels of inefficiency and adverse distributional consequences that are socially unacceptable. Second, it forecloses serious consideration of options that might strengthen regulation and improve industry performance. If the failure of regulation is assumed, then the only debate is over how fast to phase out or eliminate price-earnings controls.

To avoid these pitfalls, this chapter will endeavor to present a comprehensive analysis of the emergent roles of market structure and regulation in telecommunications, together with a critique of recommendations for reform and an assessment of these proposed changes in terms of both efficiency and equity criteria. As a first step, significant landmarks in the development of the telecommunications industry and regulatory policy will be placed in historical perspective. This will be followed by a detailed examination of the forces promoting and negating competition in telecommunications. Since the form of regulatory intervention is a function of the nature of market failure, the imperfections inherent in telecommunications markets along with a revised theory of the behavior of the regulated firm serve as a basis for evaluating so-called first approximation reforms (such as price caps) and proposals for controlling cross-subsidization. Finally, a more comprehensive proposal endeavors to integrate cost-based controls over price discrimination and cross subsidization with a greater opportunity for managerial initiative.

A Synopsis of Changing Structures and Policies

The issue of market structure has plagued the telecommunications industry for more than a century. Following the invention of the telephone in 1876, there was a period of intense rivalry between Western Union and the infant Bell Company as each firm sought to establish a position of dominance in the field. This conflict was resolved by mutual agreement in

1879, with a division of the market along voice and record lines. Western Union withdrew from telephone service and Bell agreed to stay out of the telegraph business. Stability prevailed until the expiration of the basic Bell patents in 1893 and 1894, after which a large number of independent telephone companies entered local exchange markets. The entry of the independents was swift and the fall in Bell's market share and profits was dramatic. Bell's share of the total exchange market dropped from 100% in 1893 to 62% in 1900, and to 51% in 1907. Bell's profits declined from an estimated 46% return during the patent monopoly to 8% by 1907 [1].

The movement toward competition was dramatically reversed when the legendary Theodore Vail returned to AT&T after an absence of 20 years from the company. As chairman, he took immediate steps to deny the independents access to the interexchange network by refusing to give them interconnection privileges. At the same time, he stepped up an aggressive program of acquisition and price warfare. It was during this period that Vail's famous pronouncement, "one system, one policy, universal service," set forth his vision of an optimal structure for the telecommunications industry. In addition to restricting the growth of the independents, Vail proceeded to acquire Western Union, and with it control over all forms of electronic communications.

Vail's aggressive programs prompted a three-pronged reaction on the part of government. The Post Office renewed calls for government ownership, the U.S. Attorney General moved against AT&T on antitrust grounds, and the Interstate Commerce Commission (ICC) was given authority to regulate interstate telephone service. At the state level, a number of new state regulatory commissions were also given authority over intrastate telephone service. With considerable tactical skill, Vail indicated that AT&T would divest itself of Western Union, stop acquiring independents, and allow interconnection. These terms were outlined in the Kingsbury Commitment (1913), and agreed to by the Attorney General. At the same time, Vail indicated that AT&T would accept regulation — but he argued persuasively that competition and regulated monopoly were inherently incompatible. The stage was set for a period of growth and stability characterized by AT&T market dominance that would last for 45 years.

Despite the Kingsbury Commitment, AT&T continued to aggressively acquire independent telephone companies until its share of the exchange market reached 80% by 1930. It also controlled virtually 100% of the interexchange market. When new technology threatened to disrupt the status quo, AT&T was successful in working out compromises that did not jeopardize the firm's dominance. For example, in 1920, when the invention of the vacuum tube and radio communications threatened to destabilize the industry, a cross-licensing arrangement was worked out, which allocated radio telephones between AT&T, General Electric, and RCA.

The concept of natural monopoly in telecommunications was given wide credence. The philosophy of Theodore Vail was not seriously challenged by either government or the independents. The Federal Communications Commission (FCC), created in 1934 to replace the largely ineffectual efforts of the ICC, focused on rate uniformity, Western Electric pricing, and the control of excessive profits through price reductions. The FCC was particularly active with respect to price reductions. Between 1935 and 1940, the Commission negotiated four successive rate reductions for interstate tolls amounting to $95 million on a cumulative basis by the end of 1940. In 1941, the FCC announced another reduction of $14 million, with further interstate rate reductions following in 1943, 1944, 1945, 1946, and a $50 million reduction in 1950.

The FCC's rate reductions created an imbalance between intra- and inter-state long-distance rates, which cast the state commissions in an unfavorable light. At the same time, the state agencies began to contest the allocation of local exchange costs between intrastate toll, interstate toll, and local exchange services. The states argued that the board-to-board allocation assigned a disproportionate amount of local costs to local exchange service, and they pushed aggressively for a so-called station-to-station allocation, which assigned a greater share of joint/common costs to toll service. Through a series of concessions, the FCC permitted costs to be transferred to interstate toll service. This willingness to concede to revenue transfers constituted a first error in FCC policy that would eventually undermine the credibility of natural monopoly because it had the effect of raising long-distance rates at the same time that microwave technology was creating opportunities for new sources of supply.

In 1949, the U.S. Department of Justice (DOJ) charged AT&T with violating the Sherman Act and sought divestiture of Western Electric. The DOJ was not challenging the concept of natural monopoly as much as it was challenging Vail's corporate structure, which reflected both horizontal and vertical integration. In the settlement, which resulted in the 1956 Consent Decree, AT&T agreed to freely license its technology and restrict its activities to common carrier services in order to maintain its end-to-end voice monopoly and vertical integration in manufacturing. But hardly had the Consent Decree been filed when exogenous technological pressures began to assert themselves. Microwave transmission had created new options for entry into telecommunications. Furthermore, economies of scale were apparently not significantly pervasive in micro-wave technology [2].

The traditional land-line transmission/distribution network, which was the cornerstone of comprehensive natural monopoly, had been challenged. In the Above 890 case (1959) [3], the FCC opened the radio frequency spectrum above 890 megacycles to new entrants. Microwave technology lent itself to the establishment of both private systems and specialized common carrier systems such as Microwave Communications, Inc. (MCI). MCI applied for authorization to provide private line microwave service between St. Louis and Chicago. MCI's application was approved by the FCC in 1969 [4]. Thereafter, an influx of new entrants into the specialized private line market appeared, including Southern Pacific, Western Telecommunications, and Datran. Parenthetically, it should be noted that all of these original applicants are now gone except for MCI.

AT&T reacted quickly after the Above 890 decision. It moved in two areas: First, it employed pricing strategies that involved selective forms of price discrimination. Second, it sought to circumscribe the new carriers by restrictions on interconnection. In response, the FCC committed its second major error by permitting open entry in the private line market without first establishing pricing guidelines that would constrain price discrimination and cross subsidization. As a consequence, the agency floundered when it had to come to grips, on a case-by-case basis, with AT&T's TELPAK A,B,C, and D, the Series 11000 Tariff, the Hi-Lo Tariff, the Dataphone Digital Service Tariff, and the Multiple Schedule Private Line Tariff. A common feature of these pricing strategies involved selective discounts to retain markets perceived as potentially competitive.

A third error in FCC regulatory policy was the belief that a hard-and-fast demarcation could be established between major telecommunications services in the face of rapid technological change. In 1971, the FCC issued its specialized carrier decision allowing open entry and competition for specialized services [5]. It was assumed that a clear demarcation could be made between such services and switched message toll telephone service (MTS). However, MCI moved to circumvent this distinction when major financial losses in 1971 and 1972 in the private line network forced MCI chairman William McGowen to shift his strategy to foreign exchange service (FX) [6]. MCI subsequently expanded its private line and FX services throughout 1974 and 1975, and renamed "Execunet," it became a virtual substitute for AT&T's MTS service. In effect, by blending FX and private line service, MCI had created a rival to AT&T's MTS. The

FCC ordered MCI to drop Execunet, but the court ruled in Execunet I that the FCC had failed to demonstrate that specific restrictions on entry into the MTS market were needed to promote the public interest. In Execunet II the FCC ruled that AT&T was not obligated to interconnect with carriers providing the functional equivalent of MTS. MCI appealed this decision and won. The MTS market was now open to entry by the so-called other common carriers (OCCs) [7].

At the same time, the FCC was confronted with an emerging boundary problem between regulated and nonregulated services. The question was raised whether the FCC should regulate data processing or hybrid services when message switching was an incidental factor in an integrated data processing service. In the Computer I decision (1971), the FCC decided not to regulate such hybrid services, but it did regulate data processing when it was incidental to message switching [8]. In Computer II (1980), the FCC adopted a definition that distinguished between "basic" and "enhanced" services [9]. Basic service was a common carrier offering to move information. Enhanced service combined basic service with processing applications that acted upon the format or content of the information. The Commission ruled that AT&T and GTE would have to offer enhanced services through separate subsidiaries.

AT&T president John deButts made the last defense of regulated natural monopoly in an address before the National Association of Regulatory Utility Commissioners (NARUC) in 1973. It was an eloquent plea to retain the industry structure envisioned by Vail — but somehow deButts lacked Vail's insight and capacity to reinstate the supremacy of the dominant firm. (It is interesting to speculate how Vail might have reacted in a comparable situation. One suspects that he would have incorporated IBM as an affiliate of AT&T at an early date!)

A further effort to reinstate a monopoly market structure was made in the Consumer Communications Reform Act of 1976 (popularly known as the Bell Bill). Supported by AT&T, the independents, and NARUC, this bill would have allowed AT&T to adopt incremental pricing, raised barriers to entry in the long-distance market, and given responsibility for customer premises equipment (CPE) to state regulators — all in the interest of protecting universal service. The Bell Bill did not pass Congress, and to further exacerbate matters, AT&T suffered a major defeat in its efforts to retain CPE within the framework of natural monopoly. In the Carterfone case (1968), the FCC opened the CPE market to entry. AT&T tried to forestall entry by requiring the use of a protective device for non-Bell equipment. In 1972, the FCC adopted a program of certification setting technical standards in lieu of protective devices. The court upheld the FCC in 1977 and the certification program became fully operative in 1978 [10].

AT&T faced another antitrust assault when it was compelled to respond to an antitrust suit filed by the Attorney General in 1974. DOJ's case was based on the belief that AT&T's vertical integration of regulated and nonregulated services was inherently anticompetitive. The case went badly for AT&T as the record became filled with evidence of failures to interconnect with new carriers and examples of predatory pricing practices. In 1982, in a landmark settlement between AT&T and the DOJ, AT&T accepted divestiture of the Bell operating companies in exchange for the right to compete freely in the new telecommunications markets [11]. The government rescinded the restrictions of the 1956 Consent Decree and the breakup of AT&T took place in 1984.

The divested Bell operating companies (BOCs) were reorganized into seven regional Bell holding companies (RBHCs). Seven thousand local exchanges were incorporated into 161 Local Access and Transport Areas (LATAs). Once again, a market demarcation policy had emerged. AT&T and the OCCs, such as MCI, would be free to compete in the interLATA, interexchange markets. The BOCs, perceived as natural monopolies, would be limited to intraLATA service consisting primarily of providing local exchange, short-haul toll, and access service. The BOCs would be prohibited from diversifying into nonregulated activities, including equipment manufacturing and interLATA telecommunications. Relaxation of these restrictions would be gained only by a judicial waiver granted by presiding Judge Harold Greene.

Almost immediately, the RBHCs applied for a succession of waivers in order to diversify into a variety of nonregulated activities — including real estate, international operations, and cellular mobile phones. For the most part these waivers have been granted and the only major restraints that still apply to the BOCs are the restrictions on interLATA service and equipment manufacturing.

Divestiture has led to a dramatic restructuring of telecommunications pricing. In the old format, long-distance service consisted of MTS, WATS, and private line service. Nationwide rate averaging largely ignored cost-of-service differences in favor of uniformity within the mileage bands. Local rates were based on value of service; that is, price varied according to the type of user and size of the exchange. Statewide averaging again tended to ignore cost-of-service differences. Local telephone plant jointly used for toll and local calls was assigned through separations and division of revenue procedures. Subscriber plant factors had the dramatic effect of assigning revenue requirements to the interstate services that were greater than actual minutes of use by a multiple of approximately 3.2.

Divestiture removed the old integrated approach to pricing and revenue/cost allocations. Interexchange tariffs and services have proliferated, while local exchange pricing has reflected a concerted effort on the part of local exchange carriers (LECs) to substitute local measured service for flat rates. Without question, however, the biggest single change was the introduction of access charges to compensate the BOCs and independent LECs for access provided to the interexchange carriers (IXCs). Since the OCCs were initially given an inferior grade of access (Feature Group A, B), relative to the premium access afforded AT&T (Feature Group C) the OCCs were granted about a 55% discount on access charges. With the completion of equal access, both AT&T and the OCCs would pay the same access charge.

By 1988, virtually all of the legal barriers to interexchange/interLATA markets had been removed. Only the constraints on the BOCs remained, and in a brief filed with Judge Greene, the DOJ recommended that restrictions on the BOCs pertaining to equipment manufacturing, information services, and entry into interLATA markets be removed (except for service originating and terminating in the BOC's own territory). In effect, the DOJ had reversed the position it took in the original 1974 antitrust case against AT&T. Judge Greene did not agree with the DOJ's position [12]. In passing, it should be noted that in the Computer III decision (1986) [13], the FCC dropped its requirements for separate subsidiaries for dominant carriers seeking to diversify into nonregulated activities. Henceforth the FCC would rely on cost accounting standards to segregate revenues and costs between regulated and nonregulated services.

Despite the removal of most of the legal barriers to entry (except for those still in force against the BOCs and restrictions on entry into the local exchange and some intraLATA toll markets), the question remains whether the emerging telecommunications markets are effectively competitive and whether any of the firms retain sufficient market power to practice price discrimination and cross subsidization.

The Case for Competition

If deregulated markets are to supplant economic regulation, they must be capable of inducing competitive behavior, diminishing market power, and compelling innovative performance. Achieving these objectives depends primarily on liberalized entry. There are three factors that could support successful entry in the interexchange, interLATA markets. First, the benefits of rapid technological advance are available to both the new entrant and the incumbent firm. In fact, the entrant may actually possess an advantage in that it is not burdened by a high-cost, old plant. US Sprint could make this claim by pointing to the fact that it has installed more investment in fiber optics plants than any other IXC, including AT&T [14]. Second, sustained high rates of growth will facilitate entry. Since 1970, the average annual rate of growth of MTS has been in excess of 12%; overseas communications services have grown at 16% or more, and local exchange growth approaches 9%. With the rapid expansion in digital transmission and the proliferation of new service offerings after AT&T's divestiture, it is reasonable to assume that these growth rates will not only be sustained, but will probably increase. Third, there are increasing doubts about the validity of economies of scale as a barrier to entry. Past econometric studies by Mantell, Waverman, et al., cast serious doubt on the existence of scale elasticity estimates much greater than 1.0 [15]. Furthermore, scale economies alone may not be a barrier to entry if they can be achieved by both the incumbent and entrant alike.

Proponents of deregulation believe that entry has been highly successful in the interexchange markets. They note the proliferation of different types of firms and services. These include 1) the nationwide facilities based carriers (FBCs), such as AT&T, MCI, US Sprint, and Western Union; 2) the regional carriers' carriers, such as the National Telecommunications Network (NTN), which build networks linking cities in particular regions and may therefore be considered regional FBCs; 3) resellers that compete directly with AT&T and MCI for new accounts (these resellers can buy capacity from the nationwide FBCs or from the carriers' carriers); and 4) value-added networks (VANs) such as Tymnet and Telenet, which link microcomputers with leased lines to offer packages for data transmission and protocol conversion for end users. On the international scene, MCI has acquired Western Union International and threatens to challenge AT&T by offering service to 60 countries. US Sprint reaches 62 countries. In addition, five projected fiber optics carriers' carriers would challenge satellites in the Atlantic basin.

At the local exchange level, proponents of deregulation argue that the BOCs and the independent LECs are vulnerable to potential entry. Despite franchise restrictions on entry, exchange carriers are susceptible to bypass and diversion. Private microwave systems, rooftop satellite antennas, shared tenant services, and alternative operator services are cited as evidence of contestability. Indeed, the fear of bypass is so strong that it has been introduced as justification for assigning all of the nontraffic sensitive local loop costs to the end user as a fixed monthly access charge.

Market Infirmities and Competitive Failures

The case for competition appears far too optimistic when examined in greater detail. There is strong evidence that entry is of limited effectiveness, and that the persistence of market dominance by the FBCs together with fundamental demand and production economies, market segmentation, and interdependence between firms, constitute major obstacles to pervasive competition.

Potential and Realized Entry

Although concentration remains high in all of the major common carrier markets (excluding CPE), the possibility that entry can discipline the incumbent firm's behavior must be considered. Entry can take two forms: 1) potential or hit-and-run entry, as embodied in the theory of contestable markets; and 2) actual or realized entry, which diminishes the market share of the incumbent firms. The contestability theory argues that if the incumbent firm is vulnerable to potential or hit-and-run entry, it will not engage in price discrimination or cross subsidization, nor will it be able to sustain monopoly profits. Actual or realized entry constitutes a significant loss of market share by the established firms, which will serve to reduce profit levels and diminish the market power of these firms.

W. G. Shepherd states that contestability requires that three conditions be satisfied: 1) Entry must be free and without limit; 2) an entrant must be able to establish itself before the incumbent can make a major retaliatory response; and 3) entry must be perfectly reversible (i.e., sunk costs must be minimal) [16]. Shepherd also notes that entry barriers influence profits through their effect on market shares (i.e., ease of entry can reduce market shares and therefore influence profitability). For entry to be successful in this regard, four conditions must be met: 1) An opening of entry must be so substantial that the remaining barriers become negligible. 2) Entry must be rapid and sharply depress market shares in the utility's prime markets in order to be an effective constraint. 3) The new entrant must be able to capture at least 15–25% of the market to be viable and preserve independent behavior. 4) To be an effective constraint on profits, the market share of the dominant firm must fall below 40% and this loss of market share must be permanent [17].

Contestability has very limited applicability in most interexchange markets served by FBCs. A new FBC must incur substantial investment and the burden of sunk costs in the event of failure can be monumental. For example, in 1985 IBM was required to absorb $400 million in outstanding debt in order to divest itself of Satellite Business Systems. In 1986, GTE had to write off $1.3 billion in Sprint, and United Telecommunications had to write off $170 million in its long-distance service when they were merged to form US Sprint. In 1988, Western Union had to write off $603 million to withdraw from the long-distance telephone business. The attractiveness of hit-and-run entry is also greatly diminished by the existence of excess capacity in the interexchange market. In 1986, US Sprint and MCI each had enough fiber optic transmission capacity in place to accommodate the total volume of domestic interLATA traffic [18]. The existence of excess capacity was also a major factor causing Fibertrak (a consortium composed of the Norfolk Southern, Santa Fe, and Southern Pacific Railroads) to suspend its plans for a nationwide carriers' carrier fiber optic network. Finally, potential entry will be deterred by the low levels of profitability of the OCCs (to be discussed later) and the clear and growing willingness of AT&T, the dominant firm, to strike back immediately with a variety of promotional pricing practices at any perceived threat to its market hegemony.

At the local exchange level there is overwhelming evidence to suggest that most markets are not contestable. Duplicative local service would entail massive investments in local loops which are sunk costs with little resale value. Bypass technology such as rooftop antennas serve only to connect pairs of points and cannot handle diffused traffic. Cellular radio is too costly in terms of both initial investment and monthly operating charges. CATVs would have difficulty entering the market because they are typically not designed for two-way communications and they would encounter major problems in interconnecting with neighboring cable systems. Of course, a potential entrant might duplicate some of the local plant and rely on the LEC for the balance, but this would not give such an entrant a cost advantage — the subscriber would have to assume the burden of subadditivity. Only in the case of shared tenant services would the potential entrant appear to enjoy some intra-building cost advantage, but this could soon disappear when subscribers wanted to make outside calls and had to sacrifice control over their telephone traffic to an unregulated agent.

Where would contestability seem to apply in telecommunications? Aside from the CPE markets where imports have made major inroads, the answer would appear to be in the enhanced services and brokerage functions. Resellers, VANs, and enhanced service providers have the option of buying capacity from FBCs or carriers' carriers. By the same token, however, they are vulnerable to pricing and service strategies of the vertically integrated FBCs. As evidence of this concern, the largest reseller, ALLNET, now called ALC, has moved to create its own switching centers, and, like other resellers, would be quite pleased to become an FBC. Contestability in these markets will be a function of the ability of regulators to control price discrimination and cross subsidization. At present this depends on the successful implementation of open network architecture (ONA) and Part 64 of the FCC Rules.

Insofar as actual or realized entry is concerned, Shepherd's criteria have not been satisfied at the interstate, interexchange level — even though the private market has been free of legal restrictions to entry since the early 1970s and the interstate switched services have been free since 1978. AT&T still retains approximately 70%–80% of the switched market, and a parallel high share of the private line market [19]. Whether measured by revenues or toll minutes, MCI's market share appears to be about 8%–10%, US Sprint about 4%, and all other OCCs about 4%. Thus, after a decade the OCCs have not met Shepherd's minimum market share conditions individually, and collectively come nowhere near capturing a share of the market sufficient to constrain AT&T's profits. By comparison, the independents at the turn of the century captured 40%–49% of the local exchange market after the expiration of the basic Bell patents in 1893–1894.

In the intraLATA, interexchange market, the BOCs clearly dominate. Huber estimates that ". . . each BOC carries close to 100% of the intra-LATA toll traffic in its area" [20]. In passing, it should be noted that many states still forbid or discourage intraLATA toll competition.

In the international markets, AT&T accounted for 95% of the overseas telephone market (measured in revenues) in 1986, while MCI and US Sprint lagged far behind with 3.3% and 0.8% respectively [21]. The international record carriers appear to constitute a diminishing threat as Telex and public message telegraph service decline in relative importance.

At the local exchange level, loss of market share due to the bypass of the BOCs and independent LECs appears to have been negligible. The analysis of bypass is complicated by the need to differentiate between economic and noneconomic bypass as well as service and facility bypass. For the seven RBHCs, the ratio of bypass-lost revenue to total revenue is 6% (using carrier 1988 filings). However, L. Selwyn and P. Montgomery argue that these estimates are too generous and bypass measured on the basis of the share of transmission circuits retained by BOCs is closer to 2%–4% [22].

Unfortunately, one crucial area where adequate market concentration data are not available involves the rapidly proliferating new promotional services. These include optional calling, 800-WATS, and virtual telecommunications network service (VTNS). If AT&T has a dominant share of these emergent services, then the prospects for new entrants are grim indeed.

If the OCCs are to increase their market share at the expense of AT&T, it is clear that they will have to develop strong earnings growth, incur substantial advertising expenditures, and maintain a price spread sufficient to attract customers. On each of these points, present trends do not have much basis for optimism.

AT&T's interstate earnings still remain under rate base/rate-of-return (RBROR) regulation, with an allowed overall rate of return of 12.2% on regulated services. In 1987, AT&T earned a 14.4% return on average equity (including regulated and nonregulated business). With price caps, AT&T hopes that it can earn a target 20% return on equity [23]. In contrast, the OCCs have had a dismal earnings record. To date, all of the OCCs except MCI have reported substantial annual losses. For 1987, MCI earned an overall rate of return on net plant, before income taxes, of 4.5%. (To review the pattern of MCI revenues, expenses, and income from 1982 through 1987, see Appendix.) In passing it should be noted that Western Union's annual deficits became so burdensome that the carrier withdrew from the long-distance telephone business in 1988 [24]. Also in 1988, GTE drastically reduced its holdings in US Sprint (from 50% to 20%) by selling a majority interest to United Telecommunications. This decision was undoubtedly influenced by GTE's loss of $577 million on its Sprint investment in 1987. A continued pattern of negative or depressed OCC earnings over time would result in a higher cost of capital, reduced investment, a failure to expand plant and attract new customers, and an eventual decline in market share. On an optimistic note, MCI reported higher earnings for the first half of 1988, noting the growth in large business accounts as a major contributor. Ironically, this is the same market that AT&T is moving to target with its new Tariff 12 and 15 offerings designed for large customers.

Advertising expenditures and price spreads will also be required to achieve an OCC growth in market share. In 1986, AT&T's advertising expenditures were $3\frac{1}{2}$ times greater than those of MCI and two times greater than those of US Sprint. Yet as a percentage of sales, AT&T advertising was $\frac{1}{2}$% as opposed to 1% for MCI and $3\frac{1}{2}$% for US Sprint [25]. Sustaining large advertising outlays will clearly place a relatively greater burden on the OCCs. Price spreads between AT&T and the

OCCs have consistently narrowed as the OCCs have been compelled to pay progressively higher access charges as more local exchanges are converted to equal access. While it is difficult to generalize about current price spreads because of the complexity of rate structures, it appears that MCI and US Sprint's rates were about 5% lower than those of AT&T in 1987 [26]. Perhaps more significant is AT&T's price leadership in the interexchange long-distance markets, which places immense pressure on the OCCs to maintain a spread in the face of AT&T price reductions. This point will be considered later.

Fundamental Demand and Production Economies

It is evident that the emergent industry structure in telecommunications will be characterized by the coexistence of FBCs (whether national or regional) and a group of enterprises that can be collectively designated as enhanced service providers and brokers [27]. The former have certain basic demand and production characteristics that are typical of public utility industries; the latter are essentially customers of, and at the same time competitors with vertically integrated, multiproduct FBCs. This breakdown ignores private networks which may have an influence on demand, but if private networks become carriers' carriers they should be treated as regional FBCs.

An FBC's long-run market dominance will be a function of its ability to achieve 1) a high load factor (high average demand relative to peak demand); 2) a high diversity factor (high noncoincident peaks relative to the system peak); 3) a high capacity factor (high levels of plant utilization); 4) a long-run cost function that reflects subadditivity based on economies of scale and joint production and an aggregate level of output sufficient to realize these economies; and 5) technological gains that equal or exceed those of potential rivals. To the extent that the FBC attains these goals, its dominance will be secure. High levels of average demand will assure full utilization of plant and low fixed unit costs; high levels of total output will permit exploitation of scale and joint production economies; and the entire average cost function over time will demonstrate subadditivity. Conversely, a failure to achieve the required usage patterns will cause a retreat backward on the short-run average cost function that could easily negate any of the scale-technology gains. The successful FBC could be challenged only if a new entrant employed a lower cost, new technology that the FBC was unwilling to adopt, or if inept corporate pricing policies or public regulation held prices sufficiently high to encourage inefficient entry.

Regrettably, there have been no major empirical efforts to integrate all of these factors into a comprehensive study of the demand-production process. However, there is selective evidence with respect to individual factors, such as the impact of fiber optics on the cost of transmission. Fiber optics has dramatically lowered transmission costs, as shown by comparisons of the installed cost per circuit mile of cable, microwave, and fiber optics [28]. The effects of technology are also evident in the decline in average plant investment per circuit mile from 1960–1985 [29]. T. Pryor and C. Weaver believe that the impact of fiber optics may be so great as to reinstate natural monopoly [30]. Huber believes that short-haul fiber loop costs per unit of traffic decline so sharply as traffic increases that it gives the LECs "...a very favorable — perhaps overwhelmingly favorable — position..." in such traffic [31]. Studies have also shown that technology has reduced switching costs and that it may be reducing the distinction between switched and private line services.

L. Selwyn has made the most progress in integrating an analysis of demand and minimum efficient size. In a study of intrastate telecommunications in Michigan, Selwyn introduces the concept of minimum efficient market share (MEMS) [32]. (MEMS is essentially the same concept as minimum efficient size, Scherer's minimum optimum scale, or Salop's minimum viable scale [33].) As economies of scale and scope increase MEMS relative to the size of the market, prospects for successful entry and competition diminish. Conversely, as MEMS decreases, entry and competition become more viable. When MEMS is over 50% only one firm can efficiently produce the output. A substantial growth in demand can reduce MEMS and facilitate entry, but this requires that the new growth must be captured in large part by the new entrant. History indicates that the incumbent will take strong steps to prevent this from happening.

To calculate MEMS, Selwyn quantifies demand for switched and private line services in a series of different markets, and the underlying switching, transport, and access costs. His results indicate that MEMS for switched services ranges from 35% in the Detroit LATA to 80% or higher in the less dense LATAs. For dedicated private lines, MEMS is consistently at or close to 100%. For interexchange, intraLATA switched services, such as Lansing to Jackson, Michigan, MEMS is 80%. In all of these cases his empirical studies show that demand would have to increase very substantially (e.g., by a multiple of 300%) to have a significant impact on MEMS. His empirical results also show that there are substantial economies accruing to the FBC that is able to utilize multiple switches and routes, and that integrating services (i.e., the same carrier providing switched and private line services in exchange and inter-exchange markets) is highly cost effective.

Market Segmentation

Demand characteristics in telecommunications markets reflect significant concentration among business and residential users. For example, 4% of business customers (excluding the federal government) account for 62% of total interstate long-distance business billings, while 20% of the business users account for 90% of business billings [34]. Similarly, 10% of the residential customers accounted for 50% of all long-distance interstate residential billings in 1983 [35]. There is also a strong geographical concentration of usage between major cities. The 16 largest metropolitan areas contribute 33% of all business MTS and WATS revenues; the top 100 contribute 70%. The top 20 LATAs contributed almost 50% of all residential long-distance revenues in 1986 [36].

Clearly, these usage patterns lend themselves to market segmentation. They also encourage the design of tariffs and rate structures that fully exploit each market segment to achieve the potential demand and production economies just described. It becomes easy for management to rationalize a system of price discrimination, cross subsidization, and limit-entry pricing that will promote the full usage of plant at lowest cost in such a setting. Segmenting customers with differing elasticities of demand and then designing price structures for that classification becomes, in the eyes of astute management, a contribution to both the firm's long-term viability and the public interest.

AT&T has moved more effectively than any other firm to exploit these demand characteristics. To appreciate this accomplishment, one need only examine the variety of niche markets that are included in the spectrum of offerings encompassed by MTS, Reach-Out-America, Pro-America, WATS, MegaCom, and SDN, or the refinements in customer classifications embodied in expanded 800 services (Ready Line 800 service for small users, regular 800 service, and MegaCom 800 service for large users). The new AT&T Tariff 12 offerings mark a further step, with the introduction of Virtual Telecommunications Network Service designed for specific large customers (e.g., General Electric, DuPont, and Ford).

Effective market segmentation has obvious detrimental effects on entry and competition. If segmentation and price discrimination become highly sophisticated and large numbers of consumers have little or no opportunity for arbitrage, then the prospects for contestability or across-the-board entry are minimal.

Interdependent Action

Interdependence among firms in the telecommunications industry has emerged at at least three levels. First, there is a need for cooperation and coordination to establish uniform standards for ONA and the Integrated Services Digital Network (ISDN). This will require that the BOCs, independent LECs, IXCs, and specialized user groups reach agreement on specific standards and facilities. A second form of interdependence has emerged as a result of the divestiture of AT&T. Even though the old monolithic structure is gone, there is a clear interdependence between AT&T and the BOCs, brought about by their buyer-seller relationship. In 1987, approximately 25% of the BOCs' operating revenues came from access charges paid by the interexchange carriers. Given AT&T's over-whelming market share, it has become the largest single customer of the BOCs. Conversely, about 50% of AT&T's costs stem from the payment of access charges. In such a setting, the BOCs cannot jeopardize their relationship with their largest single customer without fear of AT&T reprisal in the form of bypass of the local exchange. On the other hand, AT&T is vulnerable to BOC access pricing strategies. It could be hurt by increases perceived as discriminatory, but it could also benefit substan-tially if the BOCs (with deregulation) were to institute some form of promotional access pricing through declining block rates. With both parties so closely dependent upon each other, it is difficult to envision head-to-head price competition between them in every major tele-communications market.

Another factor that will mitigate AT&T/BOC aggressive pricing com-petition is the unique structure of interexchange revenues. Each of the seven regional Bell holding companies (RBHCs) controls no more than 15% of the nation's total access lines. At the same time, Huber estimates that "... from any one region's (RBHC's) perspective, 80% of all interexchange calls do not touch it at all" [37]. In other words, each regional holding company would have to incur costs to interconnect its BOCs with six other regional holding company BOCs when the potential benefits could appear to be dubious. It would make more sense for an RBHC to concentrate on the private line, dedicated facilities markets and selected toll markets within its region than attempt to contribute toward building a rival nationwide network. If it were to attempt the latter, the RBHC would again face AT&T retaliation. In effect, a new market shares policy could emerge by consensus between the RBHCs and AT&T with price competition focusing primarily on large customers for whom custom designed systems would appear to be most attractive.

A final dimension of interdependence exists in the pricing strategies of AT&T and the OCCs at the interexchange/interLATA level. For example, on June 1, 1986, AT&T reduced rates for MTS by 10%–12%, WATS by 12.8%, SDN by 11%, and MegaCom by 12%. On July 1, 1986, MCI followed with a 10% across-the-board decrease, and on August 1, 1986, US Sprint reduced rates by 9%. A similar pattern followed in response to FCC-ordered AT&T price reductions on January 1, 1987, July 1, 1987, and January 1, 1988. Price leadership extends not only to reductions in average prices, but also to changes in rate structure design (e.g., peak and off-peak rates) and price increases (e.g., MCI simultaneously mirrored AT&T's 1988 voice grade channel increases). Under these conditions, it is not unexpected that MCI would advocate that the FCC give AT&T greater freedom to set its own prices on the grounds that this "... would make the industry more orderly" [38]. It would permit the dominant firm to establish patterns of price leadership with which the OCCs could coexist and reduce the immense and continuing pressure on OCCs to lower prices in order to keep a sufficient price spread to attract customers. It should be noted that evidence of price leadership and interdependence has appeared at both interstate and intrastate levels [39].

Failure of Markets to Minimize Costs

The emergence of selective competitive pressures and increased uncertainty has given rise to a set of management strategies that will prevent markets from equilibrating in a fashion that minimizes costs and sustains competitive pressures. There will be a strong incentive to expand plant and create demand and supply imbalances so that markets will not clear at minimum cost. The interexchange carriers have an incentive to expand capacity, given the pressures to capture market share and achieve high load and diversity factors. This incentive is reinforced by the low incremental cost of applying fiber optic technology and a belief that market growth will compensate for overbuilding. The unregulated solution to chronic excess capacity is, of course, predation and entry foreclosure in the short run, followed by mergers and consolidations in the long run until demand and supply are brought into balance.

A similar investment incentive exists with respect to ISDN, where the creation of a broadband network is assumed to enhance the position of both the LECs and the IXCs by permitting them to offer more services, thereby diminishing the attractiveness of exchange bypass and alternative private networks. The difficulty is that there may be an artificial stimulus insofar as ISDN is concerned if the carrier can engage in cross subsidization. Doubts about the contribution of ISDN are reflected in a popular rephrasing of the acronym: "innovations subscribers don't need."

A second factor affecting least cost supply is the unwillingness of the incumbent firm to interconnect with potential rivals. The public utility industries have had a long history of refusals to interconnect, and it is difficult to see how corrective measures would appear in the absence of direct government intervention. Failure to interconnect could frustrate innovative state programs designed to minimize the costs of expanding additional telephone plant by recourse to competitive bidding [40].

A Revised Theory of the Regulated Firm

Two generic market structures have emerged in telecommunications. First, there are those essentially monopolistic markets in which consumer options are few, demand is inelastic to price increases, and consumer usage patterns readily lend themselves to segmentation. Second, there are those competitive markets in which buyers have options, demand is elastic to price decreases, and arbitrage may be prevalent. The FBCs will serve both types of markets with plant and facilities that are often interchangeable or fungible between services, and with a cost function in which common and joint costs are a high proportion of total costs. How will the FBCs react in such a setting? The Averch-Johnson model sought to explain the behavior of the regulated firm in terms of the constraints imposed by rate base/rate-of-return regulation (RBROR) [41]. Whenever the allowed rate of return was greater than the cost of capital, A-J argued that there was an incentive to gold plate, to invest in noncompensatory services, to create excess capacity, and to avoid low-cost sources of supply that added nothing to the rate base. The objective was to camouflage monopoly profits by inflating the rate base until the ratio of utility operating income to net rate base was brought into line with the allowed rate of return. The result was a distortion of inputs in favor of capital relative to other factors, an expansion of service at less than long-run marginal cost, and the cross subsidization of peripheral markets by monopoly markets. The Averch-Johnson model assumed that the regulated firm occupied essentially a monopolistic position and that competition was essentially a fringe issue. But with the new market structures characterized by the coexistence of monopoly and competition and the growing disenchantment with RBROR regulation, modification of the original A-J model is called for.

Imperfect Markets as a Determinant of Behavior

In the current market structure, the regulated firm is no longer free to pursue a policy of overinvestment to camouflage monopoly profits. Gold plating, redundancy, and refusal to consider low-cost options are no longer feasible management strategies. Such practices would preclude the FBC from competitive markets and would jeopardize its cost advantage in monopoly markets.

Assuming that the regulated firm wants to perpetuate a position of market dominance, it must realize all of the demand and production economies previously described, but it can go much further by effectively employing price discrimination, cross subsidization, deregulation of profits, and diversification. If successful, these tactics would permit the firm to reposition itself to take maximum advantage of changing market conditions.

The propensity to engage in price discrimination and cross subsidization is carried forward from the original A-J model, but the motivation is no longer a function of rate-base regulation. Rather, the firm will seek to employ price discrimination and cross subsidization to take advantage of differentiated markets and assure growth in gross revenues and profits over time. Effective price discrimination will increase gross revenues by raising prices in markets where demand is inelastic and lowering prices in markets where demand is elastic. Cross subsidization provides a perfect complement by shifting common and joint costs between markets on the basis of elasticities. Whenever possible, a higher proportion of common and joint costs will be allocated to inelastic markets. A more subtle form of cross subsidization can be achieved by denying the savings from new technology and joint production to monopolistic markets and, instead, flowing these benefits to competitive markets.

Price discrimination and cross subsidization become highly attractive practices from the standpoint of the firm. In addition to increasing gross revenues, as noted above, they permit the firm to be "kept whole" by recovering past depreciation reserve deficiencies through price increases in inelastic markets where there will be a comparatively small decline in sales. Cross subsidization is also attractive because it reduces the risk associated with entry into competitive and nonregulated markets. If such entry fails, the firm will still recover those costs, which cross subsidization has allocated to residual monopoly markets. Finally, cross subsidization will permit the FBC to recover the overhead costs associated with projects such as ONA and ISDN in a manner that minimizes the dampening effect on traffic growth.

The firm will seek to complement price discrimination and cross subsidization with aggressive programs in three areas. These include: first, a general relaxation or removal of constraints on profits; second, vigorous resistance to any efforts that might impose a full-cost allocation standard on the carrier; and third, removal of all restrictions on diversification. Removal of profit constraints would be justified on the grounds that enhanced profits serve as an inducement for greater efficiency and innovation. Avoidance of full-cost standards would be necessary to remove any interference with cross subsidization and the allocation of common and joint costs on the basis of relative demand elasticities. In this regard, the firm could argue that the emergence of competition requires different standards of accountability from those which prevailed in the past, and this requires a shift to incremental costs as a test for judging minimum compensatory prices and a more general acceptance of demand-based rates. Removal of restrictions on diversification into nonregulated industries would be justified on the grounds that distinctions between markets are rapidly disappearing and such diversification is necessary in order to maximize the continued growth of total revenues.

Diversification is interesting because it again demonstrates a new aspect of the strategy of the FBC attempting to adjust to new market structures. It represents an important opportunity to make use of heavy cash flows and to participate in any operational synergism that may arise from integrating traditional telephone functions with new services such as cellular radio, data processing, or electronic publishing. From the standpoint of management, it also affords an opportunity to achieve any financial synergism that may arise through an improved risk/return trade-off when the stable growth of utility services is integrated with the higher growth rate of speculative ventures [42].

Cross subsidization can play a key role in the strategy of the firm seeking to promote diversification. By aggregating its overall rate of return, the firm is able to utilize the low cost of capital to the public utility to offset the higher cost of capital that would normally be associated with competitive, nonregulated activities. This bundling process understates the required return needed to enter a competitive market so that these markets take on an artificial attractiveness. The willingness of the regulated firm to enter competitive markets for a lower overall return places it at a comparative advantage relative to its rivals in these markets. On the utility side, however, consumers will overpay because they are being assessed a revenue requirement that reflects an average overall return that partially incorporates the proportionally higher risk associated with nonregulated activities. Needless to say, the rate payer will be burdened even more if the diversification program fails and the average, bundled cost of capital is increased. This form of cross subsidization will arise when the FBC serves both regulated and nonregulated markets; it can be repeated when the entire utility enterprise becomes a subset of a new holding company.

A new set of distortions in output and income distribution will result from this revised model of the regulated firm operating under conditions of partial deregulation and imperfect markets. Cross subsidization will depress output in monopoly markets and lead to overexpansion of output in competitive markets. Resistance to experimentation with lower prices in monopoly markets will reduce income for this class of consumer, while many of the benefits of joint production, new technology, and price experimentation with lower rates will accrue to customers in competitive markets. These strategies will also tend to adversely affect competition in nonregulated markets and create a greater degree of instability in basic telecommunications markets.

Firm Behavior in Practice

There is strong evidence that the revised model of regulatory behavior typifies reality. On the matter of costing and pricing strategies, IXC and LEC procedures tend to shift a significant portion of common costs to monopoly markets. At the interexchange level, this is demonstrated by AT&T's endorsement of the net revenue test whereby a competitive or promotional service is judged compensatory if its revenues cover its incremental costs. By definition, this approach assigns some part of common costs to residual monopoly services [43]. At the LEC level, the BOCs have long used embedded direct analyses (EDAs) to compare revenues from local exchange service with the embedded direct cost of the local exchange. In the calculation of EDAs, all access-related costs are assigned to the local exchange. These costs are designated as non-traffic sensitive (NTS) since they allegedly do not vary with volume within the limits of their capacity. This process is used to justify raising exchange rates when the EDA studies show a poor revenue-to-cost ratio. The EDA studies ignore the fact that both intra- and interstate toll are provided over the same local NTS facilities.

To cover revenue requirements, the BOCs typically calculate rates for competitive services together with their incremental costs and any related avoided costs. Then each competitive or discretionary service is reviewed in terms of its ability to generate prospective revenues and cover these costs. The BOC subtracts the revenues expected from the proposed rates for competitive services from its total revenue requirement. The residual portion is then recovered from the basic exchange service customer [44]. This form of residual rate-making is consistent with the revised model of the behavior of the firm, and it will certainly continue as long as the LECs offer basic exchange service under monopoly conditions.

In passing, it should be noted that residual rate-making can be expected to distribute to the basic exchange service much of the cost of future network modernization associated with the conversion to a digital telephone system. The irony is that the residual telephone customer using the analog system will probably benefit very little from such a modernization program. This prospect suggests that the test for modernization should be: Does such a program lower average costs (and prices) significantly to all classes of customers when compared to system costs before modernization? That is, is everyone better off and no one worse off?

The incumbent carriers at both the exchange and interexchange levels have also moved aggressively to promote the deregulation of profits and individual services. By late 1987, 22 states had enacted 25 general statutes to deregulate telecommunications services or service providers. Most of these statutes retain regulation over local exchange rates while giving the state commission discretion to determine the adequacy of competition insofar as other services are concerned, but two actions deserve special attention. Nebraska eliminated economic regulation of the local exchange on the condition that rate increases do not exceed 10% for any consecutive 12-month period, while permitting the carrier to retain its local franchise. Vermont's Social Contract eliminated controls over the carrier's rate of return while imposing price caps for local exchange service for five years. Intrastate toll rates were also deregulated. This arrangement must be renewed in 1992, and the telephone company is expected to provide adequate service.

The most significant federal step toward relaxing telecommunications regulation has come in two notices of proposed rulemaking (NOPRs) issued by the FCC in August 1987 and May 1988 [45]. These NOPRs would apply to interstate telecommunications services and would impose price caps on AT&T and qualifying local exchange carriers. Telephone companies would be free to select either rate-base regulation or price caps. AT&T is a proponent of price caps, and the NOPR would cap all AT&T existing services except Tariff 12 offerings and new services. The latter would presumably be capped eventually and would be held to the net revenue test (i.e., net revenues from a service must equal or exceed its incremental cost). AT&T capped services would be placed in two "baskets" — i.e., switched network services (MTS, WATS) and private line services. An estimate of aggregate revenue-weighted rates within each basket would be used to calculate a composite price cap for that basket. The results would then be adjusted on a periodic basis by an inflation index and a productivity offset (the latter, set at 3%, would include a "Consumer Productivity Dividend" of 0.5% per year). The price caps would go into effect on April 1, 1989.

It is not surprising that in the face of strong pressures to deregulate profits and services, relatively few fully distributed cost studies have been made at the state level to examine interservice cross subsidization. The FCC has reinstated fully distributed cost in Part 64 of the FCC Rules to segregate plant between regulated and nonregulated services. It requires carriers to file cost allocation manuals that separate costs of regulated and nonregulated services, but this process does nothing to control cross subsidization between regulated services. Costs are assigned directly whenever the dedicated use of equipment or a basic service can be identified. Common costs are assigned in proportion to the direct costs to which they are related. Any residual common costs are then assigned through a general allocator. Undoubtedly, the carriers have accepted Part 64 as the price for freedom to diversify.

As the model anticipated, the BOCs, AT&T, and the independent LECs have pursued diversification with great enthusiasm. The CEO of Bell Atlantic stated in 1988 that, "we have to get into non-regulated businesses to really grow." He continued, ". . . by the end of 1991 we see ourselves as a strong industrial corporation with a utility core." By that time, he added, one-half of the company's revenues will come from unregulated businesses [46]. The most active diversifying telephone company remains Bell Canada Enterprises, with more than 82 nonregulated subsidiaries, but US West is moving rapidly to close the gap with over 40 such subsidiaries.

First Approximation Reforms

With the coexistence of monopoly and competition and the involvement of multiple levels of government intervention, it is doubtful that flash-cut, across-the-board deregulation in telecommunications is a serious option. Instead, one may anticipate increasing demands for reduced or relaxed regulation in the expectation that full competition will eventually appear. Proponents of this position usually start with a recitation of the flaws of RBROR regulation. These deficiencies include the perverse allocative and X–inefficiencies associated with the A-J model, the adverse effects of profit controls on innovation, a lack of responsiveness to exogenous factors (such as inflation), and inflexible retail rates that reflect historic accounting costs rather than current resource costs. RBROR regulation is also condemned for its failure to detect and control anticompetitive strategies of the regulated firm.

In view of the concerted effort being made to replace RBROR regulation with price caps, the basic question must be asked, will price caps do a better job? Social contracts are essentially a variant of the price cap concept and can be considered to have the same strengths and weaknesses.

Price Cap Regulation

With respect to efficiency, it is possible to argue that ceiling prices imposed on monopoly markets will tend to discourage rate-base padding and conscious overinvestment to the extent that such caps lower the rate of return vis-a-vis the cost of capital. But as noted previously, this problem has largely disappeared in the telecommunications industry.

There are a number of reasons why one can doubt whether price caps will be conducive to efficiency. If the agencies establishing price caps accept uncritically the existing rate structure, there is no assurance that the resulting rates will promote efficiency. Indeed, there is little merit in condemning the distortions inherent in RBROR regulation and then accepting a rate structure derived from the application of RBROR regulation. It is also evident that price caps would do little to eliminate past over-investment or impede the recovery of redundant, obsolete plant by depreciation. In submissions to the FCC in Docket 87–313, *In the Matter of Policy and Rules Concerning Rates for Dominant Carriers*, none of the proponents of price caps have indicated a willingness to write off past depreciation reserve deficiencies as a concession for introducing price caps. Rather, they insist on being made whole (i.e., full recovery of capital), and the courts would undoubtedly support this contention. At the same time, adoption of price caps would eliminate the prudence, used-and-useful criteria normally used to evaluate whether plant and equipment should be included in the rate base.

There are important negative incentives associated with price caps. These include the inducement to cross subsidize, the incentive to denigrate basic service, and the stifling effect on experimentation with new price and service innovations in the residual monopoly markets. Some question can also be raised as to whether the productivity offset will be a sufficient stimulus to innovation and efficiency. The British Telecom experience casts doubt on the simple belief that productivity must increase and that service will never be allowed to deteriorate [47]. In addition, one must include the negative effects associated with index-driven price increases that are independent of market conditions. There is ample evidence in the natural gas industry of the disastrous effects of inflation-indexed price adjustments that drove up gas prices in the face of an oversupply of gas. The same demand/supply imbalance could arise in telecommunications — except that the burden would fall primarily on monopolistic services.

The ability of price caps to constrain cross subsidization and price discrimination can be challenged. A ceiling on prices will do very little to prevent discrimination within and between markets at prices that are below established ceilings. This problem will be aggravated whenever broad service categories are used, such as the FCC proposal to cap only two baskets (switched services and private line services). Yet even with properly defined services, the problem of cross subsidization can still arise when demand growth, scale effects, and advances in technology lower costs faster than the productivity offset. In such cases, monopoly markets will participate less in the gains than markets perceived to be demand elastic and competitive. The latter will benefit from price reductions and promotional marketing; the former will bear the burden of inflationary increases minus any average productivity offset.

From the standpoint of constraining anticompetitive pricing strategies, price caps contribute very little. They provide no insight into the status of competition in specific markets, the anticompetitive bundling of services, tie-in sales, appropriate cost standards for minimum prices, proper constraints on cross subsidization, or the ability of the firm to manipulate joint and common costs. In short, price caps fail to come to grips with many of the issues associated with the barriers to competition previously described.

Proponents of price caps argue that caps will curtail extortionist pricing while providing new incentives to lower the general level of prices. A study made in 1987 by the Federal Trade Commission purports to show that states with price caps have lower intrastate toll rates than those without them [48]. A Bellcore Study (1988), prepared to endorse the

FCC's NOPR on price caps, allegedly demonstrates that switched access prices would have been 1% lower if price caps had been in place since 1984 [49]. Both studies are adversarial submissions seeking to provide support for the Reagan Administration's position. Clearly, it remains to be demonstrated that price caps are neutral with respect to equity and income distribution.

In fact, it can be argued that price caps contain features that will bias income distribution against monopoly/basic service customers. For example, if actual FBC costs fall more than the productivity offset, then these savings will accrue to demand elastic/competitive markets through price reductions or to shareholders through higher profits. Similarly, if price caps are too high, then excessive profits will be recovered from monopoly markets and either paid to shareholders or dissipated through under-pricing in competitive markets. Under a price cap regime, there would typically be no hard and fast determination of the appropriate level of earnings, and no formal mechanism to recapture profits perceived to be too high. Further, if there were a significant drop in a cost-of-service component omitted from the price cap formula, the firm would receive a windfall profit. On balance, it is not difficult to understand why firms enjoying current or prospective high levels of profit from market growth and technological advance would support the price cap concept [50]. It is also questionable whether such profits will provide a strong stimulus for improving efficiency and lowering prices for basic service.

Finally, the question can be raised whether price caps constitute a step toward greater administrative simplicity. There are so many debatable features that it is difficult to see how the concept can gain broad acceptance or provide adequate answers to the problems emerging in the telecommunications industry. Fundamental points involve the selection of an appropriate measure of inflation and a productivity offset. Using the CPI or PPI or a general level of productivity has no substantive or theoretical merit. It can only be justified on grounds of expedience or simplicity. Indeed, applying such general indices to highly dynamic industries, such as telecommunications, can be a most abusive form of averaging. All that can be stated with certainty is that there will be continuous debate over the selection of proper indices. Price caps, in practice, may be the most ambiguous regulatory tool since fair value.

Price caps will not reduce regulatory agency work loads, the burden of litigation, or the need to resolve conflicting arguments. There will be demands for comprehensive investigations and cost studies to set initial rates, demands for full hearings every time a cap is changed, and full reporting requirements to monitor changes. Furthermore, reports of poor

quality of service, excessive profits, price discrimination, or low productivity will lead to efforts at greater refinement which, in turn, will move
toward comprehensive rate-base regulation. This may be the scenario for
British intervention if future price caps have to be adjusted for inadequate service, narrower market baskets, excessive rates of return, and a
more appropriate index of inflation. It would be ironic if Great Britain
should move toward the U.S. model at the same time that the U.S. is
moving to adopt a variant of the initial British approach [51].

In summary, price caps, as usually proposed, do not hold the promise
of either correcting fundamental flaws in RBROR regulation or of providing a superior option for dealing with the host of new problems in
the telecommunications industry. Essentially, the concept, like the social
contract, does little more than revisit all of the shortcomings associated
with franchise regulation at the turn of the century.

Options for Controlling Cross Subsidization

Corporate strategies for achieving market dominance through cross subsidization have grown as the incumbent firms feel increasingly threatened.
But the growth of the problem has not been matched by parallel progress
toward a workable solution. The FCC has struggled with cross subsidization since 1964, when the original Seven-Way Cost Study was made. In
successive efforts, the Commission adopted an ex post fully distributed
cost (FDC) approach, an ex ante FDC approach, then a highly simpli-
fied three-way fully distributed cost manual based on historical usage
patterns. Along the way, the Commission rejected AT&T's burden test
but accepted (at least tentatively) AT&T's net revenue test — which was
even less rigorous. To prevent cross subsidization between regulated and
nonregulated services, the FCC at first adopted separate subsidiaries,
then rejected them for the FDC methodology embodied in Part 64.

The development of some reasonably acceptable methodology for
controlling cross subsidization is going to be a prerequisite for either
partial deregulation or a major strengthening of regulation.

Academic economists have proposed a conceptual framework for
defining and controlling cross subsidization. The conventional wisdom
argues that there is no cross subsidization if the maximum price for a
service does not exceed its stand-alone cost and the minimum price for a
service is not less than its incremental cost [52]. Stand-alone cost is an
estimate of the cost of a single-purpose system designed to serve a specific
market or provide a particular service. It is typically applied to a residual

monopoly service. Incremental cost is typically defined as the additional cost in plant, labor, and materials to add or expand a service. It is applied to competitive services. Proponents of this position argue that elaborate cost studies are unnecessary because conscious cross subsidization (i.e., prices greater than stand-alone costs) would be reflected either in excess profits or sales at prices below incremental costs.

There are significant problems with this approach. First, if prices are set to cover stand-alone costs in the monopoly market, then consumers in this market will be denied all economies of joint production and scope. Second, the concept creates a strong incentive to assign all economies of joint production and scope to competitive services, and while such an allocation may not constitute cross subsidization as defined by proponents, it does create an incentive to shift gains from one class to customer to another. Third, the concept disregards the historical fact that none of the services would have been produced exclusively on a stand-alone basis. Fourth, incremental cost is not a precise term, and it becomes particularly arbitrary when it involves the assignments of common plant, thereby facilitating limit entry pricing. Fifth, the argument that cross subsidization can be detected either by excessive profits or by sales below incremental cost is unrealistic because excess profits can be camouflaged and incremental cost is far from precise. It should also be noted in passing that if price caps are applied, then the regulatory agency will, by definition, be barred from passing judgment on what constitutes excess profits.

There have been a number of efforts by W. Bolter, Richard and David Gabel, M. Jamison, and W. Melody to rehabilitate the stand-alone concept. Bolter has attempted to estimate the stand-alone cost for a number of local exchange services [53]. These stand-alone costs have then been used to allocate common costs between various local exchange offerings. Bolter estimates the stand-alone investment on the assumption that exchange, intra-exchange, and interstate toll services would be offered separately and then he allocates the savings from joint production in proportion to the stand-alone investment. He states that the objective of stand-alone methodology is to distribute the benefits of joint development "in an equitable manner by assigning them to each service in direct proportion to the costs that the services would incur operating independently" [54]. What distinguishes Bolter, et al., is the belief that the stand-alone approach is a step in the process of allocating common and joint costs rather than an end result in and of itself.

A significant improvement in the allocation process could be made with the adoption of the alternative justifiable expenditures theory as developed by Martin G. Glaeser and applied by the Tennessee Valley

Authority. This model proceeds as follows:

Assume two services, A and B
1. Estimate total cost of providing both A and B from a common operation
   – Direct Cost of A
   <u>– Direct Cost of B</u>
   Common/Joint Cost to be Allocated
2. Stand-Alone Cost of A
   <u>– Direct Cost of A</u>
   Benefits from Joint Development Accruing to A
   Repeat for B.
3. Allocate common/joint costs on the basis of the relative benefits accruing to A and B from joint development.
4. A pays direct cost of A plus allocation developed above. Repeat for B.

The Glaeser model has a number of important advantages. It recognizes that a service is typically offered in a setting where it can realize economies of joint development, and it assigns common and joint costs in direct proportion to these benefits. It also reflects cost causation and marks a step in the direction of a cost-of-service price ceiling that can curb cross subsidization.

Critics could argue that the Glaeser model is vulnerable when services or customer classes cannot be defined with sufficient specificity to permit direct and stand-alone costs to be identified. But this argument is fallacious. If services or customer classes cannot be identified or segmented, it follows logically that they are not candidates for exploitative pricing or cross subsidization. Of course, the model is also vulnerable to the wearisome criticism that it involves an arbitrary allocation of common costs. However, this approach does have a consistent rationale. To the extent that the spread between stand-alone and direct costs is great, the benefiting service is asked to pay a larger relative portion of common costs. To the extent that the spread is minimal, then the service is assigned little or no common cost. Further, it must be emphasized that any costing process, once it goes beyond short-run marginal cost, can be accused of being arbitrary [55]. Even the estimation of the stand-alone cost of a single service for purposes of establishing a price ceiling implicitly assigns common costs when it denies economies of scope to that service.

A Positive Program for Reform

An alternative to the deregulation/relaxed regulation syndrome would involve taking a holistic view of the task of public control of enterprise in the context of emerging industry structures. The general elements would involve 1) examination of each of the major telecommunications markets or services to determine the degree of market power and concentration (the Landes-Posner measure of monopoly is preferred since it incorporates market concentration, entry, and demand elasticity); 2) estimation of MEMS for major FBC services with adequate allowances for future growth in demand and adjustments to reflect the importance of load and diversity factors; 3) use of the Glaeser model to isolate direct costs and allocate common/joint costs by major services; 4) application of the divisional cost of capital (whether calculated by pure play or accounting betas) to estimate the rate of return by service; and 5) estimation of operating expenses. For a monopoly service, the regulator would then have the basis for computing the relevant revenue requirement (i.e., allocated rate base plus associated rate of return plus assigned expenses). From this information, a reasonable cost-of-service rate ceiling could be derived for each monopoly service. To provide a stimulus for experimentation, a system of incentives and penalties for monopoly services could be developed. For example, performance ranges could be introduced and tied to the divisional return on equity. With this overall approach to controlling cross subsidization and identifying risk and return by service, the firm could be given considerable pricing latitude in competitive markets, freedom to initiate new services and product lines, and relaxed limits on total firm earnings.

This type of reform seeks to retain the best features of rate-base regulation while recognizing the growth of competition. It will also change in response to any realignment of the mix of monopoly and competitive markets. However, specific problems such as adequate service for low-income consumers or conscious predation will still have to be handled on a case-by-case basis.

Establishing pricing guidelines for access to the LEC will also become a pivotal part of regulatory reform since this phase of telecommunications will remain a monopoly focal point. Access charges must compensate the BOCs and independent LECs for services provided, be neutral with respect to rival IXCs, and promote efficiency/equity objectives. At present, traffic sensitive plant, such as switching equipment, is allocated to the IXCs on the basis of usage, and nontraffic sensitive plant, such as the local loop, is apportioned between the IXC (through a carrier common line charge) and the end user (through a flat monthly subscriber line charge). A heated debate has raged since divestiture over the apportionment of NTS costs. One faction argues that the cost of access is a separate identifiable incremental cost that should be levied directly against the end user as a charge for the ability to place and receive calls. It is further argued that all costs of access are NTS and should be recovered through a fixed customer monthly charge. An opposing faction argues that access is essentially an input and should be priced on the basis of the relative use of local plant by individual services. Accordingly, recovery of access costs should be based on usage rather than on a flat charge. Proponents of this view hold that imposing access fees on the IXCs will accomplish this objective, and at the same time permit the assignment of access costs to individual services on a cost-causation basis reflecting the fact that enhanced data services require more sophisticated access facilities than local telephone service.

Regulatory reform will have to resolve this debate. It seems reasonable that access costs should be assessed as a flat monthly charge against the end user whenever 1) the charge is customer specific (i.e., adding or subtracting a customer affects the cost in direct proportion); 2) an access line is used exclusively by a given customer; 3) the cost of the line is unrelated to the volume of use within the line's capacity; and 4) the cost per access line is independent of the design of the total distribution network. However, if access costs are affected by the time of use, volume of use, and type of use, then they are an integral part of the transmission-distribution plant and should be priced on a usage basis reflecting peak/off-peak, cost-causation criteria. Improper treatment of access costs could bias plant design in favor of a cost configuration that can be shifted more readily to demand inelastic end users.

The cumulative impact of these reforms on performance could be substantial. Management would have a clear understanding of the working rules within which it must operate. Limits would be placed on the extent to which monopoly markets could be exploited. Risks and rewards derived from competitive markets would be borne by shareholders. Incentives and penalties would impact performance in monopoly markets, and, interestingly, one of the few uncompensated benefits would accrue to monopoly customers whenever successful diversification projects had a large spread between stand-alone and direct costs because the expanded activities would bear an increasing proportion of common and joint costs.

This set of reforms seems preferable to an artificial system of indexed price caps, conjectural productivity offsets, or a retreat from regulation in the hope that unfettered competition will somehow emerge.

Appendix

MCI Revenue, Expenses, Earnings ($ Millions).

	1987	1986	1985	1984	1983	1982
Revenues from Sale of Communication Services	$3,939	3,592	2,542	1,959	1,521	907
Local Interconnection (Access Charges)	1,963	1,636	874	480	262	143
Sales, Marketing, Operations, General Expenses	1,107	1,097	835	696	487	308
Facilities leased from other carriers	163	267	280	343	274	104
Depreciation	471	451	343	265	159	89
Operating Income (before interest & payment of income taxes)	235*	(444)	52	125	340	262
Net Income	88	(448)	113	59	203	151

* Estimated return on *net* rate base for 1987

$235 ÷ 5,284 = 4.5%

Asset write down of $585 in 1986.
Source: MCI annual reports and MCI analytical abstracts.

References

1. For a discussion of the early rise and fall of competition, see Trebing, H. M. "A Critique of Structure Regulation in Common Carrier Telecommunications." *Telecommunications Regulation Today and Tomorrow*, edited by E. M. Noam. New York: Harcourt Brace Jovanovich, 1983, 127–134.

2. For an analysis of microwave scale economies, see Waverman, Leonard. "The Regulation of Intercity Telecommunications." *Promoting Competition in Regulated Markets*, edited by A. Phillips. Washington, D.C.: Brookings Institution, 1975, p. 221.

3. *Allocation of Frequencies Above 890 Mc.* Report and Order, 27 FCC 359 (1959).

4. *Microwave Communications, Inc.* Decision, 18 FCC 2d 953 (1969).

5. *Specialized Common Carrier Services*. First Report and Order, 29 FCC 2d 870 (1971).

6. Foreign exchange service was originally offered by AT&T. It provides a dedicated private line from a customer's premises to an interexchange switchboard and finally a local line to complete the connection. As adapted by MCI, it permitted an Execunet customer to dial MCI's local number, gain access to MCI's long-distance circuits, and then dial directly any number in another city.

7. In Execunet I, the Court of Appeals held that the FCC could not exclude MCI and other competitors from the interstate MTS market without determining that the public interest would be served by establishing AT&T as a monopoly in that market. See *MCI Telecommunications Corp. v. FCC*, 561 F. 2d 365 (D.C. Cir.), *cert. denied*, 434 U.S. 1040 (1977). For Execunet II, see *MCI Telecommunications Corp. v. FCC*, 580 F. 2d 590 (D.C. Cir.), *cert. denied*, 439 U.S. 980 (1978).

8. *Regulatory & Policy Problems Presented by the Interdependence of Computer & Communications Services & Facilities*, 28 FCC 2d 267 (1971).

9. *Second Computer Inquiry*, 77 FCC 2d 384 (1980).

10. For FCC actions, see 35 FCC 2d 539 (1972); 56 FCC 2d 593 (1975). Also, *North Carolina Utilities Commission v. FCC*, 552 F 2d 1036 (4th Cir.), *cert. denied*, 434 U.S. 874 (1977).

11. U.S. District Court for the District of Columbia, *U.S. v. American Telephone and Telegraph Co.; Western Electric Co., Inc., and Bell Telephone Laboratories, Inc.*, Civil Action Nos. 74–1698, 82–0192, and 82–0025. Final judgment entered August 24, 1982.

12. Judge Greene retained restrictions prohibiting BOC entry into the interexchange/interLATA markets as well as prohibiting BOC/RBHC entry into the manufacturing of CPE, network, and central office equipment. See first triennial review of the Modification of Final Judgment, U.S. v. Western Electric Co. et al., Civil Action No. 82–0192, *Opinion*, dated September 10, 1987.

13. FCC, Docket No. 85–229, *Report and Order*, June 16, 1986.

14. By the end of 1987, US Sprint had an approximate investment of $1.275 billion in fiber optics. AT&T's investment was $1.125 billion, and MCI's was $474 million. See Kraushaar, J. M. *Fiber Deployment Update, End of Year 1987*. Federal Communications Commission. January, 1988, table 2. However, AT&T had more route miles of fiber optics than US Sprint (19,000 vs. 17,000) and more fiber miles (456,000 vs. 323,000) in 1987. *Ibid.*, table 1.

15. For example, Mantell estimated AT&T's scale elasticity at 1.04 to 1.16 in 1974. See Mantell, L. *An Econometric Study of Returns to Scale in the Bell System*. Staff Research Paper. Office of Telecommunications Policy, Washington, 1974. Comparable results were obtained by L. Waverman and others in studying Bell Canada. See Trebing, op cit., pp. 136

and 169 for a futher discussion. Of course, all of these econometric studies predate the introduction of fiber optics networks.

16. Shepherd, W. G. " 'Contestability' vs. Competition." *American Economic Review.* 74 (September 1984): 572–87.

17. Shepherd, W. G. "General Conditions of Entry." *Regulation and Entry*, edited by M. W. Klass and W. G. Shepherd. East Lansing: MSU Public Utilities Papers, 1976, pp. 35–60, esp. pp. 48–50.

18. Porter, M. E. *Competition in the Long Distance Telecommunications Market: An Industry Structure Analysis*. Monitor Company, Inc., 1987. Submitted as Appendix A to comments of AT&T before the FCC in CC Docket No. 87–313, October 19, 1987, p. 3.

19. The Huber Report estimated AT&T's market share in the interexchange, inter-LATA market at 80%–85% on the basis of revenues and 84% on the basis of toll minutes for 1985, MCI's share at 5%–8% and 8%, and US Sprint's share at 4% and 3.5% for the same year. See: Huber, P. W. *The Geodesic Network, 1987 Report on Competition in the Telephone Industry*. Washington, D.C.: U.S. Government Printing Office, January 2, 1987, p. 3.3. The FCC estimated AT&T's share of the switched, interstate market at 70%–72% for 1987 based on total switched access minutes, and 73%–77% based on premium (equal access) switched access minutes. The FCC estimate includes conventional long-distance calls and WATS-type calls. It excludes private-line calls and closed end WATS calls. See FCC, *AT&T's Share of the Interstate Switched Market, Fourth Quarter, 1987*. Washington, D.C., March 21, 1988, at table 3. There are no current data on market shares in the private-line market, but between 1968 and 1980, AT&T's share of the intercity private-line market revenues actually increased from 81% to 85% reflecting a decline in the share of Western Union. The specialized carriers' share increased from 0% to 4%. See Trebing, op. cit., p. 140.

20. See Huber Report, op. cit., p 3.5. IntraLATA, interexchange switched traffic accounts for about 30% of all switched toll traffic and about 25% of all switched toll revenues.

21. See FCC, *Trends in the International Communications Industry 1975–1986*. Washington, D.C., December 1987, table 4. Interestingly, AT&T's share of all overseas communications revenues (voice, record, etc.) has actually grown from 58.7% in 1975 to 72.8% in 1986.

22. See Montgomery, W. P., L. L. Selwyn, and S. M. Baldwin. *Analysis of Local Exchange Carrier April, 1988 Bypass Data Submissions*. Boston: Economics and Technology Inc. August 24, 1988, esp. pp. 1–7 and tables 1, 6, and 7.

23. Statement of L. Prendergast, AT&T Corporate Vice-President and Treasurer, at a shareholders meeting in Columbus, Ohio. Prendergast also reported that AT&T has retained 80% of the long-distance market. *UPI Wire*, 5/18/88.

24. See "Western Union Sets $603 Million Charge to Leave Long-Distance Phone Business." *Wall Street Journal*. May 24, 1988, p. 2.

25. See Porter, op. cit., figures 23 and 24.

26. Ibid., figure 22.

27. The Canadian Department of Communications uses the same classification, referring to Type 1 facilities-based carriers and Type 2 enhanced services.

28. See Porter, op. cit., figure 80.

29. Ibid., figure 81.

30. Pryor, T., and C. Weaver. "The Future of Competition in the Telecommunications Industry." *Public Utilities Fortnightly*. March 5, 1987, pp. 28–32.

31. Huber Report, op. cit., p. 2.20.

32. L. L. Selwyn and Associates. *Telecommunications Competition in Michigan and Regulatory Alternatives, Volume I: Market Structure and Competition in the Michigan Telecommunications Industry.* A Report to the Michigan Divestiture Research Fund Board, Boston: Economics and Technology, Inc., April 1988.

33. See: Scherer, F. M. *Industrial Market Structure and Economic Performance.* Chicago: Rand McNally, 1980, p. 91. Also, S. C. Salop. "Measuring Ease of Entry." *The Antitrust Bulletin.* 31 (Summer 1986): 551.

34. Porter, op. cit., figure 41.

35. Ibid., figure 67.

36. Ibid., figures 42 and 68.

37. Huber Report, op. cit., pp. 3.10 to 3.11.

38. "MCI Eases Its Position on Deregulation of AT&T, Signaling Major Policy Shift." *Wall Street Journal.* March 1987, p. 7. Of course, MCI and US Sprint will continue to be protected in interexchange, interLATA markets as long as the BOCs are prohibited from providing interLATA service. Denying BOC entry will serve to reinforce AT&T's role as a price leader.

39. Some insight into deregulated price leadership and interdependence may be obtained by examining Virginia's intrastate, interLATA toll market, which was deregulated in 1984. Approximately 87% of all access lines had been converted to equal access as of December 1987. Beginning in early 1986, MCI's toll rates began to track, but remained below AT&T's rates, but after early 1987, MCI's rates became virtually identical with those of AT&T for daytime, evening, and night-weekend MTS. US Sprint's rates, on the other hand, remained below those of AT&T and MCI for evening and night service but higher for daytime service until the fourth quarter of 1987, at which time they also became identical to those of AT&T and MCI. The Virginia Commission staff noted ". . . There is effectively no price competition for MTS between the 'Big Three' in Virginia." Measured in calls, AT&T has 77% of the market, MCI 15%, and US Sprint 6%. These rate and market-share patterns do not include IXC large-scale promotional rates, private line rates, or custom services. Virginia does not permit intraLATA competition. See Virginia State Corporation Commission. *The InterLATA Market in Virginia, 4th Quarter, 1987.* July 1, 1988. Evidence of intrastate price leadership was also found in Iowa. See Murphy, J. W. *The Demand for Message Toll Service: An Empirical Analysis of Iowa, 1985–1986.* Iowa State Utilities Board, INU-86-4, June 1988, p. 33.

40. See Maine's proposal to utilize competitive bidding to ensure that additions and replacements to the interexchange network will be provided at the lowest possible cost. *Proposed Rulemaking on the Provision of Competitive Telecommunications Services.* Maine Public Utilities Commission. Docket No. 87–31, February 18, 1988.

41. Averch, H., and L. Johnson. "Behavior of the Firm under Regulatory Constraint." *Amer. Econ. Rev.* 52 (December 1962):1053–1069. The real-world shortcoming of RBROR may not have been its tendency to distort inputs, as the A-J model suggests, but rather its inability to compel innovation and the retirement of obsolete plant. Since divestiture, ". . . AT&T has taken a total of $13.4 billion in pretax charges to account for write-downs of obsolete long-distance facilities and telephone products and for factory consolidations, inventory adjustments, layoffs and accounting changes." A further write-off or accelerated depreciation of $4–5 billion is contemplated as AT&T converts its domestic, switched traffic entirely to digital transmission by late 1990. See J. Guyon. "AT&T's Third-Quarter Net Rose 17%; $5 Billion Write-Off Possible for Year." *Wall Street Journal.* October 21, 1988, p. A-2. One can question whether these steps would have been taken under FCC application of RBROR.

42. There are significant doubts about the private benefits from financial synergism due to conglomerate diversification. See Trebing, H. M. "The Impact of Diversification on Economic Regulation." *J. Econ. Issues*. 19 (June 1985): 463–474.

43. In 1988, AT&T asked the FCC for a declaratory ruling applying the net revenue test to customized Tariff 12 offerings. The Commission had already accepted this test in Docket 84–1235 for optional calling plans. One can assume that this residual approach to pricing (i.e., new services cover incremental cost while residual services cover the balance of the revenue requirement) will result in higher monopoly prices, but its proponents argue that it could result in lower prices than would otherwise be possible. In either case, residual pricing would not be possible if intense competition existed in every market.

44. For a more detailed discussion of local exchange costing and residual pricing, see Public Utility Commission of Ohio. *Addendum to Staff Report of Investigation, In the Matter of the Application of GTE North, Inc. for an Increase in Rates and Charges*. Case No. 87–1307-TP-AIR, p. 6–24. This addendum was prepared by Walter Bolter (hereafter referred to as Bolter Report).

45. See FCC. *In the Matter of Policy and Rules Concerning Rates for Dominant Carriers*. CC Docket No. 87–313, Notice of Proposed Rulemaking, August 21, 1987. Also see the revised Further Notice of Proposed Rulemaking, May 23, 1988.

46. Ballen, K. "Report Card on the Baby Bells." *Fortune*. June 20, 1988, pp. 88, 93.

47. The British price cap based on RPI-3% was applied to British Telecom in 1984. From 1984 through 1987, there was no productivity gain in the local network and there have been frequent complaints about the poor quality of service. See Director General of Telecommunications, Office of Telecommunications. *The Regulation of British Telecom's Prices, A Consultative Document*. January 1988, pp. 9 and 10.

48. Mathios, A., and R. P. Rogers. *The Impact of Alternative Forms of State Regulation of AT&T on Direct Dial Long Distance Telephone Rates*. Bureau of Economics, Federal Trade Commission, Working Paper Series No. 159, December 1987.

49. *The Impact of Federal Price Cap Regulation on Interstate Toll Customers*. Prepared by Bellcore, March 17, 1988 (mimeographed).

50. AT&T has proposed a form of flexible regulation that would approximate price caps in Indiana. The staff report of the Indiana Commission discloses that AT&T intrastate operations in Indiana (intrastate toll) earned a rate of return of 32% after operating taxes in 1987. A decline in intrastate access and billing expense was an important contributor to this level of return. See Pilalis, L. E. "Observations on the Joint Submission of U.S. Sprint, MCI and AT&T communications of Indiana of a Settlement Agreement." *Staff Report*. Indiana Utility Regulatory Commission, Case Nos. 37557, 37559, 37911, June 23, 1988, p. 8.

51. In the initial 1988 report (see Footnote 47, *supra*), the Director General of Telecommunications invited comments about the feasibility of incorporating targets for productivity and quality of service into the British Telecom price caps. He also invited comments on the need to redefine market baskets and the proper treatment of profits and the cost of capital. In the final *Statement*, the Director General tightened the control from "RPI-3" to "RPI-4½" with a freeze on price increases until August 1989. The new rule would last four years. No targets for quality of service were introduced, but some refinements were made in the market baskets and an extensive discussion of the interrelationship between price caps and the rate of return was included in the *Statement*. He concluded: ". . . I believe that a price-cap should be chosen on the criterion that it is likely to produce a trend in rate of return that brings rate of return to a satisfactory level for the risk of the business concerned, allowing for some time to be taken about the process so that the benefits of efficiency can be retained for a reasonable period." In effect, the price cap should be set to yield a "reason-

able" rate of return (including earnings growth and the cost of debt) together with a regulatory lag as an incentive for efficiency. The door was kept open for future revisions. See Director General of Telecommunications. *The Control of British Telecom's Prices*. London: July 7, 1988.

52. For a further discussion, see Baumol, W. J. "Minimum and Maximum Pricing Principles for Residual Regulation." *Current Issues in Public-Utility Economics*, edited by A. L. Danielson and D. R. Kamerschen. Lexington, Mass.: D.C. Heath, 1983, 177–196.

53. Bolter Report, op. cit., pp. 22.

54. Ibid., p. 27.

55. For example, long-run incremental costs can be defined narrowly as the avoided cost no longer incurred when a specific service is dropped; or incremental cost could be defined to include a share of common plant needed to expand the service. So-called full incremental cost goes even further to include the additional cost associated with all similar services that use some or all of the major items of telephone plant in common.

The alternative justifiable expenditures model was developed by Martin G. Glaeser to allocate joint costs on dams of the Tennessee Valley Authority. The assignment of costs was necessary to estimate revenue requirements for reimbursable (e.g., power) and nonreimbursable (e.g., flood control) functions. This method was reviewed and approved by Congress. For a detailed discussion, see Clemens, E. W. *Economics and Public Utilities*. Appleton-Century-Crofts, 1950, pp. 619–622.

Commentary by Basil L. Copeland, Jr.

Professor Trebing has written a stimulating and provocative précis of the regulatory dilemma arising out of the rapid rate of technological change in telecommunications. I've always been impressed with Professor Trebing's ability to distill and synthesize material from a variety of sources. But he does more than merely synthesize the work of others. He invariably stamps it with his own insight and observation, and usually in a way that cautions us from a too-easy acceptance of the latest fad in the economics of regulation. He has done it again here, in his cautionary tale of two theories, the theory of unfettered markets on the one hand (or whatever you want to call the theory of "contestable markets"), and the theory of the regulated firm on the other.

It would serve the reader no purpose at all for me to simply offer my own synopsis of Professor Trebing's paper. The paper speaks for itself, and deserves to be read for the breadth and depth of the analysis that it contains. I would rather direct my comments toward illustrating some of the provocative insights I derived from the paper, in the hopes that the readers might be stimulated to approach the paper with the hope of discovering for themselves that there is still much to be said and learned about the policy implications of technological change in telecommunications.

Many will pick up on Professor Trebing's attempt to articulate a "revised theory of the regulated firm." This is no doubt his concession to neoclassical orthodoxy, which has long considered the A-J hypothesis to be the accepted model of the regulated firm. I've never been a strong advocate of the A-J model. While it offers *one* rationale for why regulated firms overinvest, I've never been persuaded that it is the only rationale, or even the most likely. But that is beside the point. What Professor Trebing argues is that even *if* one accepts the A-J model as a starting point, it quickly loses its appeal as an explanation of the behavior of regulated firms, which operate in segregated markets, where the demand for its products or services is monopolistic in some markets and subject to competitive forces in others. Professor Trebing offers as a revised theory, a picture of regulated firm behavior that exploits the differences in monopolistic and competitive markets by engaging in price discrimination and cross subsidization. Actually, there is nothing particularly new or novel about any of this. The picture of firm behavior that Professor Trebing paints is one that could be drawn with the broad brush of neoclassical price theory for any *unregulated* firm that simultaneously operates in markets that can be segregated along monopolistic and competitive lines. In other words, it is not so much a revised theory of the regulated firm as it is the conventional theory of the unregulated firm applied to a firm that ought to be regulated but isn't. Even orthodox neoclassical price theory will predict adverse and anticompetitive behavior under the conditions demonstrated by Professor Trebing to exist in current markets in telecommunications. The real question, then, is whether we retain the insights of the old price theory, or sacrifice them on the altar of the new "contestable markets" theory. Professor Trebing has done an able job in assessing the weaknesses of the contestable markets literature, and in calling attention to the fact that the older price theory may yet have a thing or two to say about the behavior of regulated firms operating in dual monopolistic/competitive markets.

If we reject the applicability of the contestable markets theory to the continuing problems of telecommunications regulation, which I think we must in all but a few trivial cases, then we have to confront head-on the problems of price discrimination and anticompetitive firm behavior that Professor Trebing so ably describes. How are we to do this? The current fad is to recommend the substitution of price caps for traditional rate-of-return/rate-base regulation. Professor Trebing does a good job of assessing the problems with this approach. It is doubtful that the substitution of price caps for the frustrations of cost allocation seriously represents a major social advance. Professor Trebing would thus encourage more effort in the development of adequate cost allocation procedures. He is well aware of the fact that cost allocation is not the solution normally favored by orthodox economic theory. That may be more a reflection of the inadequacies of orthodox economic theory than it is of Professor Trebing's analysis. Traditional theory has no theory of cost allocation: it is solely a theory of cost *recovery*. In the world of traditional economics, firms do not set prices, the market does. Thus cost allocation is always an "irrelevant" exercise. But since firms *do* set prices, as anyone but an economist knows, it is not surprising that economic theory has little to offer the regulator in the way of advice as to how to allocate costs between competitive and monopolistic markets.

Professor Trebing proposes a theory of cost allocation based upon Martin Glaeser's work for the Tennessee Valley Authority (TVA). It is certainly a proposal worth taking seriously. The economists of Glaeser's generation were far more sensitive to the importance of cost allocation, especially when considering the social and public policy implications of firm behavior. In addition to reconsidering Glaeser's approach, today's economists could learn a thing or two from John M. Clark's *The Social Control of Business* or his *Studies in the Economics of Overhead Costs*. At least Glaeser and Clark realized that cost allocation was inherent in any resolution of the problem of the social control of business when markets fail. It is not very helpful for economists to criticize cost allocation and recommend reliance upon market forces, when the need for it arises out of market failure to begin with. If they truly believe that all cost allocation is arbitrary, they no longer have anything to say to public policy-makers and regulators, and if they have nothing to say, then they ought to say nothing at all.

While I consider the Glaeser model worth serious consideration, there is another possibility that I think deserves equal consideration. Professor Trebing notes that one of the problems inherent in the firm that serves both monopolistic and competitive markets is the temptation to utilize the low cost of capital of the monopolistic or utility service to offset the higher cost of capital that would normally be associated with the services offered in a competitive, unregulated market. As a sometime financial economist and rate-of-return witness, I believe that the problem alluded to here is more intractable than perhaps even Professor Trebing realizes. The problem is not merely a differential cost of capital that can be exploited by the regulated firm. The problem is also that there are fundamental differences in capital requirements, and in the rational allocation of capital between reinvestment and payout, for firms operating in mature and immature markets. Firms that specialize in innovative technologies and new markets typically retain a high portion of their earnings and pay out very little in the way of dividends to investors. It can be easily demonstrated that systematic risk is a mathematical function of the earnings retention ratio: the higher the earnings retention (or reinvestment) rate, the more volatile the stock price. Investors in such securities forgo present income for a speculative, but potentially higher, future return. The rate of retention, and potential stock price appreciation, are a function of the potential growth of the final product market for the new product. If you have an innovative technology with significant (but speculative) growth prospects, it would make no sense at all for the firm to pay out a high portion of current earnings (if it has any!) in dividends, merely to have to turn around and sell new shares to raise the capital required to finance its growth. In other words, retention policy is far from arbitrary and can hardly be divorced from the intrinsic characteristics and opportunities of the final product market under consideration.

We have to turn these factors around when we look at monopolistic markets. By their very nature, they tend to be stable and mature. Since growth prospects are limited in relation to the total cost of equity capital, we tend (and expect) to find such firms retaining only a small fraction of total earnings, and paying out the rest to investors as current dividend income. When we compare monopolistic markets with competitive markets, we not only find that the cost of capital is higher in the latter, we find that the two markets call for very different approaches to the tradeoff between earnings retention and dividend payout. If we combine the two into one, the opportunities for exploitive behavior are even more severe than Professor Trebing might imagine. We not only have the problem of utility ratepayers being burdened with an average cost of capital that is higher because of the presence of high-risk unregulated ventures, we have the problem of cash flows from the utility operation, which should be paid out to investors as dividends being diverted as a source of capital for the unregulated venture. There is a significant potential here for resource misallocation because capital is being reallocated from a low-risk market to a high-risk market, not by the marketplace, but by the administrative decisions of utility managers. While it is true that the price of the utility stock should adjust to reflect the expected return of *whatever* bundle of investments management chooses to make, that is not the same thing as saying that the outcome is economically efficient. After all, the stock price of an unregulated monopolist would eventually be driven up to the point where the marginal investor receives no more than the cost of capital. That wouldn't make the allocation of resources any more efficient. Efficiency and equilibrium in capital markets does not insure efficiency and equilibrium in product markets if resource allocation in product markets is not subject to true competitive pressures.

I have long been a critic of utility expansion into unregulated or competitive markets. Not only does such expansion create numerous administrative difficulties, many of which are enumerated by Professor Trebing, I also think that it is inherently inefficient. If utility executives wish to be entrepreneurs or captains of industry, let them resign their utility posts and seek jobs elsewhere. The managerial tasks of a stable public utility are far different than the visionary requirements of a technological innovator. Entrepreneurs exist to create markets; public utilities exist to satisfy customer requirements in markets that already exist. That certain industries may go through a period of technological innovation before they mature to public utility status goes without saying. And some industries may evolve from public utility status to a more competitive market structure. But that is not what we are talking about here. We are talking here about the problems inherent in a multiproduct environment where one product (or bundle of products) represents a mature, monopolistic market, and the other product (or bundle of products) represents a competitive, and possibly innovative market. I am simply not convinced that it is possible to regulate such a firm. Since deregulation is out of the question (because the monopolistic side of the firm still begs to be regulated), I think that the best course to follow is to prohibit entry into competitive markets by firms that have a substantial presence in monopolistic markets.

In other words, if the cost allocation procedures recommended by Professor Trebing are objectionable, we could always eliminate the problem entirely by forbidding the regulated firm to operate in competitive, unregulated markets. I mean that suggestion to be taken seriously. I'm well aware of the immediate objection: What if there are economies of scope or of joint production? Doesn't this deprive society of these economies? Not necessarily. If there are economies of scope or joint production to be realized from the capacity required to serve monopoly markets, simply have the utility auction off the right to that output to the highest bidder. In other words, rather than have the utility compete directly in the final product market, simply permit it to auction off its "excess" capacity as an intermediate product to other suppliers in the unregulated market. If there is a truly competitive marketplace for these alternative services, there will be any number of participants in the market willing to bid for this capacity. The price they bid will be based upon their avoidable cost, making this a market-based method of arriving at something analogous to a true "stand-alone" cost test. The only problem that regulators will then face is that of allocating the "profits" from the sale of "excess" capacity. Like the problem of cost allocation, any proposal along this line is subject to the charge of arbitrariness. But I should think that regulators would prefer to be faced with the task of allocating profits, rather than costs. Even if there are incremental costs associated with the achievement of economies of scope or joint-production, these costs need not be allocated; the allocation would only involve revenues in excess of these costs.

I've obviously oversimplified the issue somewhat, but I've said enough to give the reader the general picture. What I hope the reader would do is take to heart Professor Trebing's critique of the present trend toward deregulation, or of the substitution of price caps for traditional rate-of-return regulation. There is no question that the presence of rapid technological change and the proliferation of new services at the periphery of a market that remains basically monopolistic places strong demands upon regulators and public decision makers. I think that Professor Trebing and I both agree that the solution is not necessarily less regulation, but more enlightened regulation. While the jury remains out on what regulatory reforms would truly make regulation more enlightened, Professor Trebing has ably demonstrated that the present infatuation with approaches that place more emphasis upon deregulation than upon enlightened regulation appears to promise more than it can deliver.

5 NATURAL GAS PIPELINES AND MONOPOLY

Curtis Cramer

The natural gas pipeline industry is no longer a protected natural monopoly. Regulation policy favors increased competition and open access
to the transportation network. Entry barriers to the commodity are not
sustainable with the emergence of an active spot market. Bypass of the
local distribution facilities by heavy users is occurring. With growing
competition, pipelines are seeking more flexible rates to keep major
customers on the system. Gas companies are shifting from a fully bundled
package of end-to-end services toward a multitude of services a la carte.
All the elements of vigorous competition seem to be in place. But this
Pollyannish view ignores the presence of significant economic factors that
support the continued social control of the industry. These factors are the
presence of a monopoly bottleneck transportation facility, decreasing
costs both short- and long-run, vertical integration, and the growing
incidence of pipeline mergers and acquisitions. The goal of this chapter is
to bring these two conflicting views into perspective. It is clear that the
problems of the natural gas industry must be evaluated from a broad
analytical approach. Accordingly, the paper will put forth 1) the historical
institutional practices that tie buyers and sellers in the industry; 2) the
emerging strategies of producers, pipelines, and distributors in a com-

petitive marketplace; 3) antitrust issues; 4) the "new" structure of the
industry; and 5) a recommendation for future public policy.

Structural and Institutional Practices

In 1978, Congress passed the Natural Gas Policy Act, which initiated a
program for phased deregulation of wellhead gas prices. In 1983, contract
carriage for the pipelines was advocated. In 1985, least cost purchasing
strategies were recommended for the distribution companies. Each of
these efforts, directed towards competition, conflicted with the industry
practice of tying together buyers and sellers through long-term contracts
both upstream and downstream from the pipelines. The upstream tie took
two forms: a "take or pay" provision, and a purchased gas pass through
to the end users of natural gas. Many gas field contracts, particularly
those negotiated during the supply shortages of the 1970s, included provisions that required the pipeline to pay for 75% or indeed 90% of a
property's gas deliverability, even if the pipeline chose not to take the gas
because of slack demands [1]. In essence, the producers holding take-or-
pay contracts could control their income by changing deliverability in the
field. The consequence of this institutional arrangement was that there
was no economic incentive for the producers to integrate towards the
transportation segment of the industry.

Further strengthening the ties upstream were the purchased gas adjustment clauses added by most transmission companies to their tariffs during
the 1970s [2]. These clauses allow a pipeline company to respond to inflating field prices by boosting rates to end users automatically, without
regulatory review. Both the take-or-pay provisions and the purchased gas
adjustment clauses ensured the transfer of risk to the downstream buyers.

In a vigorously competitive gas industry, there must be a balancing of
risk taking among the buyers and sellers in the transactions. The above
institutional arrangements shifted the risk of the economics of supply and
demand uncertainty to the transportation companies and ultimately their
customers. It is clear that these long-term contract provisions, binding
tightly buyers and sellers in order to artificially change the incidence of
risk, are incompatible with a competitive gas market. The shifting and
incidence of risk, is nothing more than a variation or form of cross subsidy. The concept of restraining any buyer and seller long-term is the anti-
thesis of competition. Stability, end-to-end business relationships, and
cross subsidies are results of regulation, not competition.

Equally significant to the structural practices of buyers and sellers in the industry is the downstream contract. When a pipeline company sells to a distributor of gas or another pipeline, located further down the transportation network, the tariff contains a minimum bill clause. This provision requires a minimum payment to the pipeline irrespective of the quantity of gas taken by the buyer. The quid pro quo is a pipeline's obligation to serve the negotiated contract demand stated in an agreement of service between the pipeline and buyer. The obligation to serve and the minimum bill provisions are other instances of how the industry has bound the buyer and seller into a long-term contract.

In a period of declining demand for natural gas, these minimum bill clauses become important. A competitive market would allow customers of the pipeline, faced with lower demand or cheaper alternative supplies, to respond by lowering their takes of gas. The minimum bill obligations are an obstacle to the functioning of a competitive market, in that, they lock-in the buyer and assure that the pipeline's throughout will be sold. In another view, the minimum bill arrangements put little pressure on the pipeline to get out from under the upstream, high cost, take-or-pay contracts with producers [3].

These rigid institutional arrangements that lock-in buyers and sellers through long-term contracts both upstream and downstream are the vision of regulation. Competition and deregulation reject these long-term contracts. Perhaps the issue can be best seen by a further examination of the minimum bill debate.

The minimum bill protected pipelines from the risk of market loss due to excessive field prices and thereby kept gas prices above a market-clearing competitive level. Conversely, removing minimum bills places the risk of demand uncertainty on the pipeline and thereby gives the pipeline a strong incentive to keep the price of gas low. Further, the pipeline's customers, relieved of minimum bill obligations, could pursue a strategy of purchasing gas from the lowest-priced pipeline, leading to increased competition among pipelines.

The minimum bill provision creates a significant rate shock for residential and small commercial users. Because the minimum bill protects the inflated field cost of natural gas, large industrial and commercial users switch to alternative fuels. The result is that pipeline fixed costs must be recovered from the customers remaining. These are mainly small users. Worse still, most minimum bill provisions do not allow the customer to make up the gas in a later period and so there is a strong possibility that the pipeline will over-recover its costs [4].

The rationale for a minimum bill provision was long-standing in the industry. The pipeline, burdened by upstream institutional supply arrangements, sought to shift the risk downstream. The only way this was possible was to sell distribution companies on the need for an agency contract with the pipeline. The pipeline was to act on behalf of the distribution company by finding an assured source of supply and then transporting that supply to meet their needs irrespective of the possible demand uncertainties and variations. The pipeline was more than a transporter of gas, it performed the merchant function for the distribution companies. In addition a very significant obligation to serve was undertaken. The minimum bill was the reward for some pipeline serving as the supplier of last resort.

On May 25, 1984, the Federal Energy Regulatory Commission adopted a rule that prohibits the use of a minimum bill provision to recover variable costs that are not actually incurred by the pipeline [5]. The effect of this rule is that nonincurred purchased gas costs may not be recovered through a minimum bill. Significantly, take-or-pay payments by pipelines would not be made up. Removing minimum bills places the risk of market loss on the pipeline. Finally, the rule clearly gives pipeline customers much greater flexibility to cut back on gas purchases or shift purchases to other pipelines.

The incomplete part of the regulatory revolution concerns the obligation-to-supply standard. It should be obvious that all the downstream ties between buyers and sellers must be broken down in a competitive marketplace. If regulation is going to remove the minimum bill provisions, then, the regulatory authorities should release pipelines from their obligation to serve. Of course this does not rule out a customer choosing a premium service from the pipeline for an assured supply obligation. Rejecting the obligation-to-supply standard prevents the following circumstance from taking place. If a shortage were to occur, a full-requirement captive customer, who had been buying its full contract quantity, could be forced into a pro rata curtailment by a partial requirements customer who had essentially left the system because of a temporary lower cost supply. The partial requirement customer could return to preempt part of the captive customer's gas [6].

To foster competition in the industry is to look to a more transportation like answer. The natural gas pipeline takes on the characteristics of common or contract carriage. The pipeline phase of the industry will be similar to other traditional transportation industries.

To conclude this section, the institutional practices that tied buyers and sellers into long-term contracts and prevented competition in the industry were four contract provisions: purchased gas automatic adjustment clauses, take-or-pay requirements, minimum bill obligations, and the mandate to serve as the supplier of last resort. End-to-end service and integrated business relationships, fostered by regulatory approval, conflict with a competitive segmented industry. The ties that bind buyers and sellers are now burdensome.

Emerging Strategies of Producers, Pipelines and Distributors

The Distribution Companies

The distribution companies, facing the pressures of competition, are beginning to identify their core customers. These core customers exhibit the highest inelasticity. It is in this area that supply security is most important. Supply security arrangements have two aspects. There are the obligations to serve the variations of demand of the customer and the customer's agreement to take a certain volume of natural gas. As competition deepens, the customer's commitment to the distribution company is what will drive the public utility's purchases of pipeline gas. The merchant function performed by the pipeline will be confined only to those distribution companies that maintain a large central core of inelastic customers. It can be clearly seen that any distribution company, that places the emphasis of its purchased gas strategies on long-term gas supply commitments from the pipeline, will not be ready for the new competitive era. How much and how long the institutional arrangements of adjustment clauses, take-or-pay obligations, and minimum bill will survive depends upon the distribution companies response to competition.

The major thesis of this discussion is that the purchase and sale of gas does not represent the characteristics of natural monopoly. The only place where the natural monopoly argument might be raised is on the purchase side. Great purchase volumes may give the utilities a bargaining advantage in dealing with producers. Such economies of scale would give the utilities a competitive advantage over direct purchases by end-users. This would allow the utilities to hold their lower-value sales markets. However, for this to happen, entry to the scale advantage must be difficult. This is not the case. Many interstate pipelines have set up marketing affiliates in competition for the purchase volumes. In addition, independent marketers are rapidly entering the business of buying gas for end users. By combining with numerous customers, these marketers exploit their own economies of scale and perhaps are advantaged by greater diversities of demand [7].

The critical economic strategy for the distribution company enters from the side of access to and duplication of transportation facilities. The local distribution company faces the increased ability of an end user to take service directly from an interstate pipeline and bypass their facilities.

Bypass of the local distribution company has the potential to significantly alter the structure of the industry and the conduct of the end users. First, the cross-subsidies, which a customer employing bypass may have provided, are lost. Only by the elimination of subsidies can we be assured that the local distribution network will capture service areas where it is the most efficient provider. Rate design will have to become more cost based and offered on an unbundled basis. To maintain a large industrial user on the distribution system, the rates may have to be reduced to incremental costs. Rates to smaller, inelastic customers will have to be increased. Cost responsibility (peak load) will be shifted more to those that cause it. Energy decision making, based on improved price signals, will be more efficient.

It is clear that, as deregulation occurs and bypass grows, the protection of the local distribution company's market is substantially lessened. The regulatory answer is not for the state to prohibit bypass. This will cause industrial customers to be locked into high energy costs. As a result they could be at a competitive disadvantage relative to industries in other states. The study of direct industrial sales contracts of pipeline has shown that buyers care more about equal treatment with their competitors than about the price of natural gas [8]. In the gas industry, industrial customers are driven by an equal treatment standard so as not to be placed at a competitive disadvantage. State regulatory authorities would be well advised to consider this fact in their bypass policy.

It is a fact that the local distribution company (LDC) may have certain advantages in the competition raised by potential bypass. The distribution system has a greater diversity of supply and a stronger degree of reliability, which an individual customer may not be able to obtain. The LDC has the advantage of access to block I (old gas), which is priced substantially below the market and is reserved for the pipeline's traditional customers. Larger diameters of pipe (economies of scale) on the distribution network provide additional restraint on bypass. Perhaps the most important economic factor that favors the competitiveness of the local distribution company is that its rates are conditioned on a older, lower cost, depreciated rate base. The LDC is the low cost provider of gas distribution. The local distribution company can be very competitive as long as its rate design is cost based and unbundled.

The Pipeline Transportation Companies

The pipeline companies, facing increasing competition, are looking at the possibilities of contract carriage. Contract carriage creates an open environment in which local distribution companies and other end users will be free to purchase gas from various suppliers, with the assurance that access to the pipeline's transportation network is available to all comers. End users can buy directly at the wellhead.

What are we seeing in the industry is the separation of transportation from the commodity. This major unbundling prevents the exercise of monopoly power in the purchase of gas supply. Both producer and buyer have free access to the transportation routes to the markets. If the transportation rates are designed so that the pipeline utility is indifferent between providing gas service or providing transportation service, competition is fostered. The transportation rate form should be cost-driven not value based. Average system wide costs are not acceptable. The individual routing network and load balancing characteristics become critical to a good rate design.

The industry structure is affected by these emerging contract carriage strategies. The interconnection of facilities to neighboring pipelines will accelerate. This will allow enhanced service offerings to the buyers and sellers of gas. New gas marketing arrangements will exist. The pipelines and the local distribution companies may broker sales and then serve specific end users and industries outside their certificated market areas. For example, one could differentiate service by becoming the gas broker for the entire glass industry on a nationwide basis. Open-network architecture will become the theme of the transportation segment at the expense of end-to-end service.

The new regulatory era will force the pipelines to assume greater risks than they have in the past. It is not clear that they will be able to collect their overall cost of service. Competition may fail to provide pipelines with the sunk cost recovery that they received as a protected monopoly under rate-base regulation. At a minimum, the rate practice of shifting a disproportionate share of cost recovery to the most elastic portion of the market is over. The long period of "tilting" rates is not compatible with the new era. We now face the problem of shifting the pipeline's revenue requirement back to its inelastic load customers.

Future strategies of the pipelines will change from past practices. Rate level regulation accommodated increasing costs for new facilities by rolling these costs into the rate base and thus creating internal cross subsidization. As a result, costly new facilities were built that could not survive on a stand-alone basis. The average cost standard of rate making led to overcapitalization. Now with interfuel competition and conservation, demand has fallen far below peak levels, so that the pipeline industry has substantially more capacity to move gas around the country than is needed. This burden of excess capacity has broken down the traditional view of rigid monopoly pipeline links between supply areas and regional markets. Gas-to-gas competition has become active. As the gas markets mature, market share becomes the critical factor in survival. The risks from "cream-skimming" operations become the serious threat for interstate pipeline networks. The potential for market share losses should not be underestimated. Once lost, these markets will be very hard to recover. The natural gas pipelines must be prepared to pursue future strategies that manage this new competitive environment.

Field Producers

There are two major changes in the regulatory environment taking place in the gas field. High priced, deep gas is unmarketable. For a long time regulation allowed old gas, which was low cost, to be "rolled in" with expensive gas. Today, this expensive gas must face a market-oriented, net back determined price. Pipelines are refusing to buy any gas that cannot be marketed competitively. Higher cost gas supplies need to be allocated directly to interruptible customers. These customers have alternative fuel capability. Therefore they are the pipeline's most elastic customers. Economic principles tell us that they cannot support a high-priced supply source. The wellhead price for new gas must come down.

The second major change taking place in the field is the declining economic power of gas producers. Every producer must have access to a transportation route to take their gas from the field to the market. Most producers do not have access to an alternative transmission route. They are the captive customers of the pipeline. The pipeline operates the bottleneck facility. The pipeline companies are increasingly using their economic power to extract concessions from the producer. A separate rate for transportation service by the pipeline prevents the extension of monopoly power to the supply of gas. But there must be ultra free access by producers to this unbundled transportation service.

Selected Antitrust Issues

From the previous sections it is clear that competition has been considerably enhanced in the gas industry. The case for economic benefits is strong in the short-run from the breaking down of ties between buyers and sellers. But the long-term or structural implications may be a different matter entirely. The transportation company may see its ownership of a monopoly bottleneck (the only pipeline's transportation route out of a gas producing field) as an opportunity to capture an assured supply of gas for its pipeline capacity. The pipeline can squeeze the field price down to an acceptable marketable level since the producer has no alternative but to shut down. Meanwhile the pipeline can afford to pay its production affiliates more for their gas because pipeline regulation is based on an average cost of purchased gas standard. Their affiliate gas price is offset by the low prices of other suppliers. The presence of monopoly transportation bottlenecks to the field producing areas is likely to prevent a significant increase in the competitive nature of the gas industry.

A related antitrust matter is the monopolization of the transportation function. The dropping the of the minimum bill provisions have made this possible. The Federal Energy Regulatory Commission, by walking away from the minimum bill contracts, created an opportunity for a transportation bottleneck and its resultant monopoly power.

Colorado Interstate Gas Company Versus Natural Gas Pipeline Company of America

This antitrust case [9], decided in favor of Colorado Interstate Gas (CIG) illustrates how short-run regulatory decisions to promote competition can lead to antitrust problems. The case concerned a major gas-producing area in the western United States, the Overthrust Area of Wyoming. The issue was Natural Gas Pipeline's (NGPL) attempt to monopolize the long-distance transportation of this Wyoming gas. Natural's pipeline system had excess capacity. (Natural's pipeline system out of the Overthrust Area was called Trailblazer.) It was a new pipeline network and was built with an unusual rate condition. The allowed rate of return was dependent on the throughput of natural gas. The Federal Energy Regulatory Commission (FERC) wanted to put the stockholders at risk in case the pipeline was underutilized. At the time the new Trailblazer came on line (around 1982), the gas markets had collapsed. There was a decline in gas prices, consumption, and drilling activity. As a result, Natural was concerned about its ability to fill and sell the pipeline's capacity.

The primary competitor for long-distance transportation to eastern markets was Colorado Interstate Gas. CIG was a significant competitive threat for two reasons. It's transportation network duplicated the capital facilities of Natural. More importantly, they were the lower-cost transportation system. This lower cost result was totally the product of regulatory treatment. The nature of rate level regulation is to favor a company with older capital inputs. That is because of the depreciated rate base. From a social standpoint this may make sense. We want the older pipeline to be at capacity before the new system wins additional incremental throughput. One can see with the collapse of the gas market in 1982 that the new Trailblazer was in real trouble.

Given the circumstances of this case, the ability to create a transportation bottleneck is paramount. If one could become the only transporter for gas out of the Overthrust Area to national markets, the competitive forces could be eliminated. Then, worries about having gas to put into the system, and worries about not being able to market this gas because of high transportation rates, are overcome. We simply squeeze the producers down in price to cover the high-cost transportation and if they don't like it, the alternative is to shut-in the gas. The only problem with this scenario is the presence of Colorado Interstate Gas and its ability to offer a higher price for gas to producers.

In the natural gas industry, a significant amount of gas throughput on pipeline networks is purchased downstream by other pipelines. These purchasing pipelines could be in competition with the seller in upstream transportation routes. This was the situation in the antitrust case. A portion of the gas from the Overthrust field was transported over the CIG system and then delivered to the competing pipeline, Natural. These deliveries were necessary because CIG had no facilities near eastern markets. So to access these markets, they had to use a portion of Natural's system. At the same time, because of earlier service obligations, CIG was obligated to sell Natural a certain volume of gas. This sales transaction was subject to a minimum bill provision for 90% of the contracted demand. Around the time FERC made its "competitive" rulemaking on the minimum bill, Natural refused to take any of Colorado Interstate's gas under this sales contract. It is interesting to establish who is at risk with this strategy. The refusal to take meant a loss of 25% of the total sales of Colorado Interstate. The supply-side effect was a minimal risk to the buyers. Natural was shutting down 5% of their supplies of gas. There was another implication beside the risk differences. It was CIG's obligation to be a supplier of last resort to all its customers. This in one of the most significant duties of a public utility. Natural could walk away from the transaction, CIG could not.

Having lost the ability to transport gas for Natural, Colorado Interstate Gas sought to fill its pipeline from other sources. It is important to note that in rate-of-return regulation, a pipeline's profits would come from the transportation and use of its capital facilities, not from the sale of natural gas. The product that Colorado Interstate Gas was giving Natural was transportation more than gas. This shows why transportation is the name of the game in the pipeline industry.

In the summer of 1984, CIG was negotiating with American Natural Resources (ANR) for the transportation of ANR's gas to utilize the pipeline's capacity lost by Natural's actions. During this off-peak demand period, Natural turned on its gas take from CIG. Since Colorado Interstate Gas still has an obligation to serve Natural, its excess capacity disappeared. As a result, CIG quoted a high price for transportation gas to ANR. So ANR then went with Northwest and El Paso. As soon as this decision was announced, Natural stopped taking the gas. These actions confirm the antitrust theory. As long as minimum bills are not enforceable, but obligations to be suppliers of last resort continue, the downstream pipeline holds sway over a competitor and ties up the competitor's transportation system.

A further act of conduct at issue in the case was the situation where CIG attempted to offer interruptible service for Tennessee Gas. Because Tennessee Gas didn't have a physical interconnect with CIG, Colorado Interstate delivered gas to Natural for Tennessee's account. After signing the agreement and the commencement of service, Natural elected once again to purchase its gas service contract and refused to receive the Tennessee transportation gas. Thus CIG was forced to interrupt service to Tennessee Gas. Subsequently, Natural offered to provide an exchange of the gas for Tennessee over its Trailblazer system. Tennessee left CIG and went with Natural. Once again, CIG's ability to compete in transportation was tied up by Natural.

Considering the issues of conduct in this case, the jury decided that Natural Gas Pipeline Company attempted to monopolize the long-distance transportation of Wyoming Gas.

A further antitrust issue in the gas industry is how a pipeline treats its affiliate company's production. The abuse occurs when the affiliate is favored over other lower cost producers. In a period of declining demand for gas, the affiliate's production is not shut in. Other independent producers must either lower their prices or be shut in. The pipeline's capacity is not being filled with the lowest cost gas. This is hardly a competitive field market. Once the independent lowers its gas price, the high price affiliate's gas becomes marketable under average, rolled-in pricing. The pipeline's bottleneck facility makes this all possible.

When this issue of preference for affiliate production is raised, these factors must be determined: Has the affiliate been shut in before, and what were the amounts and length of the close-down? What were the levels of takes from affiliates compared to the total amounts of the pipeline's cutbacks? Are there third party producers in the contract, and additionally what percentage of the production is owned by the pipeline affiliate? Has the affiliate been willing in the past to reduce its price? Has the affiliate waved take-or-pay penalties? Was the gas in question "search gas" funded by the pipeline's customers? If the gas was treated before being released into the pipeline network, what were the conditions of the contract with the gas treatment plant? There factors are important before one can determine the pipeline's treatment of its affiliate company's production.

The long-run structural implications are clear. Because pipeline networks frequently parallel and cross each other, or are positioned further downstream, a substantial portion of pipeline gas sales are to other pipeline systems. With the dropping of a minimum bill obligation, at the same time that the obligation to serve is still there, the opportunity for the downstream pipeline to move upstream and enforce a transportation bottleneck is enhanced. A further consequence is that the transportation bottleneck allows them to capture the benefits of vertical integration or, through monopsony power, gain the same advantages. In the long run, the concentration of the transportation phase is the result. The goal of deregulation and competition is creating a perverse effect. Social control by antitrust law must become increasingly active. The regulatory response should be to embrace a more transportation like answer to fostering competition. The regulatory authorities should release pipelines from their obligations to serve. Then the natural gas pipeline industry will take on the characteristics of common carriage.

The New Structure of the Industry

The rigid institutional arrangements that lock in buyers and sellers through long-term contracts both upstream and downstream have a significant economic effect. They serve the same function as vertical integration in the industry [10]. These integration benefits already have

Table 5–1. Gas Pipeline Mergers and Acquisitions, 1982–1986.

Date	Parent/Acquiring Company	PGJ500 Rank*	Acquired Pipeline	PGJ500 Rank*	Cost (Millions $)	Markets Acquired**
11/82	Northwest Pipeline Co.	18	Cities Service Gas Co.	12	340	CO/KS/MO/NE/OK/TX/WY
12/82	Burlington Industries	—	El Paso Natural Gas Co.	2	1,300	AZ/CO/NM/OK/TX/UT
2/83	Goodyear Corp.	—	Mid-Louisiana Gas Co., Louisiana Intrastate Gas	67 49	830	LA
8/83	CSX Corp.	—	Texas Gas Transmission	20	370	AR/CO/IL/IN/KY/LA/MS/ OH/OK/TN/TX
9/83	MidCon Corp. (Natural Gas Pipeline Co. of America)	6	Mississipi River Trans.	41	260	AR/IL/LA/MO/OK/TX
10/83	Williams Companies	—	Northwest Pipeline Co.	12	820	CO/ID/MN/OR/UT/WA/WY
12/83	MidCon/Texas Oil & Gas	6, 17	Tatham Corp. pipelines	—	200	LA/TX
6/84	MidConTransok Inc./Houston Natural Gas Corp.	7, 47, 21	Texoma Pipeline (conversion from crude to gas)	—	130	TX

Table 5–1. (cont.) Gas Pipeline Mergers and Acquisitions, 1982–1986.

Date	Parent/Acquiring Company	PGJ500 Rank*	Acquired Pipeline	PGJ500 Rank*	Cost (Millions $)	Markets Acquired**
1/84	Phillips Natural Gas Co./Phillips Gas Pipeline Co.	—	Seaway Pipeline (conversion from crude to gas)	—	N/A	TX
11/84	Houston Natural Gas Corp.	21	Transwestern Pipeline Co.	28	390	AZ/KS/NM/OK
12/84	Houston Natural Gas Corp.	21	Florida Gas Transmission	29	390	AL/FL/LA/MS
3/85	Coastal Corp. (Colorado Interstate Gas. Co).	19	ANR Pipeline Co., 50% of Great Lakes Gas Transmission	8, 55	2,450	IL/IN/IA/KS/LA/MI/MO/OH/TN/WI/WY
5/85	InterNorth (Northern Natural)	1	Houston Natural Gas Corp.	21	2,300	TX/NM
7/85	Tenneco (Tennesee Gas Pipeline)	4	Mid-Louisiana Gas, Louisiana Intrastate Gas. Co.	71, 51	500	LA
9/85	MidCon (NGLPA)	6	United Texas Pipeline Co., United Texas Transmission	14, 39	1,400	AL/FL/LA/MS/TX

10/85	U.S. Steel	—	Texas Oil & Gas Corp.	15	3,600	TX
12/85	Occidental Petroleum	—	MidCon/NGPLA/MRT/UER	6	3,000	AL/AR/CO/FL/IA/IL/KS/LA/MO/MS/NE/NM/OK/TX/WY
5/86	Sonat (Southern Natural Gas Co.)	17	50% of Florida Gas Trans.	26	360	AL/FL/LA/MS
3/86	Arkla Inc.	13	Mississippi River Transmission	44	352	IL/MO/MS
6/86	Texas Eastern Corp.	11	Algonquin Energy Inc.	65	117	CT/MA/NJ/PA/RI
6/86	K N Energy Inc.	5	Rocky Mountain Natural Gas	—	N/A	CO
6/86	Northwest Central Pipeline	12	Williams Natural Gas Co. (Faustina Pipeline)	—	N/A	LA
8/86	Oklahoma Gas & Electric	—	Mustang Fuel Corp.	36	125	OK

* Company Rankings are for the PGJ Top 100 Gas Pipelines for the year in which the transaction occurred; rankings change from year to year.

** Markets acquired are "new" states served by acquiring company.

Source: Pipeline and Gas Journal, August 1986, p. 40.

been captured by producers and pipelines. Since gas regulatory policy historically discouraged vertical integration [11], the industry developed along a parallel benefit path.

With the movement away from minimum bills, take-or-pay, and other arrangements, a basic conflict is created. Competition and deregulation reject these long-term contracts and destroy the substitute structure form for vertical integration. It is not certain that competition will be enhanced by this policy. The industry response will be the acceleration of mergers and vertical integration with the attendant concentration of the industry. An industry best described as a "tight" oligopoly is likely.

Today, combinations of production companies and transportation companies are rapidly taking place. If for no other reason, producers see ownership of a transportation network as a way to assure that their gas will be transported to end-use markets and not be left in the field without access to a pipeline. High-priced gas producers would have the greatest incentive to vertically integrate into the transportation phase. On the other hand, the transportation company may see its ownership of a monopoly bottleneck (the only pipeline transportation route out of a gas-producing field) as an opportunity to capture an assured supply of gas for its pipeline capacity. Merger activity between pipelines is another way to concentrate the transportation routes to major markets.

In order to evaluate the trend towards a tight oligopoly in the gas industry, one should look at recent mergers and combinations and see if the deregulation era of social policy has encouraged this trend. From October, 1982, to July, 1986 — a period less than four years — there have been 23 major mergers or acquisitions involving major natural gas pipelines. These mergers and acquisitions are given in table 5–1. The ranking system used in the table is based on the *Pipelines and Gas Journal's* ordering rather than that reported by the Energy Information Administration [12].

The table shows that the gas industry is concentrating pipeline networks. Pipelines are acquiring other pipelines, and production companies are buying pipelines. Vertical and horizontal integration of the industry is rapid. If this pace of combinations were to continue, the industry soon would become a tight oligopoly. One must conclude that deregulation policy has played a significant role in this long-term structural change in favor of concentration. This does not appear to be in the public interest.

A Recommendation

It may well be that the natural gas pipeline industry is a natural monopoly. The evidence from Table 5–1 supports the view that there are
gains to be made from integration and coordination. Ownership of a
transportation bottleneck and attendant economies of scale are an effective barrier to entry. The social policy question is whether this tightness
of the transportation structure can come to dominate the increasingly
competitive end user and production phases of the industry. I think not.
But this answer requires effective antitrust enforcement and enlightened
regulatory oversight.

Looking at the antitrust issue first, the policy must recognize the growing role of a transportation bottleneck principle. Control of the essential
facility can allow favored producer affiliates to win the field competition.
Downstream from the pipeline, independent brokerage must be protected. Pipelines should not be allowed to benefit their affiliated marketing
companies. The area of most antitrust concern is raised when downstream
pipelines walk away from their contracted demands or minimum bills
while leaving their competitors with an obligation to serve. Social control
of these forms of anticompetitive behavior must be vigorous.

Regulatory policies need to encourage a transportationlike answer for
the pipelines. Contract carriage, offered on a nondiscriminatory basis,
will break the essential facility problem that can lead to monopoly power.
Ultrafree access to the economies of scale will assure a strongly competitive industry. Load balancing can be undertaken by either the pipeline
itself or by independent brokers. An obligation to serve by the pipelines
or distribution companies needs to be sold on a premium service basis.
Service offerings must be unbundled. The social agenda calls for open-
networks architecture. Every phase of the pipeline network is for sale
or usage in combination with external facilities and interconnections. The
ownership of facilities is secondary to the usage, processing, storage, and
marketing of gas. The economies of decreasing costs now serve to foster
competition. With open-network architecture, the services offered will
be customer designed and customer driven.

The final element in the social control of the gas industry is restriction
of pipeline mergers and acquisitions that substantially lessen competition.
The rapid movements toward a tight oligopoly are not in the public
interest. If our society is not successful in preventing the formulation of
a tight oligopoly, then the dominate issue for regulatory concern will be
price leadership behavior. It is hoped that in the process of experimenting
with regulatory rules and rates we don't come to this environment.

References

1. Energy Information Administration. *A Study of Contracts Between Interstate Pipelines and Their Customers*. Washington, D.C.: U.S. Government Printing Office, 1984, p. 3.

2. Tussing, Arlon, and Connie Barlow. *The Natural Gas Industry: Evolution, Structure, and Economics*. Cambridge, Mass.: Ballinger Publishing Company, 1984, p. 165.

3. Cramer, Curtis. "The Structural Implications of a Minimum Bill Provision in the Transportation of Natural Gas." *International Journal of Transport Economics*. February 1986.

4. Energy Information Administration. op. cit., pp. 24–25.

5. Federal Energy Regulatory Commission, Order No. 380, Docket No. RM 83-71-000.

6. Energy Information Administration, op. cit., p. 000.

7. For an excellent discussion of distribution company strategies, see Tussing, Arlon, and Connie Barlow. "The Restructuring of the Natural Gas Industry: Implications for Gas Distributors and Their Regulators." *Natural Gas Industry Restructuring Issues*. National Regulatory Research Institute, 1986, 7–18.

8. Cramer, Curtis. "The Non-Jurisdictional Gas Pipeline Tariff." *Industrial Organization Review*, 5:2 (1977): pp. 130–134.

9. Colorado Interstate Gas Company versus Natural Gas Pipeline Company of America. Civil Docket No. C84–0139. U.S. District Court for District of Wyoming.

10. For a similar view see Tussing, A., and C. Barlow. *The Natural Gas Industry*. op. cit., pp. 211–212.

11. Vertical integration abuses by public utility holding companies were one of the reasons for the passage of the Public Utility Holding Company Act of 1935.

12. Energy Information Administration, *Statistics of Interstate Natural Gas Pipeline Companies*, Selected Years, Washington, D.C.: U.S. Government Printing Office.

Commentary by W. W. Sharkey

The natural gas pipeline industry is a textbook case of natural monopoly. It is also an industry in which the virtues of deregulation are readily apparent. This is the tension that underlies the current debate over the proper role of regulation not only of pipelines but in other regulated industries as well, notably telecommunications. Economists have devoted substantial effort to questions such as the behavior of firms in regulated industries, desirable forms of regulation, the definition of natural monopoly, and related issues. Relatively little effort has been expended on the analysis of deregulatory scenarios. That is, arguments in favor of deregulation are typically based upon the desirable properties of perfectly competitive markets and the known inefficiencies of the regulatory process. Yet the introduction of competition into formerly regulated markets, particularly those once thought to be natural monopolies, is likely to lead to an equilibrium that can be characterized at best as a form of imperfect competition and at worst as an unpredictable hybrid of regulated competition.

Curtis Cramer does a fine job of presenting both sides of the issue. He makes several major points. First, the long-term take-or-pay contracts between the pipeline companies and their upstream suppliers, the field producers of natural gas, are an inefficient extension of natural monopoly into an otherwise competitive industry. These contracts limit the ability of pipelines to competitively shop for low-cost supplies when market conditions change, thereby locking producers and pipelines into a long-term relationship. At the same time minimum bill provisions in downstream contracts with other pipelines or local distribution companies were used to protect the pipelines and ultimately transfer risk to the final consumer. Cramer argues that these relationships were a product of regulation, which competitive or deregulated markets would rightfully reject.

There is, however, another side to the issue. Unless field producers are risk neutral, there is an efficiency gain associated with sharing risk with pipeline and their downstream customers. The incentives for vertical integration or long-term contractual relationships due to appropriability of relation-specific investments is well known [1]. These difficulties are compounded in the case of gas supply due to common pool problems. If a single pipeline serves a high-cost field with several competing suppliers, and world prices fall, each supplier may be compelled to sell at any price above production cost rather than allow competitors to deplete the pool they share. Often the efficient response would be to leave the gas in the ground until market conditions change. Masten and Crocker [2] argue that take-or-pay provisions in long-term contracts can be used to give both parties correct incentives to carry out the terms of the contract if and only if it is jointly efficient. They therefore act as a substitute for complex contingency clauses and ex post adjudication.

It is also the case, as documented by Cramer, that merger activity among pipelines and between producers and pipelines has accelerated between 1982 and 1986, years of instability in world energy markets in which the Federal Energy Regulatory Commission also curtailed use of the minimum bill provision. Cramer argues that vigilant antitrust enforcement is the appropriate social policy recommendation in order to preserve both short-run and long-run efficiency gains from competitive markets. This is a sensible proposal, but it is too early to accept it as the only solution. In the absence of any form of long-term vertical relationships between producers and pipelines, it is possible that inefficiently low levels of exploration will occur. Also the proper role of regulation within the pipeline industry is not resolved. It is possible that merger activity reflects the efficiency gains from coordination within the industry in addition to the gains from ordinary collusion. In short, deregulation of the natural gas pipeline industry raises as many new questions as it ostensibly resolves.

In the remainder of my comments I would like to do three things. First, I will argue that in many respects the natural gas pipeline industry represents an ideal test case for deregulation. Since technological change is relatively predictable in the industry and market boundaries are well defined, arguments for and against deregulation can focus on the respective properties of regulated and deregulated equilibrium. Next, I will review the arguments for natural monopoly in the transportation of natural gas via pipelines. These arguments suggest that antitrust policy may be particularly difficult to enforce since large efficiency gains may be present for horizontal mergers. Finally, I will offer some general comments on the difficulties that are associated with promoting competition in industries that supply outputs on a network, and in which production is subject to decreasing average cost.

In many respects the natural gas supply industry resembles the telecommunications industry. Both are in an intermediate stage of a process of deregulation whose final outcome is uncertain. Both industries are concerned with transporting commodities on a network of great complexity. In both industries, local distribution is separately owned and is regulated by state authorities, while long-distance transmission is partially competitive and is regulated by federal authorities. In both industries, rate structures have been designed that contain cross subsidies from industrial or business customers to residential customers and from region to region. (In telecommunications the regional cross subsidy is primarily urban to rural, while in natural gas supply it is primarily from producing states to consuming states.) Finally, in both industries selective entry and customer bypass have threatened the subsidized rate structures.

While there are no doubt important lessons to be learned in both industries from the experiences of the other, I believe that the differences are more important than the similarities. One difference concerns the nature of the commodity carried on the network. The role of the telecommunications network is to transmit an intangible commodity — information — on demand, for a large set of customers. The role of the pipeline network is to transport a physical commodity from a relatively small set of producers to a much larger set of final consumers. Since the commodity is physical, inventories can be stored and used to provide reliable service in spite of short-run peaks in demand. The most important difference, however, concerns the question of market boundaries and technological change in the industry. The telecommunications industry today is viewed in vastly different terms than it was a few years ago. The line that divides the transmission information from the enhancement of information or even the provision of new information is difficult to draw. Technologies used in transporting information, such as modern switching machines, can also be used to store or enhance that information. However, the transmission side of the industry has been traditionally regulated, while the newly developing information services industry seems inherently competitive. In contrast, the transmission of natural gas is an easily defined activity with few close substitutes. Aside from some minor questions of intermodal competition with liquefied natural gas, the boundaries of the industry are clear. Furthermore, technological change in the pipeline industry is likely to follow predictable lines. It is unlikely that an entirely new technology will replace the current one. For these reasons it is possible to consider the arguments for deregulation in a clear and uncluttered form. To put this another way, if deregulation does not work well in the natural gas industry, it is not likely to work well in other traditionally regulated industries. In this sense, natural gas supply is a convenient testing ground for advocates and opponents of deregulation.

The case for natural monopoly in the pipeline industry is relatively straightforward. It is the same case that can be made in other industries that supply goods or services on a network. However, it must be recognized that the case for natural monopoly rests primarily on technological arguments for subadditivity of an underlying cost function [3]. It does not take account of the diseconomies associated with large organizations. For example, Chandler [4] has noted that railroad executives were reluctant to expand their networks beyond systems of 500 miles of track because of the complexity of managing such a large enterprise. Eventually, improvements in accounting and control functions made it possible for larger systems to form. In the pipeline industry the basic source of subadditivity is the scale economy associated with large diameter pipe, since capacity or volume grows faster than cost, which depends on surface area. More subtle, but also more significant are the various economies due to "networking." For example, in a triangular network with vertices A, B, and C, the cost minimizing network may consist of two links, say AB and AC, in which flows from A to C must pass through B. Although the variable costs of indirect routing are higher, for moderate levels of demand they are outweighed by savings in fixed costs of right-of-way and the ability to use larger diameter pipe. For larger levels of demand a full three link network may be required to minimize costs. Thus, there is a need to project the expected demand and to coordinate the sizes of all links in the network in order to arrive at a cost minimizing configuration. Since capacity must be constructed in anticipation of future demand, there are various economies associated with coordinating the capacity expansion of the entire network. Similarly there are operational economies of alternative routing, by which unusually large point-to-point demands can be transmitted on both direct and indirect routes. The capacity of an individual link in a large network can therefore be maintained at a lower level than would be required in a smaller network to carry the same level of anticipated demands. For these reasons, it is likely that many parts of the overall pipeline network would remain under the control of a single supplier in a deregulated environment. Although point-to-point competition would exist on some routes, there would be a need for regulatory scrutiny on the remaining natural monopoly segments.

Let us now consider the nature of the equilibrium that might be expected in a deregulated pipeline industry. There are two characteristics of the technology of the industry that make competition potentially unstable. Both require some coordination among competing firms if an efficient and stable equilibrium is to occur. The first characteristic is an indivisibility in the short-run production function. A pipeline of a given size cannot transport arbitrary volumes up to its capacity. In order to operate effici-

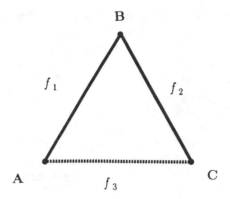

Figure 5C-1. A triangular network representation of producing and consuming regions.

cntly it must supply something close to its full capacity, or nothing at all. If two or more pipelines compete on the same route, the short-run marginal cost of each carrier is effectively zero up to capacity, when it becomes infinite. If aggregate demand is sufficient, all carriers can operate at full capacity at a price that covers their short-run production cost and contributes to the long-run fixed costs as well. In periods of slack demand, however, when all carriers cannot simultaneously operate at capacity, there may be no stable equilibrium. Competition among the carriers tends to force price to the short-run marginal cost, which is zero, due to the indivisibility problem. At a price of zero, all pipelines would choose to shut down, and so even the slack demand would not be carried.[1]

The point of the above argument is that the usual kind of competitive equilibrium fails to exist in this example. Of course some kind of equilibrium does exist. For example, in the noncooperative game with prices as strategies, the periods of slack demand would have an equilibrium in mixed strategies. An alternative possibility, however, is that firms in the industry would enter into long-term relationships with their customers so as to eliminate the instability. If the ability to form long-term relationships is limited there would be a strong incentive to merge.

The second argument regarding the need for cooperation among firms concerns the competition among firms who supply different links on a more complicated network. Consider the triangular network of figure 5C-1. Node A represents a producing region and nodes B and C represent consuming regions. Suppose that connecting links in the network can be constructed at fixed costs f_1, f_2, and f_3 respectively for links AB, BC, and AC. Assuming that $f_1 \leq f_2 \leq f_3$, the minimal cost network consists of links AB and BC. If each link in the minimal cost network is controlled by a different firm, then there is a need for cooperation since flows from A to C must travel on both links. The point of this example is that market prices cannot by themselves play that role. That is, there do not exist prices that simultaneously allow both firms in the minimal cost network to recover their costs without giving an incorrect signal for the third link AC to be added to the network. This is easily seen if each link must charge the same price to all users of that link. Suppose that each consuming market demands one unit. Let p_i represent the price for the link with cost f_i. Then the necessary constraints are

$$2p_1 \geq f_1$$
$$p_2 \geq f_2$$
$$p_1 + p_2 \leq f_3.$$

The first two inequalities are break even constraints for the active links in the minimum cost network. The third constraint must be satisfied if entry by the third link AC in order to serve customer C is to be avoided. Together these inequalities imply $f_3 > (f_1 \div 2) + f_2$ which is in general, not true. In particular if $f_1 = f_2 = f_3$, the latter inequality can never hold.

It might be thought that the failure of prices to sustain the minimal cost network is due to the inability of link AB to distinguish between short-haul and long-haul demand. This is not the case. Letting p_{iB} and p_{iC} represent the prices for customers B and C respectively, the relevant inequalities become

$$p_{1B} + p_{1C} \geq f_1$$
$$p_{2C} \geq f_2$$
$$p_{1B} \leq p_{3B}$$
$$p_{1C} + p_{2C} \leq p_{3C}$$
$$p_{3B} + p_{3C} < f_3.$$

The interpretation is that for any price vectors p_1, and p_2, and p_3 that satisfy the first four inequalities, the final inequality must also hold.[2] The first two inequalities are break even constraints for links AB and BC. The third and fourth inequalities are necessary if customers B and C are to have the incentive to use the minimal cost network instead of the alternative link AC. The final inequality states that there are no feasible prices at which the owner of link AC would wish to operate. It is assumed that since customer B does not use link BC in the minimal cost network, p_{2B} = 0. In other words, in a competitive market, link BC would be willing to carry additional traffic for customer B at any price greater than marginal cost, which is equal to zero. Any prices which satisfy the first four inequalities must satisfy $p_{3B} + p_{3C} \geq f_1 + f_2$. The set of all inequalities is therefore inconsistent if $f_3 < f_1 + f_2$. Since the final triangle inequality is likely to be satisfied on most networks it is seen that prices cannot be used as the only means of allocating resources on a network.

To briefly recapitulate, it has been argued above that the natural gas industry is a natural candidate for deregulation. The potential benefits of deregulation include enhanced competition in the production of gas and more flexible responses to changing market conditions. My comments have been primarily addressed to the potential for deregulation of the pipeline industry itself. Although nearly everyone recognizes that some sparse routes in the network are true natural monopolies, it is quite conceivable that multiple firms could coexist in the denser routes. However, the failure of the technical conditions for natural monopoly does not make the industry naturally competitive. It was argued that decreasing average costs even in the short-run production function may make the competitive outcome particularly unstable. When firms compete by supplying separate sections of an interconnected network, a similar instability may occur if firms and their customers rely only on prices to guide resource allocation. The implication of these arguments is not that competition is impossible or necessarily inefficient in network industries. Instead the arguments show that some minimal degree of coordination or cooperation is required. Thus, there is a need for models other than the standard competitive model to predict equilibrium outcomes in the industry. Until equilibrium behavior of competing firms in decreasing cost or networking industries is better understood, it would appear wise for deregulatory policies to be implemented with caution.

Notes

1. This argument is described in greater detail in Telser [5], Chapter 2 and in Bittlingmayer [6].

2. These "prices" are actually optimal dual solutions in a linear program which is related to the computation of the minimal cost network. Further details are given in Sharkey [7]. Bittlingmayer [8] and Carlton and Klamer [9] discuss related issues in network industries.

References

1. Klein, B., R. G. Crawford, and A. A. Alchian. "Vertical Integration, Appropriate Rents and the Competitive Contracting Process." *J. Law Econ.* 21 (1978): 297–326.

2. Masten, S. E., and K. J. Crocker. "Efficient Adaptation in Long-Term Contracts: Take-or-Pay Provisions for Natural Gas." *Amer. Econ. Rev.* 75 (1985): 1083–1093.

3. Sharkey, W. W. *The Theory of Natural Monopoly.* Cambridge: Cambridge University Press. (1982).

4. Chandler, A. D. *The Visible Hand: The Managerial Revolution in American Bus.* Cambridge, MA: Harvard University Press. (1977).

5. Telser, L. G. *Econ. Theory and the Core.* Chicago: University of Chicago Press. (1978).

6. Bittlingmayer, G. "Decreasing Average Cost and Competition: A New Look at the Addyston Pipe Case." *J. Law Econ.* 25 (1982): 201–230.

7. Sharkey, W. W. "Cores and Implications for Pricing in a Model of Production with Fixed Costs and Shared Facilities." Bell Communications Research Economics Discussion Paper #1. July, 1985.

8. Bittlingmayer, G. "The Economics of a Simple Airline Network." Unpublished manuscript. October, 1985.

9. Carlton, D. W., and J. M. Klamer. "The Need for Coordination Among Firms, with Special Reference to Network Industries." *U. of Chicago Law Rev.* 50 (1983): 446–465.

6 URBAN WATER SUPPLY: THE DIVERGENCE BETWEEN THEORY AND PRACTICE

Patrick C. Mann

Over two decades ago, Milliman [1] reviewed the status of urban water economics and found it deficient in many respects, especially regarding pricing and costing.[1] A prediction was made that within the next several decades, urban water economics would be subjected to substantial change, with reform occurring in such areas as rate design and costing methods. The theme of this chapter is that, unfortunately, Professor Milliman's prediction has been only partially affirmed. Important research developments have taken place in water economics; however, little activity has occurred in implementing the research results.

The historical neglect of water costing and pricing can be attributed to several factors. Historically, water service has been provided at lesser cost than other public utility services and has constituted a relatively small proportion of consumer expenditures. This cost gap has recently widened as water prices have been increasing at a slower rate than those for other public utility services. The neglect can also be linked to the traditional engineering emphasis that has prevailed in water supply decision making and the abundance in the past of inexpensive and easily accessible water supplies. Occasionally, geographical shortages have induced substantial activity to insure long-term supplies. However, the primary response to shortages has been rationing rather than pricing modifications.

However, forces of change are emerging, in part due to urban water provision becoming increasingly complex. Issues of economic growth and environmental quality have complicated the supply of urban water. Per capita usage has continued to increase with rising affluency and urbanization. Potential reservoir sites have become scarce while ground sources have become limited in availability. Increasing energy costs have elevated water provision costs. Federal and state legislation has imposed new quality standards on public water service. The traditional solution to supply problems has been to augment supplies; however, nontraditional methods such as wastewater recycling, conservation, and programs for improved system efficiency have been implemented. The numerous pressures that have affected public utility regulation have impacted upon water service. For example, inflation has recently meant rate increases at a higher frequency than in the past. Increasing consumer militancy has generated sentiment to shield low-income consumers from increasing rates. Regulatory agencies are now considering rate designs such as seasonal pricing. However, the rate innovations are beset by numerous implementation problems.

One theme of this chapter is that there have been important research developments in water demand and costing that generally have not been translated into pricing reform. That is, the water service industry continues to be characterized by inefficient rate design. This is exemplified by New York City (where unmetered water accounts for approximately 80% of consumption) and Denver (where unmetered charges cover 50% of residential usage).

The neglect of pricing and costing matters has produced the general underpricing of urban water service in the United States. That is, present practices tend to generate prices less than the real unit costs of providing urban water service. The undercosting and underpricing is a function of the use of historical accounting (rather than present or near-term future) costs in the rate-setting process, the use of average cost (rather than marginal cost) as the primary pricing standard in the context of increasing real unit costs of water provision, and consumer pressure combined with the political orientation of water rate determination. The result of this underpricing includes the postponement of both system maintenance and capital replacement.

Several caveats must be offered regarding the relatively narrow focus of this article on pricing and investment decisions in urban water supply. This focus is not intended to indicate that related issues are less important. For example, there are important issues concerning water quality both at intake treatment and sewage discharge points. There is the issue of the optimal mix of treatment expenditures and water quality. Given surface sources, there is the policy issue of trading off increased sewage treatment costs upstream for decreased water treatment costs downstream. In addition, urban water pricing can not be examined in isolation from the allocation of supplies between urban and agriculture uses, particularly in rapidly growing areas in the Sun Belt. This intersector allocation can place limits on urban growth. Furthermore, the historically inefficient pricing of irrigation water probably more than offsets any societal gains to be derived from increased efficiency in urban water pricing.

Demand Developments

Numerous studies of water demand have been completed in the past two decades. The majority have focused on either aggregate municipal demand or on residential use (only a few have examined commercial and industrial demand). The empirical results indicate that municipal and residential demands are highly price-inelastic. The exception occurs when residential demand is disaggregated into seasonal and nonseasonal components; seasonal demand exhibits higher price elasticities than nonseasonal usage.

Despite the general result of price-inelastic demands, there have been substantial variances in empirical results. Several reasons can be provided for these variances [2]. One, the use of average rather than marginal price as the singular variable in the estimating equation generates excessively high coefficients, particularly in the context of declining block rates. This problem is especially significant in the context of changing marginal prices combined with constant intramarginal rates. Two, given wastewater charges being levied on water usage, equations incorporating sewage charges produce more valid results than those that ignore wastewater charges. Three, the price impact on usage can be swamped by other demand variables (e.g., income, rainfall, and population growth) and is complicated by usage response lags. In addition, the price effect on consumption can be minimal if there is very little change in real water prices over the long run.

Most studies have employed cross-sectional data, thus yielding long-run elasticity estimates. Few studies have used time-series data focusing on locations experiencing substantial price variations over time. An exception is an analysis of Boulder, Colorado, in its transition from flat rates to metering [3].

In addition, there is lacking reliable estimates of the price elasticities of peak and off-peak demands (i.e., there is inadequate data on whether users change consumption patterns when confronted with time-differentiated rates) and inadequate information on the magnitude of these shifts.

Of the approximately 100 demand studies completed in the past two decades, several are particularly worthy of mention. Using cross-sectional data from 39 urban areas in the United States, Howe and Linaweaver [4] found the price elasticity of residential demand to be −.41. Domestic demand was price-inelastic (−.23); seasonal or sprinkling demand was price-inelastic in the West (−.70) and price-elastic in the East (−1.57). Billings and Agthe [5] employed time-series data in an analysis of residential demand for Tucson, Arizona. Two price variables were employed: marginal price and a variable measuring changes in flat charges and other nonmarginal water rates. The elasticities for the marginal price ranged from −.27 to −.49; the elasticities for the other price variable ranged from −.12 to −.14, indicating that changes in nonmarginal rates can affect water usage.

Carver and Boland [6] examined pooled time-series and cross-sectional data for 13 water systems in the Washington, D.C., area. Their non-seasonal model generated short-run elasticities less than −.10 and long-run elasticities ranging from −.62 to −.70. Their seasonal model produced short-run elasticities less than −.30 and long-run elasticities less than −.40. This analysis produced seasonal elasticities significantly lower than previously reported. Using an improved model and aggregating residential demand, Howe [7] reestimated elasticities for the data in the original Howe and Linaweaver analysis. The incorporation of intramarginal rates in the equation produced substantially lower elasticity estimates (i.e., the coefficient for domestic demand was −.06; the coefficient for seasonal demand varied from −.43 in the West to −.57 in the East).

In brief, the most reliable empirical results clearly indicate that urban water demand is highly price-inelastic, with the possible exception of seasonal (sprinkling) demand. The implication is that time-differcntiated (seasonal) rates are probably more effective in managing demand patterns than general rate increases. However, it should be noted that the various impacts of seasonal pricing may not be easily forecasted.

Costing Developments

The conventional scheme of water cost classification employs three categories. Customer costs are those costs varying with service connections. Commodity costs are those costs varying with water usage. Demand or capacity costs are those varying with system capacity. This categorization recognizes that costs vary as a function of customers, quantity produced, and required system capacity. An alternative method categorizes costs as to source of supply, treatment, transmission, distribution, customer services, and fire protection. This classification recognizes that costs behave differently across system components.

An important contribution to costing was provided by Dajani [8] via a modification of the functional classification method. This variation viewed water costs as having two components — nodal and network. The nodal component involves the production center (i.e., source of supply, transmission, and treatment). The network component involves the delivery network (i.e., distribution system). This classification is useful since the effect of scale and consumer density can differ substantially between the nodal and network components. For example, the nodal cost function is similar to that portrayed in microeconomic theory. The network cost function is more complex, being affected by the form and structure of the service area and the spatial arrangement of consumers. The two cost functions can produce different results. The nodal function may experience economies of scale offset by diseconomies of spatial dispersion in the network function. The implication is that cost minimization solutions for water systems must reflect both nodal and network costs.

There have been several recent cost analyses of water provision that are worthy of specific mention. Ford and Warford [9] employed cross-sectional data in an examination of supply costs. One conclusion was that increasing per capita usage and/or increasing user density within a service area decreased unit costs. Another conclusion was that unit costs increased with an expanding service area (i.e., both decreasing usage and decreasing density elevated unit costs).

Clark [10, 11] provided evidence that regionalization and system consolidation produce treatment economies of scale that can be offset by increasing delivery costs. An analysis of a system with a single production center indicated that unit costs increase with increasing distance from the treatment plant and decrease with increasing density within the service area. The implication is that there are limitations on the efficient maximum size of a service area. Clark and Stevie [12, 13] developed a model focusing on the cost tradeoffs between production economies and delivery diseconomies. Their model solved for the minimum cost distance from the treatment plant (i.e., there was a determination of the least cost size of service area). Two conclusions resulted. One, the minimum cost distance is not generally influenced by per capita usage and population density levels (i.e., these factors have little effect on the optimum size of service area). Two, the least cost solution is highly sensitive to population dispersion changes (i.e., density changes have a substantial effect on the point where production economies are offset by distribution diseconomies).

Turvey [14] proved that it is possible to generate adequate estimates of the marginal costs of water provision. However, he noted that the increments to production capacity are lumpy and can produce rather volatile cost estimates over time; in contrast, the increments to distribution capacity are less lumpy, thus producing more stable marginal cost estimates. Turvey's estimation method involved an incremental cost calculation based on the effects of changes in demand growth rates on system costs. Employing this method of calculating the cost effects of postponing (or accelerating) system expansion, Hanke [15] generated more refined estimates of the marginal supply costs for a water system. Mann, Saunders, and Warford [16] introduced an alternative estimation method, average incremental cost. The calculation of average incremental cost is an attempt to compromise between short-run allocative efficiency and generating correct investment signals in the long run.

In brief, the recent cost analyses clearly indicate that although increasing scale of production can lower unit supply costs, this cost reduction can be offset by increased distribution costs. This raises doubts regarding the efficiency of the declining block rate structure in water service while simultaneously indicating the need for consideration of spatially differentiated pricing. In addition, the marginal cost analyses indicate that reliable estimates of marginal and incremental cost can be generated, thus providing the foundation for both marginal cost and time-differentiated pricing.

Pricing Theory and Practice

The common rate design in water service has been the declining block rate structure. Its original justification was the water system experiencing decreasing unit costs with increasing usage (via utilization rate improvements and economies of scale). The declining block rate design passes these cost savings onto consumers. Declining block rates also enhance revenue stability (i.e., the placing of the more price-elastic demands in the tail blocks tends to dampen usage fluctuations). The major criticism of declining block rates is their failure to track costs. Already noted is the tendency of economies of scale in production to be offset by distribution diseconomies. In addition, there is evidence of diminishing scale economies for some large systems. Expansion costs are increasing due to competition between environmentalists and developers for potential reservoir sites, the extension of distribution systems to consumers more distant from production centers, and the gradual elimination of more accessible sources of supply. In addition, the cost of new facilities has increased due to increased storage requirements associated with the inverse linkage between stream flows and seasonal demands [17]. The failure of the declining block design to track costs means that small users subsidize large users. In brief, the declining block rate form is efficient only under unique conditions (e.g., all users must consume water in the same last block in each season) [18]. Prices exceeding costs in the initial blocks and prices less than costs in the tail blocks promote neither conservation nor economic efficiency.[2]

The counterpart to the declining block form, the inverted (increasing) block rate structure has recently been advocated as a form of conservation pricing. In some cases, its adoption has been solely derived from its potential to reduce water consumption [19]. Its support also comes from water systems experiencing increasing incremental costs with expansion and as a mechanism for affecting income distribution. The inverted block rate has serious deficiencies. Similar to the declining block rate, the inverted block form is efficient only under unique conditions [18]. If the inverted block rate structure does not track costs, the result is cross subsidization with large users subsidizing small users. Prices of water service below costs in the initial blocks and prices exceeding costs in the tail blocks promote neither conservation nor efficient water use. An additional problem with inverted block rates is the potential product of decreasing average demands unaccompanied by decreasing peak demands (i.e., the results include deteriorating load factors, revenue erosion, and eventually the need for rate increases).

The cost argument underlying the inverted block rate form is of questionable validity (i.e., with the incremental costs of new capacity increasing, increasing usage should be discouraged by price signals). However, the cost-causers in this case are the users responsible for the peak demands imposed upon the system, who are not necessarily large users of water service. In addition, its justification as a method for reducing income inequalities is questionable since the distributive argument is based on the premise that water consumption has a strong positive correlation with income levels.[3]

Give the conceptual deficiencies of both declining block and inverted block rates, a rate design that has acquired recent support in the water industry is the uniform (constant) commodity rate. Even though the uniform rate may not track costs with precision, its popularity is linked to its administrative simplicity and its compatibility with prevailing notions of equity and fairness.

Although the declining block form continues to dominate in water provision, more efficient solutions to problems of increasing incremental capacity costs and increasing delivery costs are time-differentiated and spatially-differentiated rates, preferably based on incremental costs.

Marginal Cost Pricing

The conceptual problems of marginal cost pricing in water service can be condensed into three components. The first is the problem of price volatility given the lumpiness associated with capacity increments. The second is the problem of attaining economic efficiency in the context of second-best considerations and nonefficiency pricing objectives. The third is the problem of the financial viability of the system. The application of marginal cost pricing in the urban water sector involves tradeoffs among price stability, economic efficiency, equity, administrative costs, and adequate revenue generation [17].

The general application problems of marginal cost pricing in water include cost forecasting, rate instability, the disposal of excess revenues, and uncertain income distribution effects. The transition from theory to practice is also confronted with specific problems such as needle peaking, shifting peaks, unanticipated cost effects, and difficulties in calculating marginal fire protection, distribution, and customer costs [20]. An application problem that has received inadequate attention is the conflict between water metering practices and the implementation of time-differentiated pricing. For example, meters are not generally read with sufficient frequency to permit prices to conform with peak demand pricing principles.

As indicated above, there are alternative ways of estimating marginal cost in water supply. The methods are similar in that they focus on future costs; the definitions differ in the extent to which they focus on short-run verus long-run allocative efficiency. Given lumpy capacity increments, prices equal to marginal cost can generate substantial excess capacity.

This problem involves the choice between short-run marginal cost (SRMC) and long-run marginal cost (LRMC). LRMC prices may provide more correct investment signals than SRMC prices, at the cost of temporary excess capacity. In essence, the elimination of the excess capacity necessitates SRMC prices [21]. For example, SRMC pricing involves setting price equal to the marginal cost that equates usage with existing system capacity. This suggests increasing prices prior to the availability of new capacity (to constrain demand within existing capacity). Then, to attain an efficient utilization of capacity when the new capacity is available, price should be decreased to the point where usage is equated with capacity; as demand increases, price should be increased periodically to constrain usage within existing capacity. When price attains the level of estimated LRMC, this is a signal for the addition of new capacity.

Seasonal Pricing

The focus on seasonal rather than on time-of-day pricing in water provision is essentially a function of system design [22]. Distribution systems are generally designed to meet the maximum flows anticipated from fire protection (i.e., maximum hour demand is not an important parameter in distribution system design). In addition, maximum hour demand is not a critical factor in the design of transmission facilities since the daily demand cycle is partially accommodated by elevated storage facilities. In contrast, treatment and source of supply facilities are designed to meet maximum day demand or seasonal variations. Thus, there is substantially more variation in the incremental cost associated with seasonal demand cycles than in the incremental cost associated with daily demand cycles.

Although time-differentiated pricing logically flows from marginal cost pricing, seasonal rates in the past have generally been based on average cost rather than on marginal cost. For example, Tucson, Arizona, and Santa Fe, New Mexico, recently replaced declining block rates with seasonal rates. Although these rate design changes may be steps in the direction of more efficient pricing, these specific changes did not appear to incorporate marginal cost principles. This is an example of the imperfect quality of rate innovation in the water sector.

Most water systems experience distinct seasonal peaks, due to weather-sensitive demands. Seasonal pricing provides recognition of the cost variance between serving peak and off-peak demands. Given the premise that prices are to track costs, seasonal rates provide price signals to consumers as to the actual cost savings that can result from changing usage time patterns. In addition, seasonal rates can avoid certain results associated with voluntary conservation (i.e., declines in average demand but not in peak demand with the result of revenue erosion and increased unit costs).[4]

Seasonal marginal cost-based pricing can be advocated on the basis that uniform rates over time induce system expansion beyond an efficient size. Rates not differentiated by time are set less than the cost of providing maximum demands and set in excess of the cost of providing off-peak demands. This cross subsidization encourages capacity expansion to serve the peak users. In sum, the averaging of peak and off-peak costs produces an involuntary subsidy to peak users from off-peak users and produces an incentive to increase system capacity.

Given highly price-inelastic demands, seasonal pricing may have a minimal effect on consumption patterns; therefore, the anticipated benefits (e.g., deferred capacity expansion) of seasonal pricing may not materialize, despite prices tracking costs.[5] Whether this is an important problem depends upon one's perspective. To the economist, it is more important that efficient prices be charged than that the benefits of rate innovation be attained. To the manager and the regulator, it is more important that the anticipated operating effects be achieved than that the correct price signals be transmitted. Fortunately, in the water sector, efficient pricing produces the anticipated benefits in many cases.

Zonal Pricing

Efficient pricing cannot be accomplished solely by reliance on time-differentiated rates. Conceptually, seasonal water rates should be complemented by spatially-differentiated (zonal) rates. Both uniform rates over time and uniform rates over space generate inefficiencies (they are both subtle methods of cross subsidization). Employing the cost-causation standard, if water provision costs vary with both time and space for a particular system, then to achieve efficiency in pricing, rate design must incorporate both time and space. Schlenger [23] developed a simple zonal pricing model incorporating prices varying by pumping district within a service area. However, it was noted that substantial design and administrative costs, minimal spatial cost variances, and consumer resistance can block the adoption of zonal rates in specific cases. There is a potential for zonal pricing in water service as well as wastewater; however, some obstacles exist to the attainment of this potential. For example, the expense of acquiring spatial cost data has limited experimentation with zonal pricing.

It must be acknowledged that many municipalities employ a variant of zonal pricing in the form of rate differentials between internal (within the city) and external (outside the city) consumers. However, these internal/external rate differences generally have been motivated by purposes such as taxing nonvoters or inducing annexation; the rate differences have not been justified by actual pumping and capacity cost differences. Recently, zonal rates have been considered in Idaho (Boise Water Company), Connecticut (Connecticut-American Water Company), and Florida (Tampa). The implementation of relatively simple versions of zonal rates has occurred in Birmingham, Alabama, and in Kentucky (Kenton County Water District). An overall assessment of these cases produces the conclusion that the major obstacles to extensive implementation of zonal pricing is managerial, political, and consumer resistance rather than the costs of acquiring spatial data and the administrative costs of implementation.

Spatially differentiated pricing is recognition that pricing policy impacts upon urban growth rates, urban land use, and urban spatial structure. That is, zonal pricing (coupled with seasonal pricing) can assist in reducing low-density growth. In contrast, water pricing that ignores both time and space can induce urban sprawl and a corresponding increase in required capacity for both water supply and sewage disposal.

Fixed Charges as a Cost Recovery Option

Lump sum or fixed (periodic) charges are an alternative to commodity charges as a method of water cost recovery. There is a need to address the issue of whether or not to have certain capacity costs recovered by fixed charges in lieu of being recovered through commodity charges. A useful way of viewing the cost recovery issue is in the context of a two-tier pricing structure. The two-tier approach recognizes that users impose three types of costs upon water systems. One, general usage causes the firm to deliver service units. Two, peak usage causes the firm to provide capacity increments. Three, customer presence in the system causes the firm to provide incremental connections. Conceptually, the cost-causation standard indicates having commodity charges recovering usage-sensitive costs and having access charges recovering usage-insensitive costs. The access charges would reflect the cost of providing entry or access to the water system (i.e., the access charges would recover the costs incurred when consumers join the system). Access charges are payments for system access regardless of usage. Admittedly, there presently exist variations of access charges in the water sector (e.g., delivery capacity charges, readiness-to-serve charges, fire protection fees, capital contribution charges, availability benefit assessments, and connection charges). However, these existing variations are generally characterized by the absence of a rational costing basis.

The substitution of fixed charges for commodity charges should be evaluated in the context of three standards: efficiency, equity, and transaction costs. A periodic access charge makes economic sense if it is a cost associated with a specific customer (i.e., if the customer withdraws from the water system, the cost can be avoided). In sum, an access charge makes economic sense if it reflects a connection used exclusively by the consumer, if the cost associated with the connection is independent of the consumer's volume of usage, and if the connection or access cost is essentially independent of production and delivery system design.

Obviously, there is a need to explore alternative methods of water cost recovery and pricing. However, even though a movement toward two-tier pricing does not involve an increase in costs recovered (but instead a redistribution of the cost burden), it will most likely be met by substantial consumer and political resistance. Thus, this exploration should take place in the context of consumer benefits and costs, if decision makers are to be expected to support substantial changes in pricing practices. In essence, an assessment is warranted regarding the institutional nature of the urban water sector and its linkage to the acceptance and implementation of pricing reforms.

An Overview

As noted above, urban water prices tend to be below that dictated by most relevant pricing standards. That is, present practices in the water sector generate prices less than the real unit costs of providing urban water service. This underpricing results in aging capital facilities combined with inadequate system repair. The problem of the deterioration of water supply facilities as well as other infrastructure elements is a serious problem confronting many urban areas, particularly those in the older industrialized regions of the U.S. The deterioration is partly a function of pricing and partly a function of municipal administrations viewing the water utility simply as a stable source of revenues (revenues that can be diverted to nonwater uses), rather than as an important component of a well-functioning urban area.

An empirical analysis lends credibility to the underpricing hypothesis [24]. For 1960–1970, real water prices in the United States remained stable for residential, commercial, and industrial users. For 1970–1980, real prices for residential and commercial users declined while the real price of industrial service increased. In sum, the rate-setting process needs to be reformed to ensure adequate financing for system maintenance and capital improvements.

The focus on pricing and investment decisions for urban water supply should not detract from the importance of concurrently making similar decisions for urban sewage disposal. Water supply and sewage systems are interrelated (e.g., a decrease in household water consumption can result in a decrease in the volume of waste). Separating their decision making can negate efficient pricing and investment policies in water supply. Coordinating water and sewage policies may necessitate sewage metering or special charges for certain types of waste. In essence, efficiency in both water supply and sewage disposal should be incorporated into water pricing objectives.

Water supply decisions historically have been implemented ignoring the linkages between water demand, costing, and pricing. For example, water supply planning in urban areas involves tradeoffs between anticipated drought damages and system costs. Specifically, a tradeoff exists between the risk of having excess capacity versus the risk of having suboptimal capacity. Solving this tradeoff requires a compromise between demand factors (i.e., the risk of water deficits and the cost of usage restrictions) and supply factors (i.e., the economic and environmental costs of increasing system capacity). Conceptually, planners should strive for a system design that minimizes the sum of system costs and expected drought damages. The design selection is complicated in that pricing and conservation strategies may be pursued that restrict usage well before the occurrence of the actual deficit or that induce usage accelerating the deficit.

As Boland, et al. [25] noted, the appropriate approach to system design selection requires the forecasting of the risks of future deficits under varying demand conditions as well as the evaluation of the various methods for coping with the supply deficits. Once the deficit probabilities are derived, then the problem is one of deciding whether the deficit probabilities (and magnitudes) warrant increased system capacity (e.g., storage). Obviously, there is no truly objective standard available for measuring the specific costs and benefits of changing from a high risk/low storage option to a low risk/high storage option, and vice versa.

Conclusion

Important research developments regarding the costing and pricing of urban water have occurred in the past two decades. Regarding water demand, the evidence is that domestic use is virtually unresponsive to price changes and that seasonal demand is substantially more price-elastic than domestic demand. An implication is that time-differentiated rates may be more effective in altering consumption patterns than overall rate increases. Regarding water costs, the evidence is that production economies of scale can be offset by distribution diseconomies and that spatial cost variances provide a rationale for zonal pricing. Regarding water pricing, recent research has reduced the magnitude of the implementation problems associated with pricing innovation. Via improved estimation techniques, the use of the marginal cost pricing standard in implementing seasonal and zonal rates is more feasible than it was two decades ago. However, due to a mixture of knowledge gaps and application problems, the average cost standard remains dominant in the water sector, even under conditions of pricing experimentation.

There has been limited pricing reform; however, there has been slow response in converting the research developments into practice. Costing and pricing practices that were adequate several decades ago need to be adapted to a changing environment. The use of the marginal cost standard in the implementation of peak demand and spatial pricing would enhance water sector efficiency. Admittedly, there are numerous implementation problems associated with these innovations. However, the application problems are not insurmountable and should not be employed as an excuse for avoiding reform.

Water costing and pricing should not be examined in isolation. Water policymakers can derive valuable insight from examining certain issues and problems in other urban service sectors. For example, two-tier pricing issues are presently being debated in electricity, telecommunications, and natural gas. The stand-alone system concept used in telecommunications should be an important factor in estimating the costs of serving in-city versus suburban users. Similarly, the stand-alone costs of providing water service absent fire protection should be a decisive factor in determining the costs of providing fire protection versus basic water service.

This paper has focused on the relative narrow issues of urban water pricing and costing, issues on which most of the recent research has focused. It is conceded that more attention needs to be given to making simultaneous pricing and investment decisions for both water supply and sewage disposal. The historical separation of decisions regarding these interdependent systems possibly has caused as much waste as inefficient water pricing. Furthermore, urban sewage cost recovery and pricing is more inefficient than water pricing. More attention also needs to be given to how water and sewage system extensions affect the larger issues of urban land-use planning and urban growth.

Notes

1. Jerome W. Milliman and Charles E. Woods read an earlier version of this paper. The author is indebted to them for their instructive comments.

2. The primary response to the increasing criticism of declining block rates has been to reduce the number of blocks as well as to decrease the price differentials between blocks.

3. Examples of the inverted block rate structure can be found in Houston, Texas (where the rate applies only to residential consumers), and in Maryland (Washington Suburban Sanitary Commission).

4. Seasonal pricing can take the form of either separate winter/summer rates or a summer excess rate applied to consumption in excess of average winter usage. Examples of the former include Spring Valley Water Company (New York) and Santa Fe, New Mexico. Examples of the latter include Dallas, Texas, and the Fairfax County Water Authority (Virginia). In some cases, municipalities have implemented special seasonal charges for sprinkling and pool-filling.

5. Feldman [26] argued for time-of-day rates as a complement to seasonal rates. He noted that although seasonal pricing may provide an incentive for more efficient lawn sprinkling, there is little incentive to avoid days of extremely high sprinkling. Seasonal pricing may therefore avoid expensive demand metering, but it may be ineffective in reducing maximum day demand in the designated peak period.

References

1. Milliman, J. W. "Policy Horizons for Future Urban Water Supply." *Land Econ.* 39 (1963): 109–132.

2. Boland, J. J. "The Requirement for Urban Water: A Disaggregate Analysis." *1979 Annual Conference Proceedings.* Denver: American Water Works Association, 1979, 57–66.

3. Hanke, S. H. "Demand for Water Under Dynamic Conditions." *Water Res. Research.* 6 (1970): 1255–1261.

4. Howe, C. W., and F. P. Linaweaver. "The Impact of Price on Residential Water Demand and Its Relationship to System Design and Price Structures." *Water Res. Research.* 3 (1967): 13–32.

5. Billings, R. B., and D. E. Agthe. "Price Elasticities for Water: A Case for Increasing Block Rates." *Land Econ.* 56 (1980): 73–84.

6. Carver, P. H., and J. J. Boland. "Short-run and Long-run Effects of Price on Municipal Water Use." *Water Res. Research.* 16 (1980): 609–616.

7. Howe, C. W. "The Impact of Price on Residential Water Demand." *Water Res. Research.* 18 (1982): 713–716.

8. Dajani, J. S. "Cost Studies of Urban Public Services." *Land Econ.* 49 (1973): 479–483.

9. Ford, J. L., and J. J. Warford. "Cost Functions for the Water Industry." *J. Ind. Econ.* 18 (1969): 53–63.

10. Clark, R. M. "Cost and Pricing Relationships in Water Supply." *J. Env. Eng. Div.* 102 (1976): 361–373.

11. Clark, R. M. "Water Supply Regionalization: A Critical Evaluation." *J. Water Res. Plan. Man. Div.* 105 (1979): 279–292.

12. Clark, R. M., and R. G. Stevie. "A Water Supply Cost Model Incorporating Spatial Variables." *Land Econ.* 57 (1981): 18–32.

13. Clark, R. M., and R. G. Stevie. "A Regional Water Supply Model." *Growth & Change.* 12 (1981): 9–16.

14. Turvey, R. "Analyzing the Marginal Cost of Water Supply." *Land Econ.* 52 (1976): 158–168.

15. Hanke, S. H. "On the Marginal Cost of Water Supply." *Water Eng. Man.* 120 (1981): 60–68.

16. Mann, P. C., R. J. Saunders, and J. J. Warford. "A Note on Capital Indivisibility and the Definition of Marginal Cost." *Water Res. Research.* 16 (1980): 602–604.

17. Hanke, S. H., and R. K. Davis. "Potential for Marginal Cost Pricing in Water Resource Management." *Water Res. Research.* 9 (1973): 808–825.

18. Hanke, S. H. "Pricing as a Conservation Tool: An Economist's Dream Come True." *Municipal Water Supply.* Edited by David Holtz and Scott Sebastian. Bloomington: Indiana University Press, 1978.

19. Martin, W. E., H. M. Ingram, N. K. Laney, and A. H. Griffin. *Saving Water in a Desert City.* Washington: Resources for the Future, 1984.

20. Mann, P. C., and D. L. Schlenger. "Marginal Cost and Seasonal Pricing of Water Service." *Amer. Water Works Assn. J.* 74 (1982): 6–11.

21. Vickrey, W. S. "Responsive Pricing of Public Utility Services." *Bell J. Econ.* 2 (1971): 337–346.

22. Hanke, S. H. "A Method for Integrating Engineering and Economic Planning." *Amer. Water Works Assn. J.* 70 (1978): 487–491.

23. Schlenger, D. L. "Developing Water Utility Cost Estimates Incorporating Spatial Factors." *Proceedings of Symposium on Costing for Water Supply.* Edited by Thomas M. Walski. Washington: United States Corps of Army Engineers, 1983, 40–55.

24. Mann, P. C. and P. R. LeFrancois. "Trends in the Real Price of Water." *Amer. Water Works Assn.* 75 (1983): 441–443.

25. Boland, J. J., P. H. Carver, and C. R. Flynn. "Supply Capacity Is Enough?" *Amer. Water Works Assn. J.* 72 (1980): 368–374.

26. Feldman, S. L. "On the Peak Load Pricing of Urban Water Supply." *Water Res. Research.* 11 (1975): 355–356.

Commentary by Alfred L. Parker

The contribution made by Professor Mann in his chapter "Urban Water Pricing: The Divergence Between Theory and Practice" is to be applauded on several counts. First, it provides a useful survey of recent research in water demand and costing, including a constructive evaluation of the strength and weakness of recent research in these areas of water research. Second, Professor Mann makes the important connection between economic research and the real-world applications of the results of water demand and costing research. The linking of research developments to pricing innovation is clearly important, providing guidance direction in the development of new research activity. And third, Professor Mann identifies specific areas where additional research on these important topics — water demand and costing — is needed. On each of these counts the work represents an important and valuable addition to the literature.

The Pricing of Water in Perspective

A recurring theme, present, but not fully developed, in the Mann chapter warrants special recognition and comment. This is the theme reflected in the author's comments to the effect that problems in the pricing of water (the setting of municipal water rates) parallels in many respects the problems encountered in natural gas, electric utility, and telecommunications pricing.

For example, early in the chapter Mann observes, "The numerous pressures that have affected public utility regulation have impacted upon water service." The impact of inflation, consumer sentiment to shield low-income consumers, and regulators consideration of seasonal pricing are cited as examples of such pressures. And near the end of the chapter Mann states, "water policymakers can derive valuable insight from examining certain issues and problems in other urban service sectors."

I believe that there is substantial support to be found for this thesis. Not only do the problems being encountered in the pricing of water appear to parallel those facing other utilities, but also the apparent solutions and the obstacles to the implementation of those solutions to water pricing problems appear to have much in common with pricing problems encountered in the pricing of other utility services.

This is evident from the discussion of time differentiated and spacially differentiated rates, which parallel the electric utility industry's "time-of-day pricing" and "measured service" in the telecommunications industry; the discussion of fixed charges as a cost recovery option, which parallels the concept of an "access charge" for the telecommunications industry; the discussion of declining versus inverted block rate structure; the recognition of the subsidization of one sector by another; the recognition of managerial, political, and consumer resistance to marginal cost pricing and more.

The commonality of problems, solutions, and obstacles to solution implementation is an important message to be delivered to those pursuing water research, those in water management positions, and regulators of water utilities.

Confusing Activity with Progress

The strength of this message (and what may be gained from it) has been somewhat diluted by other comments relative to the implementation of the results of water research. For example, the stated theme of the Mann chapter is that although important research developments have taken place, little activity has occurred in implementing these research results. The general conclusion offered by Professor Mann expresses the same view of the world as follows:

> Important research developments have occurred in urban water economics; however, little progress has taken place in implementing the research products, particularly in contrast to activities in other public utility sectors.

The review of recent water demand and costing research does appear to support the conclusion that "Important research developments have occurred. . . ." And the references to new water pricing initiatives appear to support the conclusion that ". . . little progress has taken place in implementing the research products. . . ."

But has this experience really been that much different from the experience of other regulated industries? Because there is no effort by Professor Mann to document (or support) this element of his general conclusion the reader cannot be sure just what ". . . activities in other public utility sectors" he has in mind.

Care must be exercised to be certain that we do not confuse *activity* with *progress*. More simply stated, the deregulation of a previously regulated industry (or some portion thereof) and/or the attention that regulators have placed on the measurement of marginal costs has not necessarily resulted in better utility pricing (i.e., pricing that effectively promotes allocative or productive efficiency).

While it has become a common practice of regulators to require and for regulated firms to develop estimates of the marginal cost of the services they provide, the price structures approved by regulators generally do not appear to be closely tied to these estimates of marginal cost. Political considerations generally limit price adjustments to a level or form designed to achieve results considerably less ambitious than those generally associated with the economists concept of marginal cost pricing.

Thus, it may be suggested that the pricing of water parallels the pricing of other utility services *not only* with respect to the nature of the problems, the form of the solutions offered, and the obstacles to the implementation of these solutions, but also in the lack of success in implementing the results of existing research.

The Economists Ego

The concern expressed over the fact that there has been little in the way of implementation of the results of water demand and costing research may also simply be a reflection of what I will call "the economist ego." This is a common malady among economists and other social scientists — it is our strong tendency to assume that once we have completed our research, drawn our conclusions, and defined the correct solution that it is reasonable to expect the industry, regulators, and/or legislative bodies to respond quickly and appropriately to our work. Of course, the correct response is to adopt our recommendations and implement our solutions because they are empirically, mathematically, and logically correct. Perhaps fortunately, this is not the way things work in the real world.

This phenomenon is clearly illustrated in an incident I was privileged to observe some years ago in a unique regulatory environment. In the mid-1970s a major natural gas utility was seeking a rate increase for natural gas service being provided to residential and commercial customers located on an Indian reservation located in the southwest. The Tribal Council (duly elected by members of that tribe) was the regulatory body with jurisdiction to hold hearings and approve or reject the utility's request for such a rate adjustment.

On the day designated for the hearing of this matter several bright, confident executives from the utility's home office in another state were flown onto the Indian reservation to meet with the Tribal Council and present their case for the proposed rate increase. They arrived at the hearing in their pin-stripped suits, their leather briefcases bulging with data, analyses, and testimony supporting their position that the existing utility rates did not meet the utilities revenue requirements and that a rate increase was required, in fact was long overdue. (It should be noted that the existing gas rate structure had been in place unaltered for more than a decade.)

The utility executives were confident that they could and would make their case. After several hours of testimony and still more hours in which Tribal Council members were provided an opportunity to ask questions, a recess was taken. The utility executives expressed concern, that in spite of their considerable efforts to be responsive to the questions asked by Tribal Council members, they did not feel that they were making any real progress in convincing the Tribal Council of the need for (or that the gas company deserved) a rate increase. The fact that Tribal Council members had adopted the practice of asking the same question that had been asked but a few minutes earlier by another member of the Council was cited as evidence that no real progress was being made.

The utility executives seemed to be incapable of understanding just exactly what was going on. The Tribal Council was willing to listen courteously (if not attentively) for an indefinite time to testimony offered by company executives, and the Tribal Council would continue to ask questions that would suggest a desire on their part to learn all that these emissaries had to offer, but *the Council was not going to approve any rate increase*.

Sure, the facts as expertly developed and presented to the Tribal Council indicated that a rate adjustment was justified, but the Council had no intention of raising the gas utility bills of their relatives, friends, and neighbors.

This was clearly not a situation that the company executives had anticipated. From their perspective the facts (revenue and cost data) clearly indicated the need for a rate increase; they expected the Tribal Council to respond correctly to the overwhelming weight of the evidence. There was no such response forthcoming. (A rate increase was approved at a later date by the courts.)

Economists are frequently (if not generally) guilty of the same poor judgment. We economists perform our research from an unbiased perspective, using the best data available (or generating our own data if none is available), applying the appropriate research techniques, using the best statistical and/or econometric methodology, drawing only those conclusions that are clearly supported by the results of our analysis. How can regulators, regulated industries, or legislative bodies dare to ignore the results of our labor?

A Different Perspective

There is a more constructive perspective from which to view the important research developments and the parallels noted between the pricing of water and pricing of the services provided by other regulated industries. This perspective, rather than expressing concern over the failure to implement what has been learned, encourages us to explore the experience of other utility sectors in an effort to learn from their experience in wrestling with remarkably similar issues. Such an effort may succeed in accelerating the implementation process — moving the pricing of municipal water toward a more efficient and rational solution — a solution consistent with society's interests and the results of economic analyses.

Those pursuing water demand and costing research and/or those concerned with the implementation of the results of this research must take advantage of this opportunity to learn from the experience of other regulated industries. This is not to suggest that the results of pricing applications and experiments in the electric and gas utility industries or the telecommunication industry are directly applicable to the pricing of water, but I am confident that there is a great deal to be learned from the careful examination of the experience of these other utilities.

Mann has identified the traditionally low cost of water service relative to other public utility services, the traditional engineering emphasis in water decisionmaking and the availability in the past of inexpensive and easily available water supplies as factors contributing to the historical neglect of water pricing and costing. It appears likely that these same factors *plus* developers resistance to zonal pricing and consumers general resistance to higher water bills will remain obstacles to the implementation of more rational pricing strategies.

Factors promoting the implementation of such pricing strategies include the growing awareness of water quality problems, increased efforts by city planners to discourage low-density growth (to encourage construction on vacant lots within already developed areas), greater awareness of cross subsidization present in existing rate structures, and the highly visible pricing innovations being studied and implemented in other regulated industries.

While there remain important gaps in water pricing and costing research (e.g., demand studies using time-series data for consumers who have experienced substantial variation in water prices over time), a strong case can be made for a careful review of the pricing strategies that are being considered and applied in other regulated industries. The results of their innovation and experiments in the pricing of other utility services may provide results, insights that are directly applicable to water pricing and may thus encourage the movement toward more rational water pricing strategies.

7 NATURAL MONOPOLY MEASURES AND REGULATORY POLICY

Douglas Gegax

Western economic thought during the eighteenth and nineteenth centuries has been characterized as an explanation and justification of an unfettered market system. More recently concern over the potential failure, in some circumstances, of such a system to achieve socially desirable goals has broadened the scope of economics. Out of this concern has emerged a new set of justifications — that which emphasizes the need for government intervention or regulation. Although the justification for regulation can, and often does, stem from legal or political concerns, the purpose here is to stress the economic rationale for regulation. Of specific concern are the conditions under which monopoly — production by a single firm — accompanied by some degree of regulation is a *desirable* form of market organization.

The economic desirability of a market comprised of a single firm stems from technical aspects of cost. Given the technology used to produce some level of output, if it is less costly for production to be concentrated in the hands of a single firm rather than a multiplicity of firms, then a natural monopoly is said to exist. In situations such as these, a market structure comprised of a single firm may be desirable. To avoid potential consumer exploitation, however, the issue of regulation, both of degree

185

and form, must be addressed. This latter issue is also intertwined with technical cost relationships.

What follows is a summary of the conditions under which a monopoly market structure is desirable or "natural" and the considerations that help guide the decision regarding government intervention or regulation.

Natural Monopoly in the Single-Product Firm

Relationships Between Subadditivity, Declining Average Cost, and Declining Marginal Cost

Since the economic rationale for regulation is intertwined with technical aspects of cost, it is necessary to define precisely the term *natural monopoly*. Essentially, if a single firm can produce a desired level of output at lower total cost than any output combination of m firms ($m \geq 2$), then a natural monopoly is said to exist. Baumol [1] formalizes this point by introducing the concept of subadditivity. A cost function, $c(q)$, is subadditive over a relevant range of output q (or up to q) if and only if

$$c(q) < \sum_{i=1}^{m} c(q_i)$$

for all

$$m \geq 2, \quad q_i > 0 \quad i = 1, \ldots, m$$

such that

$$\sum_{i=1}^{m} q_i = q. \tag{7.1}$$

That is, subadditivity exists if any level of output produced by one firm costs less than if subsets of that output level are produced by more than one firm. Moreover, a firm is said to be a natural monopoly if and only if the firm's cost function is subadditive. The benefits of a natural monopoly (or "benefits of subadditivity") are given by the difference between the total cost of a multiplicity of firms producing some level of q and the total cost of a single firm producing that output level.

Although the historical development of the term *natural monopoly* has yielded different definitions, the concept of subadditivity, intuitively, is the simplest and most appealing. Baumol, Panzar, and Willig [2], in remarking on the nature of subadditivity add:

[subadditivity] surely, is what anyone has in mind, at least implicitly, when speaking of a monopoly being "natural," and that is what economists were undoubtedly groping for when they (as it turns out, mistakenly) identified natural monopoly with economies of scale.

Indeed, the economies of scale definition of natural monopoly is still pervasive in textbooks.

A single-product firm exhibits economies of scale if and only if its long-run average cost function is decreasing. Figure 7–1A shows an average cost (AC) function that is decreasing up to q_0. A firm with such a cost function would be said to exhibit economies of scale up to output level q_0. Figure 7–1A shows that for all $q < q_0$

$$\frac{c(\alpha q)}{\alpha q} < \frac{c(q)}{q} \tag{7.2}$$

where $1 < \alpha < 1 + \epsilon$, and where ϵ is a small positive number. Multiplying both sides of 7.2 by αq yields the following formal definition of economics of scale. A cost function exhibits economies of scale at q if and only if

$$c(\alpha q) < \alpha c(q) \tag{7.3}$$

for all α such that $1 < \alpha < 1 + \epsilon$.

Figure 7–1B shows the benefits of subadditivity for a particular level of output. Suppose that total market output is given by q_1. If a *single* firm were to produce q_1, then total cost would be given by the area of the rectangle $oacq_1$ (recall that $AC \cdot q = $ total cost). If, on the hand, total market output was divided equally between *two* firms, then each firm produces q_2 ($q_2 = 0.5q_1$) with the total cost incurred by each firm from producing q_2 given by the area $obcq_2$. Note however that the total cost incurred by all firms in the market is twice $obcq_2$ or simply the area $obdq_1$. Therefore, the benefits of subadditivity (in this example being the difference between the cost of two firms splitting q_1 and the cost of one firm producing q_1) are given by the area $abde$.

To use the concept of economies of scale as a definition of natural monopoly is, however, misleading because it is too strict. While it is true that a cost function that exhibits economies of scale up to some level of q is subadditive up to that output level, a cost function may also be subadditive up to q and exhibit diseconomies of scale (i.e., increasing average cost). Put another way, decreasing average cost (DAC) implies subadditivity (SA),

$$DAC \Rightarrow SA, \tag{7.4a}$$

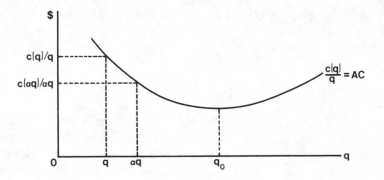

Figure 7–1A. Economies of scale.

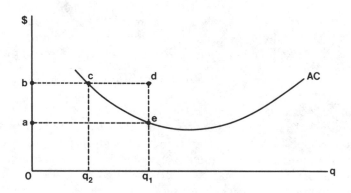

Figure 7–1B. Benefits of subadditivity.

but subadditivity does not imply decreasing average cost,

$$SA \nRightarrow DAC \tag{7.4b}$$

To illustrate this, compare two different market arrangements for producing some level of output q: 1) one firm producing all of q, and 2) two firms producing $\bar{q}$ and $q - \bar{q}$ respectively. Assume that all firms have the same cost function. Appealing to inequality 7.1, if the cost function were subadditive up to q, then

$$c(q) < c(\bar{q}) + c(q - \bar{q}). \tag{7.5}$$

For simplicity (and without loss of generality) let $\bar{q} = q/2$, so inequality 7.5 becomes

$$c(q) < c\left(\frac{q}{2}\right) + c\left(\frac{q}{2}\right)$$

or

$$c(q) < 2c\left(\frac{q}{2}\right)$$

or

$$\frac{c(q)}{q} < \frac{2c(q/2)}{q}. \qquad (7.6)$$

Note that the left-hand side of the inequality 7.6 represents the average cost of one firm producing q while the right-hand side represents the average cost of the two firms, in total, producing q.

Figure 7–2 illustrates both of these relationships.[1] This figure shows that for all levels of q less than q^*, inequality 7.6 holds; that is, $c(q)$ is subadditive up to q^*. The figure also shows that for levels of q between 0 and q_0, $c(q)$ exhibits decreasing average costs and subadditivity (i.e., 7.4a). However, note that for levels of q between q_0 to q^*, $c(q)$ exhibits subadditivity and increasing average costs (i.e., 7.4b). A formal proof of statement 7.4 is given by Berg and Tschirhart [4].

The traditional textbook relationship between marginal cost (MC) and average cost — where marginal cost rises monotonically to the right of

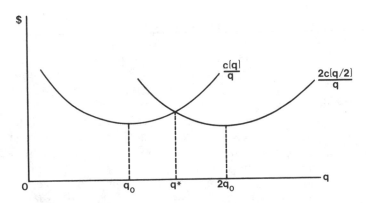

Figure 7–2. Economies of scale and subadditivity.

the minimum of average cost — can yield useful insights as well. For average cost to be declining (DAC), it is only necessary that marginal cost be less than average cost; that is, marginal cost may be decreasing (DMC) or increasing. But when marginal cost is greater than average cost, both are increasing. The relationship between AC and MC can be summarized as follows

$$DMC \Rightarrow DAC, \tag{7.7a}$$

$$DAC \nRightarrow DMC; \tag{7.7b}$$

so combining statements 7.4 and 7.7 we find that

$$DMC \nRightarrow DAC \Rightarrow SUB, \tag{7.8a}$$

$$SUB \nRightarrow DAC \Rightarrow DMC. \tag{7.8b}$$

Natural Monopoly and Regulatory Policy

In order to set guidelines for regulatory policy it is necessary to distinguish between instances of decreasing average cost and instances in which costs are subadditive but average cost is increasing. Since the former is a stronger condition, a firm that exhibits decreasing average cost will be referred to as a strong natural monopoly. A firm whose costs are subadditive but whose average costs are increasing will be referred to as a weak natural monopoly.[2] In addition to this distinction, it is necessary to establish a benchmark (welfare maximizing) price-output combination.

If we assume that the appropriate measure of society's welfare is the sum of consumer surplus and producer surplus, the single price that maximizes welfare is one that equals marginal cost.[3] Let q_w denote the level of output implied by this pricing rule. The unregulated profit maximizing monopolist, however, produces a level of q such that marginal revenue (MR) equals marginal cost (MC) with the resulting price greater than marginal cost. Let q_m denote this profit maximizing level of output. Figure 7–3 compares these two levels of output and, given the inverse market demand function $p(q)$, the corresponding levels of price.

Figure 7–3 shows that, compared to welfare maximization, the monopoly profit maximizing solution yields a higher price and lower output level resulting in lower total welfare. The welfare (or deadweight) loss due to monopoly profit maximization is given by the area of triangle cde. The monopoly profit maximization solution, is said to yield allocative inefficiency (measured by the deadweight loss) in that too few resources are allocated to the industry in which the monopoly resides. Here, output

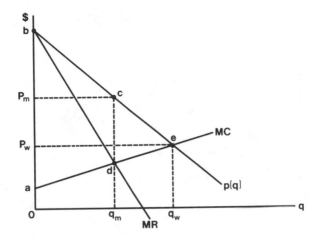

Figure 7–3.   Monopoly deadweight loss.

is too low relative to both the value consumers place on the good and the cost of expanding service. Figure 7–3 shows that for additional output units from q_m to q_w, consumers are willing to pay a price (as given by the inverse demand curve) at least as great as the extra costs of producing the additional units (as given by MC). Under unregulated monopoly, however, the expansion of service from q_m to q_w is not realized. Note that area cde could also be viewed as the potential (allocative efficiency) benefits of regulation, if the objective of the regulatory body were to maximize welfare.

The appropriate degree and form of regulation will depend upon whether, given demand conditions, the firm is a strong or weak natural monopolist. Figure 7 4A illustrates the case of a weak natural monopoly. Here the efficiency benefits of regulation are given by the area aeb. Moreover, the welfare maximizing level of output q_w, renders a viable firm earning a profit equal to area dP_wbc. Since the firm is earning a profit, other firms may desire to enter the market and produce some of q_w. But because costs are subadditive, a multiplicity of firms producing q_w would be less desirable than a single firm producing q_w. Thus, protecting the monoplist from competition would be required and, from a total production cost perspective, justified.[4]

The role of the regulatory body, however, changes under the strong natural monopoly situation illustrated in figure 7–4B. Here, the efficiency benefits of regulation are given by the area aeg, but under welfare

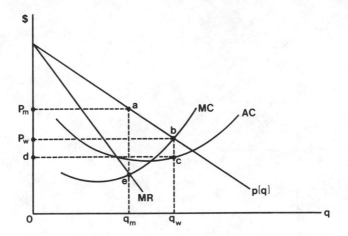

Figure 7–4A.   Weak natural monopoly.

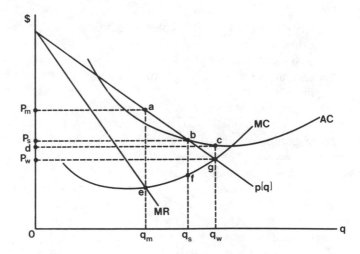

Figure 7–4B.   Strong natural monopoly.

maximizing conditions the firm is not viable. Given the output level of q_w, the regulated monopolist would face a deficit equal to area $dcgP_w$. This situation is often referred to as the "natural monopoly dilemma."

Two methods have been suggested that deal with the potential deficit.

First, price remaining equal to marginal cost and the resulting deficit would be covered via subsidies generated from an external source. Hotelling [5] suggested that if these subsidies were paid via lump sum taxes, no wedge would be driven between prices faced by consumers and those received by producers; thus, no distortions would enter the economy. Although the distribution of income would be affected by such a scheme, the total level of income would be left unaffected. And, Hotelling asserted, with the redistribution if the net gainers outweigh the net losers, there is potential for the losers to be compensated. This analysis requires either an interpersonal comparison of utilities (if a compensation scheme is not available) or that a viable compensation scheme actually exist. Furthermore, one of the taxes suggested by Hotelling was the income tax — which is not of the lump sum type.

If deficits from marginal cost pricing are not covered by external funds, the average level of rates must be raised to the level of average cost. Satisfaction of this "budget constraint" necessitates some departure from the optimal (i.e., *first-best*) marginal cost pricing rule. For example, if customers are to be charged the same (single) price, then welfare is maximized (subject to total revenue being at least as great as total cost) by setting price equal to average cost. Figure 7–4B shows this arrangement. Here, the single price, P_s, generates enough revenue so that the deficit is eliminated. However, with the benefits of (average cost pricing) regulation equaling the area *aefb*, there is still a deadweight loss equal to the area *bfg*. Therefore with the addition of the above revenue constraint, we are in a *second-best* situation.

The average-cost pricing rule, while eliminating deficits, has been shown to be inferior to other pricing rules, which involve either price discrimination across customers and/or varying price for a given customer.[5] Like average-cost pricing, such schemes can also eliminate deficits but, as compared to average-cost pricing, such schemes will generate smaller deadweight losses. An example of price discrimination across customers is given by the so-called Ramsey rule and is discussed here as an alternative to average-cost pricing.

One possible solution to the natural monopoly dilemma is found in an answer to a slightly different problem originally tackled by Frank Ramsey [9], which he stated as the following:

[If] a given revenue is to be raised by proportionate taxes on some or all uses of income, the taxes on different uses being possibly at different rates; how should these rates be adjusted in order that the decrement of utility be a minimum?

Ramsey's second-best solution to this problem required that gross prices (i.e., prices including the tax) be increased the least for those services that have the most elastic demands, and the most for those with the least elastic demand.

Baumol and Bradford [10] applied Ramsey's problem to the case of the strong natural monopolist. Their work shows, perhaps most clearly, how the Ramsey rule is derived and some of its implications for allocative efficiency. A rough sketch of the calculus is given here for a consumers' surplus definition of welfare. Although Baumol and Bradford assert that the social welfare function maximized in their paper is unspecified, Mohring [11] demonstrates that this "unspecified utility function actually had the properties of the consumers' surplus measure." Therefore, it is felt here that such a measure of welfare is representative of the work done by Baumol and Bradford.[6]

Let the natural monopolist supply n customer classes, and let the inverse demand curve and measure of consumers' surplus for the ith customer class be represented by equations 7.9 and 7.10 respectively.

$$P_i = p_i(q_i) \tag{7.9}$$

$$S_i = \int_0^{q_i} p_i(q_i) \, dq_i - p_i(q_i)q_i \tag{7.10}$$

That is, consumers' surplus is the area under the inverse demand curve, less the consumers' expenditures (firm's revenue).

The problem is how to minimize the losses in welfare, W, while allowing the firm to charge a price for each customer class above the respective marginal cost of serving that class. This problem can be alternatively stated as:

$$\max W = \sum_{i=1}^n S_i \tag{7.11}$$

subject to the constraint that:

$$\sum_{i=1}^n p_i(q_i)q_i \geq \sum_{i=1}^n c_i(q_i) \tag{7.12}$$

where the left-hand side of 7.12 is merely the total revenue generated from all the customer classes, and the right-hand side of 7.12 is the total cost of serving all customer classes. The number of customer classes is given by n.

From the first-order conditions of this constrained optimization problem, the following results are obtained:

$$\left[\frac{P_i - MC_i}{P_i}\right] E_i = \frac{\alpha - 1}{\alpha} \qquad i = 1, \ldots, n \tag{7.13}$$

where α (< 0) is the lagrangian multiplier, E_i is the demand elasticity (in absolute value) of the ith customer class, MC_i is the marginal cost of serving the ith customer class, and $(P_i - MC_i)/P_i$ is the percentage deviation of price from marginal cost for the ith customer class. Thus, for any two customer classes, i and j:

$$\left[\frac{P_i - MC_i}{P_i}\right] E_i = \left[\frac{P_j - MC_j}{P_j}\right] E_j. \tag{7.14}$$

Note that 7.14 is the Ramsey rule. If, for example, $E_i > E_j$, then for 7.14 to be maintained as an equality, it must be the case that $(P_i - MC_i)/P_i < (P_j - MC_j)/P_j$. In other words, class i receives a smaller percentage markup above marginal cost than does class j, although both receive a price greater than marginal cost.

Finally, the first-order conditions can be manipulated in order to yield the following approximation:

$$\frac{\Delta q_i}{q_i} \simeq \frac{(1 - \alpha)}{\alpha} \qquad i = 1, \ldots, n \tag{7.15}$$

where the left-hand side of 7.15 represents the percentage decrease in service to class i (in absolute value) resulting from a price to that class above its marginal cost.

For two different customer classes, i and j, 7.15 implies that

$$\frac{\Delta q_i}{q_i} = \frac{\Delta q_j}{q_j} \tag{7.16}$$

or that social welfare is maximized, subject to the revenue constraint 7.12, by setting prices P_i and P_j such that the percentage decrease in output is the same for the two customer classes. This is shown in figure 7–5. Here, the demand curves for customer class i and j are given by the lines D_i and D_j respectively. For illustrative simplicity, the marginal costs of serving the two customer classes are both equal to the constant MC_0, with the first-best (i.e., $P = MC$) level of output identical for both.

In figure 7–5 it is clear that the demand curve of customer class j is less elastic than that of customer class i. In order for the percentage change in output to be the same for the two classes, the figure shows that the price increase above marginal cost for j will have to be greater than that for class i; i.e., $(P_j - MC_j) > (P_i - MC_i)$.

Essentially, then, the Ramsey rule maximizes welfare subject to the

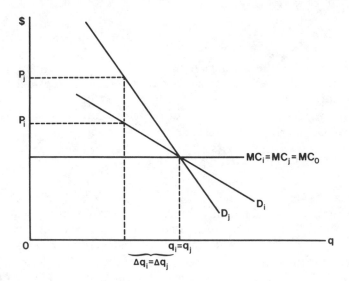

Figure 7-5. Ramsey rule.

revenue constraint by choosing the set of prices $(P_i, i = 1, \ldots, n)$ such that *distortions in output are minimized*. Furthermore, the role of relative demand elasticities across the different customer classes is crucial to the choice of prices. Here, the second-best solution is one in which the relative price deviation from marginal cost for each customer class is inversely proportional to the elasticity of demand. A large deviation from marginal cost is applied to the customer class for which there would be little change in demand — resulting in a small distortion from the first-best consumption level yet generating a significant addition to revenue. At the same time, the customer class that is most sensitive to price receives the smallest mark-up and therefore a large reduction in the optimal consumption amount is avoided. Finally, since the differences in price are not reflective of differences in cost, but rather differences in demand elasticities, the Ramsey rule is an example of price discrimination.[7]

It should be noted that price discrimination *does not* imply that those customers who pay a higher price are subsidizing those customers who pay a lower price. Although price discrimination can yield cross-subsidies from one class to another, price-discrimination as defined here (see Note 5) does not guarantee cross-subsidization. Consider the following example where a student is sitting next to a business passenger on a half-full airline. Suppose the student's maximum willingness to pay for the service is $200 while the business passengers maximum willingness to pay is $500 (e.g., the student has a higher demand elasticity). Since the plane will fly regardless of whether or not the student flies and since the plane is not at capacity, the marginal cost of serving the student is low — say $10. Suppose that the student gets a $150 fare while the business passenger receives a $300 fare. Does the fact that the business passenger is paying twice as much as the student imply that the business passenger is subsidizing the student? By the student flying, the airline incurs an additional $10 in cost. Clearly the student is more than covering these directly attributable costs. The additional $140 is therefore either contribution to either profit or coverage of fixed costs. If the student is asked to pay a fare equal to the business passenger, the student will not fly ($300 > maximum willingness to pay) and, therefore, the fixed costs must be retrieved from some other source (perhaps by higher fares to business passengers). Only if the student pays a price lower than the marginal cost of being served is the issue of cross-subsidization relevant. Remember that under Ramsey pricing all customers get a price above marginal cost with the degree of mark-up depending on demand elasticities.

The Ramsey rule can also be viewed from another perspective. Suppose that initially the strong natural monopolist is just covering all its costs by engaging in average-cost pricing as discussed above. From this initial situation suppose that the firm moves to Ramsey pricing. Such a change in the firm's pricing structure implies that prices would go up in the inelastic demand markets and down in the elastic demand markets [6, 13]. With respect to the implications of this type of price discrimination, Kahn [6] concludes that:

> ... [f]ollowing such a rule would have the effect of favoring the [elastic demand customers] over the [inelastic demand] customers [representing] a decision to distribute the major part of the benefits of the increasing returns to the [elastic demand customers]. Such an action could be justified on the ground that, since the surplus or welfare gain that the [elastic demand] customers obtain ... exceeds what the [inelastic demand] customers lose, the former could compensate the latter. But without any arrangements for such compensation, this discriminatory pricing pattern would in effect distribute more income to the [elastic demand] than to the [inelastic demand] group.

Although issues involving compensation arrangements have been de-emphasized in the economics literature, under certain situations the existence of such arrangements (or lack thereof) can significantly affect behavior. This issue is touched on in the next section.

Natural Monopoly in the Face of Competition

Up to this point, the discussion has assumed that the natural monopoly is completely immune from the competition of rival firms. Increasingly we find this is not the case. The determination of efficient prices will be affected by either: 1) direct entry (or potential entry) by rivals using a similar technology (or mode) into the regulated firm's industry; or by 2) the growth of "firms which employ greatly differing technologies to provide services which can be viewed as imperfect substitutes for one another" [14]. The latter type of competition is referred to as intermodal competition.

Braeutigam [14] sets up a model in which there is one regulated strong natural monopolist — which could not break even if the price for each of its services were equal to marginal cost — and firms from other competitive industries offering different modes of service. Braeutigam gives railroads offering freight transportation services as being an example of the strong natural monopolist and other industries, such as motor carriers and water carriers, as being examples of different modes offering services that are close (but not perfect) substitutes for rail transport.[8]

With the addition of other modes of service, the demand elasticities for each customer class facing the regulated firm will be affected. Moreover, when Braeutigam sets up a welfare maximization problem similar to 7.11 − 7.12 but including these new rivals, he gets an interesting variation of the Ramsey rule. Specifically, from the perspective of the regulated firm the second-best pricing solution (i.e., the divergence between price and marginal cost being inversely related to the elasticity of demand) is now optimal only if such a pricing rule is also being adhered to by firms in the other (competitive) industries.

Looked at another way, if the competitive nature within these other industries drives price down to marginal cost in these industries, then the set of Ramsey prices charged by the regulated firm is no longer optimal. An implication of Braeutigam's result is that in order to ensure allocative efficiency, the regulatory body would also have to regulate the rival firms. Efficient pricing by the regulated firm would require that the rivals also charge a price above marginal cost. This would require that the regulatory body either restrict entry into the other industries or impose a set of taxes to ensure that the prices consumers pay — for all models of services — diverge from the marginal cost of serving them.

Obviously, expanding the regulatory body's jurisdiction in this manner would represent an enormous undertaking. Viewed from the theoretical extreme, unless the regulatory body is allowed to restrict entry into all industries that affect the demand elasticities of the natural monopoly, Ramsey prices will no longer be optimal. Currently, as Braeutigam points out, "under the present statutory powers, regulators are not empowered to impose taxes, even if they had sufficient information to determine the levels of the taxes required."

Under certain conditions [16], if compensation were feasible from the gainers to the losers of the regulated firm's movement from average-cost pricing to Ramsey pricing, there would be little incentive for customers to purchase the service from the regulated firm's rivals. The problem, of course, arises when a mechanism for compensation is unavailable. In this situation some individual customers class would find it cheaper to purchase the service from one of the regulated firm's rivals although the total resource costs to society would be lower if all customer classes purchased the service from the natural monopoly. Here, the set of Ramsey prices (without compensation) is said to be unsustainable or vulnerable to attack by a rival.[9]

Zajac [16] points out another instance of vulnerability, which is possible even if compensation is available. He calls this type of vulnerability game-theoretic instability. Consider a hypothetical list of costs facing a regulated monopoly who serves three different customer classes. Let $30, $48, and $75 refer to, respectively, the total costs of serving one class only, two classes jointly, and three classes jointly. Note that it is cheaper to provide services jointly rather than it is to provide them separately (i.e., subadditivity of costs prevails).[10] For illustrative simplicity, assume that the same cost structure would apply to any potential rival.

Suppose that the regulated firm is to serve all three customer classes jointly and that the costs are allocated equally among the three classes (i.e., $25 each). Eventually two of the three customer classes (say class one and two) would discover that as a group they are paying $50 but if some rival firm supplied them with the service they would, as a group, be paying only $48. As a result, class one and two would agree to be served by the regulated firm only if they were charged, say, $24 each. This, however, would mean that class three would have to be charged $27. Now class three and either one or two will discover that as a group they are paying $51 but if some rival firm supplied them with the service they would, as a group, be paying only $48.

Zajac proves that no matter how the $75 overall required revenue (i.e., the cost of the regulated firm serving all three customer classes) is apportioned between the three classes, it would always be that some two classes are contributing in excess of $48. Therefore, they would have an incentive to purchase the service from a rival firm. Finally, Zajac points out that the notion of "gainers" compensating "losers" simply means a change from one possible apportionment of total costs to another. Therefore, under some circumstances, even if compensation is available, Ramsey prices would be unsustainable.

What makes the above list of costs ($30, $48, $75) "unstable" is that even though average total costs are falling throughout, the incremental costs of serving an additional customer class fall from zero to two but then rise from two to three. If incremental costs were also to fall throughout (e.g., if the list of total costs was: $30, $55, $75), then the game-theoretic instability observed above would not exist. Although by statement 7.8a both situations describe a natural monopoly, in the ($30, $48, $75) situation the regulatory body is faced with the question of how to deal with competitors undermining the benefits of subadditivity (perhaps by protecting the natural monopoly from entry) while in the latter situation it is not. This example also underscores an important point: The existence of viable competitors does not imply that the regulated firm is no longer a natural monopoly.

Natural Monopoly in the Multi-Product Firm

In the section "Natural Monopoly in the Single-Product Firm," a set of sufficient conditions for a single-product natural monopoly was given. For example, it was stated that declining average cost — or economies of scale — while not a necessary condition, guaranteed subadditivity and hence the existence of a natural monopoly. One might be inclined to use the same relationships developed in the previous section when defining natural monopoly in a multiproduct firm; or, one might be inclined to aggregate the outputs of a multiproduct firm into a single-output measure. As we will see, following inclinations such as these could be a serious mistake. Cost relationships in the single-output firm simply *cannot* be used when discussing the existence of a multi-output natural monopoly. We shall therefore, proceed initially by developing definitions analogous to those in that section. The unique relationship between these definitions and subadditivity in a multiproduct firm, however, will necessitate the development of cost definitions *unique* to a multiproduct firm.

In what follows q will denote a vector, or combination, of n distinct outputs. In general, superscripts will denote a specific output combination, or bundle, while subscripts will denote particular products. For example if, q^i denotes the ith combination of 2 distinct outputs then $q^i = (q_1^i, q_2^i)$; where q_1^i denotes the amount of output q_1 in output bundle i and

q_2^i denotes the amount of output q_2 in the bundle. Finally, $c(q^i) = c(q_1^i, q_2^i)$ would denote the total cost of producing output bundle i.

Cost Definitions

Let $q^i = (q_1^i, \ldots, q_n^i)$ be a vector of n different outputs for *any* bundle $i = 1, \ldots, m$. Then a cost function exhibits global subadditivity if and only if

$$c(q^1 + \ldots + q^m) < c(q^1) + \ldots + c(q^m). \qquad (7.17)$$

As in 7.1, m can be interpreted as a particular number of firms. Given *two* output vectors of n different goods $q = (q_1, \ldots, q_n)$ and $q' = (q_1', \ldots, q_n')$ then from 7.17 it follows that c is *globally* subadditive if

$$c(q + q') < c(q) + c(q') \qquad (7.18)$$

for any two output vectors q and q'. Sharkey [3] defines subadditivity in a way which follows directly from 7.18. He states that a cost function that is subadditive for all output vectors q (i.e., all q less than or equal to the maximum possible demand) may be more simply characterized by

$$c(q) < c(q') + c(q - q') \qquad (7.19)$$

for all $q' < q$. Note that what 7.17, 7.18, and 7.19 have in common is that the output vectors on the right-hand side of the inequality sum to the output vector on the left-hand side of the inequality.

A cost function may not be globally subadditive but still exhibit sub-additivity of cost over a specific region (i.e., locally). For a cost function to be subadditive at $q^* = (q_1^*, \ldots, q_n^*)$ the sum of the costs of separately producing *any* two output vectors, when added together to yield q^*, must be greater than the costs of producing q^* in a single firm. This is given formally by the following:

$$c(q^*) < c(q^i) + c(q^j) \qquad (7.20a)$$

where

$$q^* = q^i + q^j; \quad q^i, q^j \neq 0 \qquad (7.20b)$$

Again q^*, q^i, and q^j represent output vectors, or combinations, of n different outputs.

For example, consider a two-product cost function $c(q_1, q_2)$ that is subadditive at $q^* = (2, 2)$. Note that at q^*, $q_1^* = 2$ and $q_2^* = 2$ and for integer values for q_1 and q_2 there are four possible situations that satisfy

7.20b. They are:

$$q^* = (2, 2) = (0, 1) + (2, 1)$$
$$= (0, 2) + (2, 0)$$
$$= (1, 0) + (1, 2)$$
$$= (1, 1) + (1, 1)$$

Given subadditivity at q^*, then by 7.20a we have:

$c(q^*) = c(2, 2) < c(0, 1) + c(2, 1)$		(7.21a)
$< c(0, 2) + c(2, 0)$		(7.21b)
$< c(1, 0) + c(1, 2)$		(7.21c)
$< c(1, 1) + c(1, 1)$		(7.21d)

Economies of scope (SCOPE) is a restricted version of subadditivity. A cost function is said to exhibit economies of scope at q^* if and only if

$$c(q^*) < c(q^i) + c(q^j), \qquad (7.22)$$

where

$$q^* = q^i + q^j,$$

and where the dot product

$$q^1 \cdot q^j = \sum_{k=1}^{n} q_k^i \, q_k^j = 0.$$

Again n denotes the number of different products in the bundles. Appealing to the above numerical example, for economies of scope to exist only inequality 7.21b need hold. For 7.21b, $q^i = (0, 2)$, $q^j = (2, 0)$ and

$$\sum_{k=1}^{2} q_k^i \, q_k^j = 0.2 + 2.0 = 0$$

Given 7.21b, it is less costly to produce q^* in a single multiproduct firm than to produce the *same* level of each of the two outputs in two *specialty* firms. Note that subadditivity implies economies of scope, but economies of scope do not imply subadditivity, i.e.,

$$\text{SUB} \Rightarrow \text{SCOPE} \qquad (7.23a)$$

$$\text{SCOPE} \nRightarrow \text{SUB} \qquad (7.23b)$$

Using the relationships developed earlier when defining natural monopoly in a multiproduct firm can be a serious mistake. This is easily shown by way of the following example. Consider the following two-output cost function[11]:

$$c(q_1, q_2) = q_1 + q_2 + (q_1 q_2)^{0.5}$$

This function exhibits economies of scale in each output *separately* and so by inequality 7.4a it might be expected to be subadditive. Note however that $c(1, 0) + c(0, 1) = 2$ while $c(1, 1) = 3$ so this function does not exhibit economies of scope and, therefore, by 7.23a is not subadditive. The problem here is that, while economies of scale exist in each output separately, there are no benefits in producing the two goods jointly. Therefore, for a multiproduct firm to be subadditive there must be some type of economies of joint production. It is this idea of "jointness" that distinguishes multiproduct natural monopoly from single-product natural monopoly. Moreover, while economies of scope is a result of benefits of joint production, recall that economies of scope is still only a restricted version of subadditivity in a multiproduct firm.

While in the single-product firm there existed a straightforward relationship between scale economies and average cost (i.e., economies of scale was equivalent to decreasing average cost), this is not the case with a multiproduct firm. The problem with multiproduct production is that there is no unique denominator over which costs may be averaged: We have a problem of adding up oranges and apples. In a multiproduct firm, the ideas of economies of scale and decreasing "average" cost become distinct, but related, concepts. Let us first define economies of scale.

Like the single-product firm (recall inequality 7.3, except that here q represents an output bundle), a multiproduct cost function exhibits global economies of scale if for all output vectors q

$$c(\alpha q) < \alpha c(q) \text{ for all } 1 < \alpha < 1 + \epsilon \qquad (7.24)$$

For example, consider the function $c(q_1, q_2) = q_1 + q_2 + (q_1 q_2)^{1/3}$. This function satisfies the condition given in inequality 7.24 since

$$
\begin{aligned}
c(\alpha q_1, \alpha q_2) &= \alpha q_1 + \alpha q_2 + (\alpha q_1 \alpha q_2)^{1/3} \\
&= \alpha q_1 + \alpha q_2 + \alpha^{2/3} (q_1 q_2)^{1/3} \\
&< \alpha q_1 + \alpha q_2 + \alpha (q_1, q_2)^{1/3} \\
&= \alpha c(q_1, q_2)
\end{aligned}
$$

for $\alpha > 1$. Hence, this function exhibits global economies of scale.[12] This general definition of economies of scale, however, neither solves the aforementioned apples and oranges problem *nor implies subadditivity*. Note that this cost function does not even exhibit economies of scope. Hence, by 7.23a, the function is not subadditive. In fact this function is characterized by global *diseconomies* of scope since

$$c(q_1, q_2) = q_1 + q_2 + (q_1\, q_2)^{1/3} > q_1 + q_2 = c(q_1, 0) + c(0, q_2).$$

So that $c(q^*) > c(q^i) + c(q^j)$ and hence the inequality found in 7.22 is reversed. It should be apparent that in a multiproduct firm, economies of scale alone does not capture the jointness of production idea needed to characterize a natural monopoly.

In the multiproduct firm, average cost cannot be defined in the same fashion as in the single-product firm due to the "apples and oranges" problem. An alternative approach suggested by Baumal, Panzar, and Willig [2] is to fix output proportions and examine the behavior of total cost as the magnitude of each good increases. Figure 7–6A illustrates this concept for a two-product firm with a cost function $c(q_1, q_2)$.

Along the ray OR in the figure the proportion of q_2 to q_1 is fixed at some value, β. Different points on OR correspond to different "bundles" of q_2 and q_1 holding β constant. The absolute size of the bundle — or composite good q — can be measured once we decide on the specific q_1, q_2 combination that constitutes the unit bundle. Although one might be inclined to choose $(q_1 = 1, q_2 = 1)$ as the combination in the unit bundle, the choice is purely arbitrary. For example, in figure 7–6A suppose that the bundle $q^0 = (q_1^0, q_2^0)$ is assigned a value of one. Any movement up OR from q^0 amounts to increasing both q_1 and q_2 by a factor of $t > 1$. Therefore, t is the number of units in the bundle $q = tq^0$; or, since $q^0 = 1$, $q = t$. If, for example, both q_1 and q_2 are double from the unit bundle q^0, then the composite commodity gets a value of $q = 2$.

The average cost of the composite good can now be given as

$$RAC = \frac{c(tq^0)}{t} \tag{7.25}$$

where $c(tq^0)$ is a point on the total cost function $c(q_1, q_2)$. Expression 7.25 is referred to as ray average cost and corresponds to a given value of β.

Figure 7–6B is a construction that allows us to examine the behavior of total cost as we move out on the ray OR. Here, OAB is a cross section of the cost function $c(q_1, q_2)$ obtained by dropping a plane perpendicular to the q_1, q_2 plane and along the ray OR. Given point B on the cross section and point C on the q_1, q_2 plane, the slope of ray OB (equal to CB/OC) is ray average cost (RAC) at the point B. Note that RAC at point A is greater than RAC at point B indicating that, at least initially, as we move out on the ray OR (i.e., as we increase t) RAC is decreasing. Note that in this situation figure 7–6B shows that

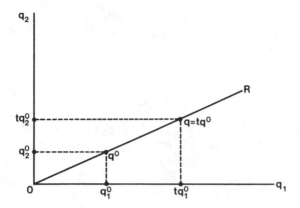

Figure 7–6A.   Fixed output proportions: The composite good.

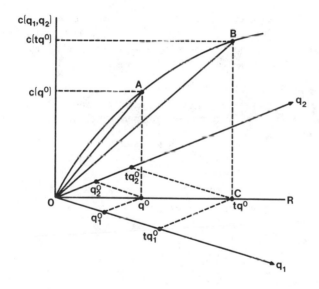

Figure 7–6B.   Decreasing ray average cost.

$$\frac{c(tq_1^0,\ tq_2^0)}{t} < \frac{c(t^0q_1^0,\ t^0q_2^0)}{t^0} \qquad (7.26)$$

where $t^0 = 1$ and $t > t^0$. The left-hand side of 7.26 represents RAC at point B while the right-hand side of 7.26 represents RAC at point A.

In general, if we consider a ray through some output vector $q = (q_1, \ldots, q_n)$ where u and w are measures of the scale of output along that ray (i.e., magnitudes of the composite commodity q), then RAC is decreasing if and only if

$$\frac{c(uq_1, \ldots, uq_2)}{u} < \frac{c(wq_1, \ldots, wq_2)}{w} \qquad (7.27)$$

for $u > w$. While RAC is a way around the apples and oranges problem, it should be noted that decreasing RAC is not necessary for subadditivity. In this respect, multiproduct production is similar to the single-product case (recall figure 7–2).

Since multiproduct firms may alter production in a way such that output proportions may change, it is useful to look at cost behavior not only along a ray such as OR but also between rays. This brings us to another cost concept unique to the multiproduct firm — transray convexity.

Essentially, if a cost function $c(q_1, \ldots, q_n)$ is transray convex through some point $q^* = (q_1^*, \ldots, q_n^*)$ then the multiproduct firm will enjoy a cost advantage over specialty firms. As Spence [17] notes, transray convexity implies that the ·

> . . . cost of producing a weighted average of a pair of output bundles q^a and q^b is not greater than the weighted average of the costs of producing each of them in isolation. That is to say, complementarities in production outweigh scale effects.

Formally, a cost function $c(q_1, \ldots, q_n)$ is transray convex through $q^* = (q_1^*, \ldots, q_n^*)$ if there exists *any* set of positive constants $w = (w_1, \ldots, w_n)$ such that for *every* two output vectors $q^a = (q_1^a, \ldots, q_n^a)$ and $q^b = (q_1^b, \ldots, q_n^b)$ that lie on the same hyperplane $\sum_{i=1}^{n} w_i \, q_i = w_0$ through q^*, we have

$$c(\alpha q^a + (1 - \alpha)q^b) < \alpha \, c(q^a) + (1 - \alpha)c(q^b) \qquad (7.28)$$

for all α such that $0 < \alpha < 1$.

Before giving an example, note the following points about this definition:

1. In order for q*, q^a, and q^b to lie on the same hyperplane there must be some set w such that

$$W_0 = \sum_{i=1}^{n} w_i \, q_i^* = \sum_{i=1}^{n} w_i \, q_i^a = \sum_{i=1}^{n} w_i \, q_i^b.$$

2. For the function $c(q)$ to be transray convex, there only needs to exist one hyperplane through q^* such that 7.28 holds — even though there are infinitely many hyperplanes through q^*.
3. A function $c(q)$ can be transray convex through one point and not transray convex through another.

Given a two-product firm, the hyperplane mentioned above amounts to a negatively sloped line through $q^* = (q_1^*, q_2^*)$. Figure 7–7A illustrates two possible lines through q^*. Note that since transray convexity requires 7.28 to hold for *any* q_1, q_2 combination on the line, the lines in figure 7–7A are extended to both axes.

Suppose that condition 7.28 holds for line AB in figure 7–7A. Transray convexity is illustrated in figure 7–7B. Let the two output vectors, q^a and q^b, be given by the two end points of the line AB. In the figure, the curve DEG is a cross section of the cost function $c(q_1, q_2)$ obtained by dropping a plane perpendicular to the q_1, q_2 plane and along the line AB. Such a cross section is referred to as a transray cross section. The line AB also represents *all* possible linear combinations of q^a and q^b; i.e., values of $q = \alpha q^a + (1 - \alpha)q^b$ for all $0 < \alpha < 1$. Therefore, the curve DEG represents all points on the cost function such that:

$$c = c(\alpha q^a + (1 - \alpha)q^b) \qquad (7.29)$$

for all $0 < \alpha < 1$. On the other hand the line DG represents all linear combinations of $c(q^a)$ and $c(q^b)$; i.e., all possible levels of cost such that:

$$c = \alpha c(q^a) + (1 - \alpha)c(q^b) \qquad (7.30)$$

for all $0 < \alpha < 1$. Note that except for the end points ($\alpha = 0$ and $\alpha = 1$), points on the line DG are not on the cost function; in fact, they lie above the cost function. Therefore, 7.29 is less than 7.30 and hence by 7.28 the function is transray convex at q^*.

A numerical example is also given in reference to figure 7–7B. Suppose that $\alpha = 0.75$. This gives us a *specific* linear combination of q^a and q^b denoted by point C on the line AB. Suppose $c(q_1, q_2)$ at point C equals 2000 while $c(q^a) = 3000$ and $c(q^b) = 1500$. Here, $2000 < 0.75\ c(q^a) + 0.25\ c(q^b) = 2625$, which is consistent with the transray convexity condition given in 7.28.

The intuition behind this illustration is that the cost of producing *any* linear combination of q^a and q^b in separate firms is greater than the cost of producing the same combination in a single firm. Thus, transray convexity incorporates the idea of jointness that simple scale economies fail to capture.

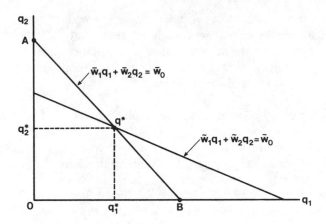

Figure 7–7A. Linear combinations of q*.

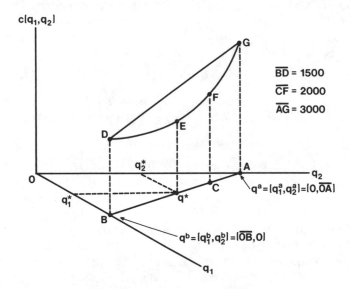

Figure 7–7B. Transray convexity.

The combination of declining ray average cost and transray convexity implies subadditivity. An example of a two-product cost function that exhibits both of these characteristics is given by $c(q_1, q_2) = q_1^{1/4} + q_2^{1/4} - (q_1, q_2)^{1/4}$ and is shown in figure 7–8.[13] In the figure, ACD is a transray

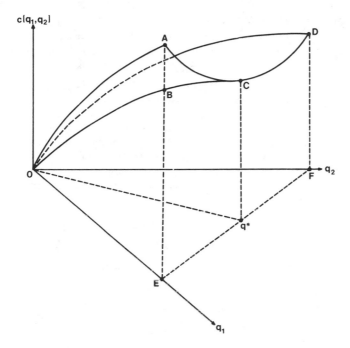

Figure 7–8. Multiproduct subadditivity.

cross section lying direct above the line EF. While OBC is a cross section lying directly above the ray oq^*. From the previous discussion, the figure shows that $c(q_1, q_2)$ exhibits (for example at q^*) both declining ray average cost and transray convexity. Moreover, this function has economies of scope at every output since

$$c(q_1, 0) + c(0, q_2) = q_1^{1/4} + q_2^{1/4}$$
$$> q_1^{1/4} + q_2^{1/4} - (q_1 \, q_2)^{1/4}$$
$$= c(q_1, q_2).$$

The combination of declining ray average cost and transray convexity implies that it is less costly for multi-output production to be concentrated in the hands of a single firm rather than a multiplicity of firms. Essentially, declining ray average cost suggests that as the *scale* of the output bundle grows, unit costs fall, hence, "bigger bundles are better." The factors that may contribute to this are similar to those that contribute to decreasing average cost in the single product firm (e.g., specialization of inputs and indivisibilities in inputs[14]). Transray convexity suggests that a single multiproduct firm producing some output bundle — q^* — has cost advantages over separate firms producing bundles that, in total, sum to q^*. That is, there are economies of coordinating production activities within a single firm (i.e., there are cost disadvantages in "splitting the bundle"). Berg and Tschirhart [4] add that:

> Here, we would expect that two (or more) outputs could share an accounting, marketing, or other administrative department and incur less cost than if each output utilize a separate department. Or, there may be some externality that becomes internalized when two (or more) outputs are brought into the same production process. Producing beef and leather hides is one classic example of shared inputs . . . daytime and nighttime electricity [is] another example.

As an example, declining ray average cost and transray convexity are consistent with cost benefits owing to, respectively, horizontal and vertical integration.[15]

The electric industry is a good example of economies of coordination. Electric utilities supply a large variety of services including varying proportions of generation, transmission and distribution of various voltages, levels of reliability, and degrees of load stability. The point that an electric enterprise is a multiproduct firm is underscored: A utility is required to provide not only current to a line, but also current that has some high probability of actually continuing to be there. That is, a utility has built generating plant and transmission plant to achieve some required level of reliability. Therefore, there are at least two products here: power and reliability.

It is traditional to separate the provision of electricity into generation, transmission, and distribution. Because of the tight physical linkage required between these elements and the necessity that the three be in continuous dynamic equilibrium, separating these three is technologically and economically meaningless. An electric power system can be thought of as a number of input nodes (generation facilities) connected to a number of output nodes (distribution points) by transmission lines. For a power system to be in equilibrium the sum of the power demanded at the output nodes must equal the sum of the power generated at input nodes (minus transmission losses). Failure to maintain this equation at any instant can result in system failure. This necessity for continuous vertical coordination can be considered as creating a vast externality problem. The externality centers around the fact that decisions made at any stage can dramatically affect system viability and reliability.

In current practice, the majority of electricity is sold by vertically integrated firms combining generation, transmission, and distribution into a single system. In these cases, the externality is internalized because the single firm bears all of the consequences of each activity. Vertically deintegrating the generation, transmission, and distribution functions among a multiplicity of firms, while maintaining current levels of system reliability and stability, at best could only happen with an enormous increase in cost.[16] Two components of the cost increase are transactions cost and outlays on transmission capacity.

As between any two nodes on a transmission grid, assuming they are the only two interconnected positions, power can flow smoothly, or relatively so, so long as generation reductions at the receiving node match the increases at the sending node and there are no, ceteris paribus, changes in electricity demand. Two contracting parties can expect that the contracted exchange in power will occur at the rate required by demand conditions. In such a case, any difficulties occurring as to transmission facilities can be handled, negotiated, between the contracting parties. Potential externalities are internalized by the contract. With deintegration and an increase in independent generation facilities the transactions costs of internalizing the externality can be expected to drastically increase.

Exchanges of power *do not occur* simply between a receiving node and a sending node, uniquely connected together. Otherwise the electric *grid* system in the U.S. would not be referred to as a grid. Contiguous utility systems are connected together in relationships, with few exceptions, that involve greater than paired transactions. Thus for any transaction between any two parties, there will virtually *always* be an involved third party or parties. A crucial potential (negative) externality to which deintegration is likely to expose the electric industry is that of loop flow.

Electricity will follow the laws of physics. Ohm's Law states that electricity will move along the path of least resistance (impedence). The result of this fact is that one observes power flowing over transmission lines that are not part of a transaction (i.e., a loop flow). This is an externality as discussed above. The third party may have to rearrange its own interchanges of electricity, and in fact, may have to build additional transmission capacity in order to protect itself from contractual flows of power to whcih it is not even a party, nor derives any benefit. With deintegration and an increase in independent generation facilities the problem of loop flow can be expected to worsen, and therefore an increase in transmission capacity would be required in order to maintain current levels of reliability.

Again, vertically deintegrating the generation, transmission, and distribution functions among a multiplicity of firms, while maintaining current levels of power and reliability can be expected to increase both transaction costs and outlays on transmission capacity.

Currently, however, there are cost savings achieved through vertical and horizontal integration. Vertical coordination between generation, transmission, and distribution may also result in cost savings at the planning stage — through the timing of needed investments — and during operation — by the scheduling of maintenance and the use of energy interchange to meet a given demand with less capacity connected to the load. In addition, horizontal integration at the regional level may result in cost savings owing to increased load diversity and a smaller fraction of spinning reserves required for a given level of reliability. Power pools are good examples of this type of coordination with the biggest single benefit of pooling involving the cost savings in reserve generating capacity. As Gegax and Tschirhart [21] point out:

> Utilities maintain generating capacity in operating reserve status to meet unexpected increases in demand, equipment failures, and maintenance. The level of reserves needed depends primarily on the size of on-line generating units and the loss-of/load probability the utility wants to achieve. An isolated utility may determine that a particular level of reserves is needed to meet the risk of excess demand; but this level can be reduced through coordination, since the risks confronted by two or more coordinated utilities are less than the sum of risks confronted by the utilities in isolation.

Note that the cost savings of horizontal and vertical integration are due to the jointness involved in producing the two products (power and reliability) and not due to the economies of scale (or lack thereof) of producing one product in isolation (e.g., generation of power).

In this section, five cost relationships unique to the multiproduct firm have been discussed.

1. subadditivity implies economies of scope.
2. Economies of scope do not imply subadditivity.
3. Economies of scale is neither necessary nor sufficient for subadditivity.
4. Declining ray average cost is not necessary for subadditivity.
5. The combination of declining ray average cost and transray convexity implies subadditivity

Of these relationships, only number 5 offers a sufficient condition for subadditivity. Declining ray average cost and transray convexity are useful constructs in which to analyze the cost advantages of a horizontally and vertically integrated firm, though other sufficient conditions for sub-additivity can be found in the literature. Indeed, other weaker conditions may be developed soon. However, to date there exists no set of *necessary and sufficient* conditions for subadditivity. Such a set would have the advantage of yielding a minimum cost requirement for the existence of a multiproduct natural monopoly.

Conclusion

The discussion in this chapter has stressed the importance of cost when analyzing the desirability of concentrated production — the focal point of the analysis being subadditivity. While the concept of subadditivity is quite straightforward, it should be pointed out that it is not easily measured. This is especially true in the case of the multiproduct firm. As Baumol, Panzar, and Willig [2] point out, "the intuitive appeal of the subadditivity concept is counterbalanced by its analytic elusiveness." For this reason it is crucial to analyze the relationship between subadditive and other (perhaps less elusive) cost concepts. It is hoped this chapter has shed some light on a few of these relationships.

It has been pointed out, for example, that testing for scale economies may be of little help in forming policy regarding natural monopoly in a multi-product firm. While this practice is common, it can lead to policy formulations that are misdirected. It should be stressed that while economies of scale offer a sufficient condition for subadditivity in the single-output firm, it is neither necessary nor sufficient for the existence of a multiproduct natural monopoly. In the latter, it is the jointness of production that may yield cost advantages to concentrated production.

While it is true that there are currently no necessary and sufficient conditions for subadditivity in a multiproduct firm, ignoring the unique cost characteristics of such production is an option we should avoid. There are conditions that are sufficient and others that are necessary. For example, the concept of *cost complementarity*, while extremely strong, is sufficient for subadditivity. If a cost function exhibits this trait, then the marginal cost of producing one good decreases as the production of another good rises. Conditions such as these can, as Baumol, Panzar, and Willig [2] point out, "yield some intuitive grasp of the more recondite properties of the concept of subadditivity."

Finally it is worth noting that the economic case for the regulation of industry is a delicate balance between the benefits of competition and the benefits owing to the potential that scarce resources are most effectively utilized (in a technical sense) when production is concentrated in the hands of a small number of firms. If, for example, the latter exists but is small in magnitude would this still justify government protection and regulation of a single enterprise? Clearly regulation itself is not a costless endeavor. On the other hand, should our focus on the virtues of competition blind us regarding the ubiquitous nature of externalities and advantages of coordination?

The question of market structure is clearly multidimensional but the economic rationale of emphasizing one market organization over another, in the end, centers around cost. Economic thought has progressed considerably in its ability to structure complicated cost relationships. In this sense, it can no longer be viewed as simply a justification for an unfettered market system.

Notes

1. A specific cost function yielding the curves found in figure 7–2 is given by Sharkey [3]. This function is $c(q) = 1 + q^2$ so that $c(q)/q = q^{-1} + q$ and $2c(q/2)/q = 2q^{-1} + 0.5q$. With reference to figure 2 it may be calculated that, given this cost function, $q_0 = 1$, $q^* = \sqrt{2}$, and $2q_0 = 2$.

2. The terms *strong* and *weak natural monopoly* are given by Berg and Tschirhart [4].

3. To show this let $P = p(q)$ denote the inverse demand curve so for some level of q consumer surplus is given as

$$\int_0^q p(q)\, dq - p(q)q$$

that is, the difference between total willingness to pay (the area under the inverse demand curve) and total expenditures paid to (revenues received by) firms. Suppose we have a single firm. In the long run, producer surplus is equal to profit, or $p(q)q - c(q)$, where $c(q)$ is the firm's long run total cost function and $p(q)q$ *is simply total revenue. Define welfare, W,* as the sum of consumer surplus and producer surplus, or (after simplification)

$$W = \int_0^q p(q)\, dq - c(q)$$

Taking the first derivative of W with respect to q and setting this derivative equal to zero yields $p(q) - c'(q) = 0$. Where $c'(q)$ is the first derivative of total cost, i.e., marginal cost (MC). So at maximum W we have $P = MC$. The components of maximum W are shown in figure 7–3. Consumer surplus is given by the area of triangle P_w be and, since long run total cost is given by the area under the long run marginal cost function, profit is given by the area of triangle aP_we. Therefore, W is given by the area of triangle abe.

4. This ignores potential inefficiencies such as the Averch-Johnson effect and X inefficiency. For an exposition of these, see Berg and Tschirhart [4] and Nowotny, chapter two.

5. For a detailed discussion of the former (i.e., price discrimination) see Kahn [6]. Kahn defines price discrimination as charging different customers different prices for essentially the same commodity where the differences in price are not reflective of differences in cost.

For a discussion of the latter (i.e., non-linear pricing) see Berg and Tschirhart [4], Brown and Sibley [7], or Willig [8].

6. Although the presentation here will assume cross-price elasticities to be zero, the notion of Ramsey optimality is useful for interdependent demands as well. See Brown and Sibley [7].

7. For a discussion regarding Caveats on applying Ramsey pricing, see Kamerschen and Keenan [12].

8. Another relevant example of intermodal competition is that which electric utilities — employing central generating plant technologies — face from industrial coegeneration. For a discussion on industrial coegeneration, see Joskow and Jones [15].

9. For a detailed discussion on the sustainability of Ramsey pricing, see Baumol, Pazar, and Willig [2], Berg and Tschirhart [4], Brown and Sibley [17], and Sharkey [3].

10. For example, if one firm provided service to two customer classes while another firm provided service to the third class, costs in total would be $78. On the other hand, if one firm provided services to all three, then total costs would be $75.

11. This example is given by Sharkey [3].

12. [3].

13. [3].

14. See Kahn [6] for a discussion on these.

15. Transray convexity can also be compared to cost benefits owing to conglomerate integration (i.e., product diversification) as well as vertical integration. Moreover, sources of economies of vertical integration can be of a technical nature (as implied here) or of a transactions cost nature. See Coase [18] and Williamson [19] for a discussion of the possible reduction in transactions costs from vertical integration.

16. See any book on electrical engineering, (e.g., Gross [20]).

References

1. Baumol, W. J. "On the Proper Cost Tests for Natural Monopoly in a Multiproduct Industry." *Amer. Econ. Rev.* 67 (1977): 808–822.

2. Baumol, William J., John C. Panzar, and Robert Willig. *Contestable Markets and the Theory of Industry Structure.* New York: Harcourt Brace Jovanovich, 1982.

3. Sharkey, William W. *The Theory of Natural Monopoly.* Cambridge: Cambridge University Press, 1982.

4. Berg, Sanford V., and John Tschirhart. *Natural Monopoly Regulation: Principles and Practice.* Cambridge: Cambridge University Press, 1988.

5. Hotelling, H. "The General Welfare in Relation to Problems of Taxation and Railway and Utility Rates." *Econometrica*, 6 (1938): 242–269.

6. Kahn, Alfred E. *The Economics of Regulation: Principles and Institutions Volume 1.* New York: John Wiley and Sons, 1970.

7. Brown, S. J., and Sibley, D. S. *The Theory of Public Utility Pricing.* Cambridge: Cambridge University Press, 1986.

8. Willig, Robert D. "Pareto-Superior Nonlinear Outlay Schedules." *Bell J. Econ.* (Spring 1978): 56–69.

9. Ramsey, F. R. "A Contribution to the Theory of Taxation." *Econ. J.* 37 (1927): 47–61.

10. Baumol, W. J., and Bradford, D. F. "Optimal Departures from Marginal Cost Pricing." *Amer. Econ. Rev.* 60 (1970): 265–283.

11. Mohring, H. "The Peak Load Problem with Increasing Returns and Pricing Constraints." *Amer. Econ. Rev.* 60 (1970): 693–705.

12. Kamerschen, David R., and Keenan, Donald C. "Caveats on Applying Ramsey Pricing." In *Current Issues in Public-Utility Economics*. Edited by Albert L. Danielson and David R. Kamerschen. Lexington, Mass.: Lexington Books, 1983.

13. Baumol, William J. "Reasonable Rules for Rate Regulation: Plausible Policies for an Imperfect World." In *Prices: Issues in Theory, Practice, and Public Policy*. Edited by American Phillips and Oliver E. Williamson. Philadelphia: University of Pennsylvania Press, 1967.

14. Braeutigam, Ronald R. "Optimal Pricing with Intermodal Competition." *Amer. Econ. Rev.* 69 (1979): 38–49.

15. Joskow, Paul L., and Jones, Donald R. "The Simple Economics of Industrial Cogeneration." *Energy J.* 4 (1983): 1–22.

16. Zajac, E. E. *Fairness or Efficiency: An Introduction to Public Utility Pricing*. Cambridge: Ballinger Pub. Co., 1978.

17. Spence, M. "Contestable Markets and the Theory of Industry Structure: A Review Article." *Journ. Econ. Lit.* 21 (1983): 981–990.

18. Coase, Ronald. "The Nature of the Firm." *Economietrica* 4 (1937): 386–405.

19. Williamson, Oliver. *Economic Institutions of Capitalism*, New York Free Press, 1985.

20. Gross, Charles A. *Power Systems Analysis*. New York: John Wiley and Sons, 1986.

21. Gegax, Douglas, and John Tschirhart. "An Analysis of Interfirm Cooperation: Theory and Evidence from Electric Power Pools." *Southern Econ. J.* 50 (1984): 1077–1097.

Commentary by Ronald R. Braeutigam

The paper by Douglas Gegax ("Natural Monopoly Measures and Regulatory Policy") in this volume discusses some of the important changes that have occurred in the characterization of and public policy toward natural monopoly in recent years. The topics alluded to in that essay have been central to public policy debates in a number of American industries undergoing regulatory reform since 1975, including among others all or parts of the airline, railroad, motor carrier, telephone, cable television, natural gas and oil industries.[1] The wave of regulatory reform is apparently extending itself energetically to other parts of the world, where terms such as privatization, liberalization, and deregulation have become commonplace.

The following questions are among those most often appearing in connection with regulatory reform. 1) What is a natural monopoly? 2) If an industry is a natural monopoly, does that necessarily mean that some form of government intervention, such as regulation, is warranted? 3) If not, what alternatives to regulating a natural monopoly might be used, and when and how might such alternatives be introduced? 4) If regulation is warranted on economic grounds, what kinds of alternatives are there, and how does one decide which to pursue in a given industry?

The Gegax article focuses on the first and (to a lesser extent) the fourth of these questions. This review will attempt to place his comments in perspective by discussing the relationships of all four questions identified above.

In his introductory section Gegax describes his paper as "a summary of the conditions under which a monopoly market structure is desirable or 'natural' and the considerations that help guide the decision regarding government intervention or regulation." Scherer [1, p. 482] describes a view of regulation and natural monopoly that prevailed at least through the 1960s, "The most traditional economic case for regulation assumes the existence of natural monopoly — that is — where economies of scale are so persistent that a single firm can serve the market at a lower unit cost than two or more firms."

As Gegax correctly indicates, the contemporary literature characterizes a natural monopoly using the concept of subadditivity instead of economies of scale. It is subadditivity, not economies of scale, that addresses the crucial question as to whether it is less costly for a single firm, as opposed to any group of two or more firms, that can produce a given set of outputs at the lowest cost. Although for a single product firm economies of scale imply subadditivity, it turns out that in general (including multiproduct technologies) economies of scale are neither necessary nor sufficient for subadditivity in the cost structure.[2]

As Gegax notes, this is one of the reasons that the traditional view of natural monopoly, which argues for regulation when there are pervasive economies of scale in a market, has been extensively questioned and modified in the literature since the late 1960s. But there are other important reasons (not discussed by Gegax) for questioning the traditional view of regulation, as the next section shows.

Public Policy: To Regulate or Not?

A finding that an industry is a natural monopoly would indicate that there is not room for competition within the market. However, the question as to whether an industry ought to be regulated does not end with a determination that an industry is a natural monopoly.

The contemporary literature characterizing a natural monopoly has suggested rather forcefully that there may be ways to introduce competition *for* a market, even if a natural monopoly structure exists within a market. Competition for the market in these instances will lead to economically efficient prices (at least in the sense of second best). The possible optimality of such competition in dealing with a natural monopoly is one of the most important ways in which the contemporary view of regulation differs from the view held twenty years ago.

There are essentially three ways in which competition for the market might be introduced in a market characterized by natural monopoly. One way is suggested by Harold Demsetz [2]. Demsetz suggests that even if competition within the market is not possible, one might still have competition for the right to operate in the market. In other words one could envision bidding among prospective entrants for the franchise rights to serve the market: This form of rivalry is often called "Demsetz competition," which may be possible if two conditions are satisfied. First, inputs must be available to all bidders in open markets at competitively determined prices. Second, the cost of collusion among bidding rivals must be prohibitively high, so that competitive bidding is in fact the outcome of the bidding process.

In the single product environment with a uniform price, Demsetz competition would lead to average cost pricing, since all excess profits would be bid away. The concept is appealing because it suggests competition may be possible even where the industry is a natural monopoly, and it is free of the usual regulatory apparatus and regulation-related incentives for firms to behave in an economically inefficient manner.

However, the approach is not entirely free of concern. The outcome of Demsetz competition is in effect a contract between a franchisor (e.g., a regulator) and a franchisee (the regulated firm). Since the firm might well adopt the short-run strategy of providing the lowest quality service possible once it has won the right to serve, the regulator may have to specify minimum quality standards for the service to be provided. It may also be difficult to include procedures for adjustments in terms of service, such as price and quality of service, as conditions in the market change over time. And finally, although the notion of a winning bid may be rather well defined for a firm offering only a single service, the determination of a winner may be difficult in a multiproduct setting, since no firm may bid the lowest price for all services to be offered.

A second way in which it may be possible to introduce competition for the marketplace has been formalized with the concept of "contestability" (see Baumol, Panzar, and Willig [3]). Although contestability and Demsetz competition are similar to each other, they are not identical. In a contestable market both entry and exit must occur in a free and frictionless manner. A firm may choose to enter a market and compete at whatever price it wishes. If it leaves the market, it can recover the full value of its assets and sell the assets or take the assets to another market. In other words, there are no sunk costs associated with entry into a market.[3]

If a number of firms with identical technologies are contemplating entry into a market that is a natural monopoly, the absence of sunk costs will lead to normal (but not extranormal) returns on investment, just as with Demsetz competition. This would occur even in a multiproduct industry; thus, contestability generalizes to the multiproduct world in a way that Demsetz competition does not. Further, in a contestable market, there is no need for the issuance and oversight of a contract awarding an exclusive franchise as is the case with Demsetz competition.

This is not to say that the theory of contestability makes the notion of Demsetz competition obsolete. The important advantage of Demsetz competition over contestability as a way of introducing competition for the market is that the former can be applied in an industry with sunk costs.[4]

Competition for the market can also be introduced in a third way, through Chamberlinian monopolistic competition (see Chamberlin, E. [4]). For example, strong "intermodal competition" among railroads, motor carriers, pipelines, and water carriers, all of whom compete for freight traffic, has often been cited as a basis for deregulation of freight transportation, even if one or more of the modes of transport appears to have the structure of a natural monopoly.

How to Regulate?

As mentioned earlier, the Gegax paper also addresses the question of how one regulates an industry if it is a natural monopoly and policy-makers decide to regulate. This might occur because competition for the market cannot be introduced, or because the second-best outcomes usually identified with Demsetz competition and contestable markets are viewed as too inefficient relative to regulatory schemes that might lead the market closer to first-best outcomes.

Gegax discusses some of the possible regulatory schemes one might employ, including external subsidies, and Ramsey pricing. To be sure, the discussion of Gegax is brief on these points. *Many* other types of regulation might be employed, including among others peak-load pricing schemes and a host of nonlinear tariff practices. A complete review of the problems in pricing and entry would also require a presentation of the many concepts of "fair" pricing, in contrast with the efficient pricing schemes addressed by Gegax. A detailed discussion of the literature in these areas is well beyond the scope of this review, and is mentioned here for completeness. For more on these topics see Brown and Sibley [5], Braeutigam [6], and Zajac [7].

The Social Contract

The final policy option for natural monopoly to be addressed in these comments is one that has received increasing attention in the past few years, the "social contract." This is not discussed in the Gegax article, but appears to be gaining support in a number of state regulatory jurisdictions and is also being studied by certain federal agencies.

The notion that regulation essentially constitutes a contract between a regulator and a regulated firm is not a new one. Goldberg [8] presented the idea over a decade ago. The concept has attracted increasing attention in recent years as regulated firms have sought to diversify into markets that are in some cases quite competitive. As a result, many regulated firms now serve a set of basic monopoly markets (call these core service markets) as well as competitive (noncore) markets.

The use of rate-of-return regulation has proven problematic under these circumstances, since there are often costs common to the provision of core and noncore services. Under rate-of-return regulation the costs of the enterprise would somehow have to be allocated to the core and noncore markets in order to determine the revenue requirement in the core markets. The process of cost allocation is arbitrary, and has led many scholars and regulators to ask about alternatives to traditional rate-of-return regulation with cost allocation.

Heuristically, the social contract embodies the notion that a regulator might reach an agreement with the regulated firm about the prices to be charged in the core markets, where the agreed upon prices are indexed over time to allow for changes in market conditions. The firm would then be able to provide service in noncore markets without regulatory oversight. The standard argument suggests that firms would enter noncore markets only if that were profitable for the firm, so that profit maximizing enterprises would have no incentives to subsidize competitive markets with revenues from core markets. The argument in favor of the social contract goes further to suggest that such entry would be socially desirable if there were cost complementarities, so that the costs of providing core services might be reduced if the firm is allowed to provide noncore services.

Research on the social contract will need to address the way in which the prices for core services are established initially, as well as the way in which they are adjusted over time through indices.

Conclusion

The connection between natural monopoly and public policy has changed significantly in the last two decades. Gegax is correct in indicating that the concept of natural monopoly has been refined to center on scale economies instead of subadditivity in recent years. But perhaps the more important change in economic arguments about public policy toward natural monopoly lies in the emphasis on competition for a market instead of competition within the market; for that reason natural monopoly is no longer seen as a sufficient economic basis for regulation.

Notes

1. See Weiss, L. W., and Klass, M. W. [9].
2. It also turns out that it may not be easy to test for subadditivity. For a discussion of some of the problems encountered in a statistical test of this property, see Evans and Heckman [10].
3. A full and formal discussion of sunk costs is beyond the scope of this paper; for more on this topic see Baumol, Panzar, and Willig [3, pp. 280–281] and Braeutigam [6].
4. The reason a market will not be contestable if there are sunk costs can be described informally as follows. Suppose Firm A (with sunk costs) enters a market without an exclusive franchise. Firm A does not know how long it will be in the market until another firm (Firm B) comes along and tries to undercut Firm A's price. Firm A will then have to recognize the possibility that it may be driven from the market and be unable to recover the entire value of the assets, and it therefore would have to charge a price higher than it would without sunk costs in order to avoid a loss. Consequently second-best pricing will not be achieved under contestability if there are sunk costs.

References

1. Scherer, F. M. *Industrial Market Structure and Economic Performance*. Chicago: Rand McNally, 1980.
2. Demsetz, H. "Why Regulate Utilities?" *J. Law Econ.* 11 (1968): 55–65.
3. Baumol, W. J., J. C. Panzar, and R. D. Willig. *Contestable Markets and the Theory of Industry Structure*. New York: Harcourt, Brace, Jovanovich, 1982.
4. Chamberlin, E. *The Theory of Monopolistic Competition*, 8th ed. Cambridge, Mass.: Harvard University Press, 1962.
5. Brown, S. J., and D. S. Sibley. *The Theory of Public Utility Pricing*. Cambridge: Cambridge University Press, 1986.
6. Braeutigam, R. R. "Optimal Policies for Natural Monopolies." In *Handbook of Industrial Organization*. Edited by Richard Schmalensee and Robert D. Willig. North Holland: Amsterdam, The Netherlands, forthcoming.
7. Zajac, E. E. *Fairness or Efficiency: An Introduction to Public Utility Pricing*. Cambridge, Mass.: Ballinger Press, 1978.
8. Goldberg, V. "Regulation and Administered Contracts." *Bell J. Econ.* 7 (1976): 250–261.
9. Weiss, L. W. and M. W. Klass. *Regulatory Reform: What Actually Happened*. Boston: Little, Brown, 1986.
10. Evans, D. S. and J. J. Heckman. "A Test for Subadditivity of the Cost Function with an Application to the Bell System." *Amer. Econ. Rev.* 74 (1984): 615–673.

8 THE CONTRIBUTION OF ECONOMIC THEORY TO THE REGULATORY PROCESS: STRENGTHS, WEAKNESSES, AND FUTURE DIRECTIONS

Marilyn C. O'Leary and David B. Smith

It is fitting that the last chapter of this book be an analysis of economic theory and its contribution to the regulation of public utilities as seen through the eyes of the regulator, the decision-maker who in the final analysis determines what the actual price or set of prices for energy, telecommunications, or water will be.

A great deal of literature including this text, has been dedicated to the economist's view of the strengths and weaknesses of the regulatory process. Economists express frustration and impatience with the regulatory process and are quick to condemn commissioners for not achieving optimal pricing conditions or for moving too slowly when considering deregulation or encouraging competition to replace regulation.

While it is true that many regulators try to make decisions that make economic sense, the average decision-maker is not concerned about optimal price paths and optimal resource allocation and in fact may not even know what the terms mean. In a word, decision-makers view the advice

---

Both authors have served as Commissioners on the New Mexico Public Service Commission.

of the economist as only one of many inputs that help to shape and direct the regulatory process. While it is true that the job of utility commissions is to act as a market surrogate and set price, that task is performed in a political and social context, and those forces also affect the decision-making process. In addition, the regulatory process integrates many other disciplines besides economics, for example, law, engineering, accounting, and finance. If economic theory is to be successfully integrated into the regulatory process economists must better understand how regulatory decisions are made.

Economics in terms of its influence probably reached its zenith during the 1970s when marginal cost pricing and variants thereof were widely accepted by regulatory commissions. Much of the glamour of cost-based pricing has diminished as commissions have turned to other issues demanding their attention. However, at the present time with the combined forces of deregulation and competition confronting the energy and telecommunications industries in varying degrees, an excellent opportunity exists for the economist to influence regulatory policies in the future. Although regulation is a precedent-based process that moves slowly and deliberately, the forces converging upon it are forcing regulators to act more quickly and to fashion innovative solutions. With a little patience, economists may once again see their influence growing.

The Price Setting Environment

It is difficult for economists to understand regulatory decision making because they usually do not understand how regulators see their role. The economist looks at the commission's statutory mandate to ensure reliable service at just and reasonable rates and is quick to point out that mandate means regulation is a surrogate for the market and should therefore accomplish similar performance standards. Regulators understand their duty to balance the interests of rate-payers and shareholders when making a decision. They understand they have an economic function to set price, but they act in an environment of inputs, constraints, and concerns that are not economic in nature. It is also important for the economist to understand that regulators, in performing the task of balancing the interests of the ratepayer and the investor, are responding to the mandate given to them by their state legislators. This mandate of "balancing" implies that the criterion of fairness be considered. This objective may not make it possible for the economic criterion of efficiency to be achieved.

First of all, commissioners do not listen only to economists before making decisions. Commissions are staffed with lawyers, engineers, and accountants as well as economists, and each of these disciplines has a role in preparing the testimony that is the basis for decisions. Next, there are a series of constraints on decision-making. Perhaps the most obvious is the legal restraint. Considering the legality of a potential decision implies the precedential basis of decision-making. Has the action under consideration been done before? Is the commission changing precedent? If so, are there compelling reasons for doing so? Has the utility been put on notice that past treatment might be changed? Does this decision comply with federal and state law?

The legal considerations that cause the regulatory process to be slow to change also cause it to move slowly. These questions involve due process. Have all the affected parties been notified of the impending case and issues? Have they had a chance to take part in the proceedings?

The political environment also is a constraint on the decision-maker. This is not to say that all commission decisions are inherently political, as some like to cynically posit, but that decisions are made in an essentially political environment, as are all decisions of public agencies. Commissioner awareness of political realities does not determine the outcome, but rather provides a background for decision. For example, has the governor, who has appointed the commissioners, made statements on particular issues? If elected, have the commissioners run on particular issues? Is the legislature interested in or considering legislating in the regulatory arena?

The utility and intervenors in a case raise other important issues. The utility argues the effect of the decision on the utility's bond rating and what effect that will have on shareholders and rate-payers. Industrial customers threaten to bypass or abandon the system if rates are set too high. Low-income intervenors argue that because of the economy they will not be able to afford higher rates. Agricultural users argue for a decision to meet their particular needs. All of these positions and more must be taken into consideration by commissioners.

Finally, commissioners bring their own backgrounds to their decision making. These backgrounds, without implying bias, may bring a certain point of view to the job. The most obvious is whether they have been consumer advocates or utility employees or even whether they believe utilities or rate-payers have been mistreated by former commission's decisions. A commissioner's profession and training will affect how he or she approaches the job. If she is a lawyer, she might be concerned primarily with the precedential support for or the legality of the decision.

A businessman might be concerned with the effect of the decision on the business climate. Regulators, then, will consider legal, economic, accounting, engineering, financial, political, and social issues when determining how to achieve a fair price. Economic theory must in fact compete aggressively with other disciplines in convincing the commission why it should receive more consideration in the final decision. Economists will probably never be fully satisfied with the extent to which economic theory is embraced by regulatory commissions. This is not to say that economics will ever be dismissed from the regulatory process as a useful and analytical tool. Economists simply must not assume that because logic demands the implementation of a certain economic concept such will be the case.

Referring to table 8–1, one can see that at the present time, approximately 11 out of 369 (.03%) regulatory commissioners have a background in economics. This fact alone helps to explains why commissioners are likely to be influenced by disciplines other than economics.

To generalize regarding what commissioners think about economics is even more difficult than generalizing regarding what economists think about commissioners. Nevertheless, the following statements can be made. Commissioners generally try to base a decision on some economic reality rather than on an economic theory. While some theories promise perfect resource allocation if implemented, commissioners are suspicious of a laissez-faire position, not because they are trying to preserve their jobs, as some economists would suggest, but because they know that the problems they must solve will not disappear merely by taking one step along the path of economic theory, for example, in the direction of deregulation. Economic theories have not completely solved allocation problems, and while they might help solve a problem, they are not the solution. It is also important to understand that commission decisions necessarily are made one at a time, and this process by its very nature goes against adopting any kind of theory all at one time in one piece.

Commissioners are becoming more educated in economic theory simply because forces in the environment in which they make decisions demand it. For this reason, economists once again have a chance to be influential if they understand their economic theories must deal with practical solutions to real problems and not with economic theories that might or might not work. To commissioners who take their jobs very seriously, the stakes are too high to rely on theory only.

Table 8–1. Commissioner Backgrounds.

Date	Attorneys	Accountants	Economists	Engineers	Business	Misc.	Unknown	Total
2/26/68	115	8	—	4	42	36	21	226
5/3/76	112	12	8	12	51	72	24	291
11/15/76	122	10	8	16	57	65	12	290
4/18/77	124	12	9	14	51	75	9	294
2/2/78	121	13	17	17	59	73	8	308
11/6/78	124	13	21	23	46	88	8	324
7/2/79	126	12	18	24	61	82	8	331
12/3/79	128	10	20	24	65	80	7	334
6/23/80	130	13	17	25	52	100	6	343
11/17/80	125	13	16	27	70	82	5	338
5/4/81	118	18	17	29	38	99	7	326
2/15/82	116	14	13	30	30	109	20	332
10/25/82	123	13	11	38	59	97	8	349
5/30/83	123	18	16	37	53	100	20	367
1/16/84	122	19	15	35	52	108	27	378
11/19/84	128	15	9	36	39	67	72	366
3/10/86	125	12	14	39	44	99	41	374
6/15/87	109	11	10	36	46	107	47	366
6/27/88	107	15	11	37	38	127	34	369

Source: NARUC Bulletin, June 27, 1988, p. 26.

The Status of Economic Theory in the Regulatory Process

While economists for the most part rarely have been appointed or elected as commissioners, considerable progress has been made by many state commissions in attempting to employ economists on their staffs. This fact is no small victory for the economics profession, as commissioners will at least be subject to economic input from their staffs. Commissioners also can rely upon their economists to conduct economic analysis of certain issues, which may become rate case issues in the future. Some state commissions have even adopted a special research and policy analysis group that is primarily comprised of economists. This is a noticeable change compared to the composition of commission staffs 15 years ago.

While economists have made their presence known at the staff level, it must be remembered that commissioners also listen to attorneys, accountants, and engineers regarding various regulatory matters. Because of the influence of these other disciplines, a final decision, while displaying some imprint of economic analysis, will also reflect the analytic impact of other disciplines.

In which areas of the rate-making process has economic theory had its greatest influence to date? This question can best be answered by looking at the basic components of the rate-making process — revenue requirements, cost allocation, and rate design.

Revenue Requirements

For the most part, the elements that constitute revenue requirements or cost of service remain in the realm of the accountant and the engineer. Economists have written on all of these components (i.e., rate base, cost of equity models, depreciation, taxes, and expenses). However, the actual computation or number crunching is left to the engineer and accountant. This statement can be verified by the fact that most economists on commission staffs either do rate-of-return analysis or rate design, while the accountant and the engineer write most of the direct testimony on rate base, taxes, depreciation, and expenses.

The economic theorist reading this chapter might ask, "How is it possible to discount the advice of the economist and give more weight to the accountant or engineer when determining revenue requirements?" Commissioners might respond by asking where economists were when commissioners were confronting two dilemmas facing the electric utility industry — high cost plants and excess capacity.

As commissioners who were faced with such problems grappled and searched for workable solutions, about all the assistance the economist could offer were such naive comments as "this sure wouldn't happen in a competitive market." The contribution of economic theory to these pressing and real issues was minimal at best. It is unfortunate that economic theory did not rise to meet this challenge since various phase-in plans that have been adopted are piecemeal plans at best with no real sustainable economic underpinnings. Decision-makers did not have the luxury to sit back and ponder what could have been or might have been. Often they were not the same people who certified the plant, and they found it difficult, some practically and some conceptually, to retrace the steps of why the plant was built in the first place. Their job was to price an asset, that is, to value a rate base and set a price based upon the value of that asset. They had to choose some subjective measure of "rate shock" and use that as a ceiling price. The entire process has been painful for both commissions and companies, and they both have vowed they will not subject themselves to this situation again. Companies are now warning of a shortage of electricity in the future because of their experience in attempting to rate base their recent plant additions. However, if commissions rely solely on the rate base rate-of-return model in the future, there is nothing to guarantee that such an event will not occur again.

While economic theory was not particularly useful in suggesting appropriate measures to resolve existing situations of cost overruns or excess capacity, it did play a useful role in pointing out the weaknesses of traditional rate base rate-of-return regulation. The problem of cost over runs and excess capacity has brought an increased recognition of the need to engage in more extensive and thorough resource planning in the future. This need has been recognized by commissions, which require companies to submit resource-planning documents on an annual basis for commission review. These resource plans contain, at a minimum, demand projections and supply options for meeting future increases in demand. This movement can be credited to microeconomic theory at least in part because it represents an effort to provide power in the future at the lowest possible cost without jeopardizing reliability. The very name of these plans, resource-planning documents, is a formal recognition of the need to achieve the goal of an efficient allocation of resources, that is, greater efficiency in the regulatory process. This process has been pushed even further in some states and by the Federal Energy Regulatory Commission (FERC) with their efforts to implement a bidding process for future supplies of electricity. The movement to adopt such plans by commissions represents one of the most significant contributions that microeconomic theory can make to the cost of service portion of rate making. This statement becomes more obvious when one remembers that taxes, rate of return, depreciation, and expenses are all a direct function of the size of the rate base. Controlling costs is much easier in the planning stage before the plant is built than after the plant is built. Therefore, economic theory can play an invaluable role in influencing the future cost of electricity if regulatory commissions will listen. Those commissions that choose to plan for the future using the standard rate base rate-of-return model that has guided policy in the past are courting with disaster.

Pricing

Cost allocation and rate design represents the area of rate making in which economics has had the most observable influence upon commission decisions to date. As competition becomes more of a reality in the energy and telecommunications industries, pricing and cost allocation will take on even greater significance while relegating the area of revenue requirements a rather minor role in the rate-setting process.

The 1970s and 1980s have seen the adoption of marginal cost pricing and variants thereof in both energy and telecommunications. Efforts by economists to provide consumers with more correct signals as to what it was costing were adopted by regulatory commissions. At a minimum, the era of declining block rates in electricity and natural gas is all but over and, at a minimum, flat energy rates are being adopted in their place.

In many ways, these costing and pricing exercises that were and still are taking place have made commissioners more aware of certain economic concepts that can prove to be of value to them in the future. Cost based pricing versus value of service, equity versus efficiency, cross subsidization, price elasticity, Ramsey pricing, and price discrimination are just a few concepts that, like it or not, commissioners will encounter in future years as the energy and telecommunications industries undergo structural change.

The movement toward deregulation and competition in certain phases of the energy and telecommunications industries will lead commissions to depend upon microeconomic theory to understand how these structural changes will affect prices. A very challenging issue for the commissions to resolve will be to determine the relevance of rate-base/rate-of-return pricing in the presence of competition or partical competition. What will be the relevance and purpose of going through an intensive nine-month rate case determining revenue requirements, cost allocation, and rate design if, in the end, some customer class *refuses* to pay that price?

Barriers and Obstacles to Implementing
Economic Analysis

Regardless of their academic training, philosophical beliefs, and personal objectives, commissioners are confronted with many obstacles during their tenures.

The Public Utility Statute Itself

What does the statute say with regard to the authority of the commission? How much power has the legislature relegated to the commission in setting "fair and reasonable rates"? How much room is there for innovation? To what extent have the legislature and court bound the hands of the commission in setting rates? While outsiders might scoff at such legal constraints, it is naive to do so and leads to the complaint that academic economists live in an ivory tower and do not understand the reality of commission decision making. It is a fact that the law sets the parameters within which commissions act. The lawyers involved in the regulatory process understand the law and use it to benefit their clients.

Time and Delay

Allowing affected parties the right to be heard is a cornerstone of our administrative adjudicatory process. Nevertheless, claims of due process can be abused in the regulatory process. Companies and other intervenors regularly challenge commission actions on the basis that their right to due process will be violated unless extensive hearings are conducted to present the pros and cons of the proposed commission action. Even disagreements over what process is due can cause delay. The issuing and implementation of general orders involve many procedural issues. What may start out as a simple, straightforward, and workable economic proposal can end up either as a hollow order or one that takes years to put into effect.

Economics and Economists Are Not Revered by
All Commissioners

While it may come as a shock to those economists who urge commissions to adopt pricing methodologies that will promote efficiency and correctly allocate resources, some commissioners are not concerned with this objective. Why? They have their own agenda. They may be concerned about the high rates industrial users are paying and devote all of their energies to changing this regardless of how it is accomplished. Others may be using the position as a stepping stone for a higher office and not wish to do anything that might jeopardize this objective. Others may be interested in developing closer working relationships with the legislature in order to help the commission attract adequate funding. Each commissioner has his or her own objective function and economic theory may not ever be a relevant input into that function. Remember the average life of a commissioner is less than three years in office. Most of their decisions will be short-run in nature with little time being permitted to sit back and undertake a long-run perspective on what the impact of their decision may have. Some economists may be shocked to learn that some commissioners don't care one way or the other about the *economic* impact of their decisions because they really do not *understand* what economics is all about. Some commissioners are also aware that while economists continue to advocate deregulation, members of the public are less than enthusiastic with its effect on them.

Fear of Breaking with the Past

A great deal of regulation is based on precedent. Legal precedent is supported by the "we've always done it this way, why change it now?" syndrome. This attitude can best be illustrated by the fact that regulators move slowly in adopting new proposals or concepts that are presented to them. There is a valid reason for this, which critics of the process really do not understand. Regulators want to be as certain as possible that if they do attempt to implement a new concept into the process it will work. Their rationale is simple: Whenever you change the price of a commodity or service you will, in most instances, initiate a response. The question is, will the response be what you hoped to elicit or will it be entirely different? If the response is not what you had hoped for, you have nevertheless set into motion a process that may take years to correct. It is interesting to note that if the commission does adopt some new methodology and the reaction is not what was predicted, there is a noted absence for a period of time of the party who advocated the change. The regulator must take the credit or the criticism of the final decision, and that goes with the territory. However, most regulators, recognizing the tremendous impact their decisions can have, will move cautiously into unchartered waters. This is a reality of regulation and should be expected.

Imperfect Information

Commissioners must make decisions based on imperfect information. This is true for several reasons. First, they are usually reacting to a proposal presented by a company in an adjudicatory hearing. Because it is likely the case will be litigated, the company adopts an adversant stance and often will file the minimum amount of information to get the case before the commission. In addition, the record may contain incomplete data, inaccurate data, or may lack data because parties were inartful in making data requests. Because they may not have specifically or correctly stated what they wanted in an interrogatory, the company did not provide what the parties really wanted. It is the nature of regulation for the company to resist providing data unless some party to the case is shrewd enough to ask for it. The data provided by the company will be the data to win a case, *not* to lose it! The company controls the flow of information, not the commission. In addition, intervenors have often taken extreme positions supported by their data that might accurately reflect the outcome of a particular decision. Therefore, to expect a commission to set an optimal price based upon incomplete and inaccurate information is naive. There is little wonder why commission orders might stray from the competitive ideal.

Removing the Barriers: Is It Possible?

Can All of the Barriers Be Removed?

The answer obviously is no. It must be stressed that regulation is an ongoing, slow moving, evolving process. There will always be political and social forces at work to persuade commissioners that self-interest goals are more beneficial for specific parties than certain economic goals that are best for all. Regulatory decisions, for the most part, are short-term decisions based upon imperfect information both in regard to the past and much more so for the future. There is not really the luxury to plan and forecast future events but instead commissioners must focus upon immediate issues and resolve them today.

While it must be recognized that there are very real obstacles that will always be present to drive commissioners to less than economically optimal decisions, economic theory has and must continue to play an important role in the price-setting process.

234

234 PUBLIC UTILITY REGULATION

Provide a Framework for Analysis

If regulators can use microeconomic theory as a frame of reference within which to base their decisions, the economics profession will have won a great victory. If the decision-maker of the future is aware of the fundamental abuses that can and do arise from monopoly power and realize that he does have the power to work within the statutes to curb and direct the conduct of the monopolist toward the competitive ideal, then a great deal will have been accomplished.

It must be shown that microeconomics is an invaluable analytical tool to evaluate the many questions that will confront commissions at the present time and in the future. How do we price in an excess capacity situation? How can industrial development rates be provided without discrimination to other buyers? How does one set price for the core or inelastic customer and customers with alternatives leave the system? How can we best plan for future generation plants and avoid the cost overrun problems encountered in the past? How can bottlenecks in transportation of natural gas be removed? What are the consequences if they are not removed? Should the states transfer regulation of generation and transmission to the Federal Energy Regulatory Commission? What will be the economic and financial impact of horizontal mergers in the electric industry? Why might a more fully integrated electric grid system lead to a more efficient use of existing and future sources of power? What are the consequences if we do not have an integrated grid systems? How do we set cogeneration rates (i.e., what is avoided cost)? Is it possible to develop efficiency measures for measuring industry performance? Should the social contract be rewritten in telecommunications? If so, what form should it take?

These problems must and will be addressed by commissions in some fashion. Once again, just as in the past, the decision-maker will receive inputs from the many disciplines discussed here. If the economist can assist the regulator in resolving these issues, economic theory may very well gain the acceptance by the regulatory community that it has been seeking.

Building an Alliance with the Legal Profession

An important fact that must be stressed at this point is that if economic theory is to continue to influence decision-makers, it must build a strong alliance with the legal profession.

Economists cheerfully like to point out in their evaluation of the regulatory process that what is needed are fewer lawyers and more economists. Those who advance such a view might do better to understand the legal underpinnings of the regulatory process before designating themselves as someone who is competent to evaluate the process. In a word, without the assistance of the legal profession, microeconomic theory will always remain at the edge of the regulatory process.

The 1970s and early 1980s represented a period of time in which economic input was sought by state and federal commissions. For decades, economists had presented the case for marginal cost pricing, and yet it took the Public Utilities Regulation Policies Act (PURPA) in 1978 to bring this economic theory into practice. Economists argued for decades about the need to deregulate the wellhead price of natural gas. It took the Natural Gas Policy Act (NGPA) Act to accomplish this goal. It took FERC Orders 436 and 451 to begin to remove obstacles to the movement of natural gas and state laws to mandate contract carriage of natural gas. Throughout the country at the present time, many state commissions are adopting orders that mandate resource planning for the electric companies under their jurisdiction. Other states like Nevada passed a statute requiring resource planning. Although unsuccessful, the New Mexico Public Service Commission tried to obtain from the legislature power over intrastate wheeling of electric power in 1984. Some states are now requiring periodic management audits, and others have actually passed statutes deregulating telecommunications or at least have bills in front of legislatures proposing deregulation of communications.

The point of this is that it took a law to enable microeconomic theory to become a reality insofar as implementing it in the decision-making process. Economic theory can provide the *rationale* for the law to either be changed or a new one to be implemented. The biggest ally the economist has is the legal staff on a commission who can look at existing statutes, general orders, and court decisions to determine the best course of action to pursue in order to implement economic theory.

The economist must realize that he needs the lawyer to forge the way through the mire of statutes and existing court precedents before there is any real possibility of his economic proposal having a chance to be applied to the regulatory process. The process will not stop at this point, however. Even if the economic proposal has enough potential to influence a commission decision, it must undergo a thorough examination by the courts if the order is appealed. If an appeal is heard by the court, the analysis will truly become a legal exercise at this point and economic theory (no matter how sound) can quickly be dispensed with if any legal inadequacy is found in the commission's order. An example of this is the suit brought against the Federal Energy Regulatory Commission (FERC) challenging FERC Order 436 [1]. The decision remanded the Order back to FERC for some modifications. It is highly probable that in some jurisdictions the notion of the social contract will be challenged by some party. The blending of economic theory with law has a satisfying order to it. The theory, if sound, will provide the rationale for a proposed change in the law and, if in fact a change does emerge, the theory will have withstood legal challenges to its credibility and substance.

The Future Contributions of Economic Theory to the Regulatory Process

What Specific Contributions Can Economic Theory Make to the Regulatory Process Now and in the Near Future?

The potential for the discipline of economics to influence regulatory policy at the present time and in the future has never been greater. Decision-makers are being confronted with more simultaneous actual and potential structural changes in the electric, gas, and telecommunications industries than in the history of regulation. Many of our state commissions have operated under the traditional rate-base/rate-of-return model and now find this traditional approach to price setting challenged. This is unsettling to them and they are now searching for another model that will guide them in setting regulatory policy. In all three industries, the combinations of actual or potential deregulation are confronting the regulator with a host of challenges never encountered by his predecessors. Many changes are occuring in the electric utility industry, such as proposed restructuring of regulation (i.e., transferring regulation of generation and transmission to the FERC). Horizontal mergers may very well create a tight oligopoly in generation if Wall Street has its way. Both the FERC and certain states are either considering or have already adopted some form of bidding format, which will be used to choose the next round of generating plant.

State regulators of telecommunications are being asked to move from traditional rate-base/rate-of-return regulation and adopt a more flexible pricing methodology (i.e., the "new" social contract). The Federal Communication Commission's (FCC) Notice for Proposed Rulemaking that on August 4, 1987, asked for comments on proposed price caps for some services while relaxing price controls on others. The FERC Notice of Proposed Rulemaking on avoided cost and bidding were issued in 1988 asking for comments from various parties including commissions. Firms in the natural gas industry are asking for more pricing flexibility to prevent bypass and to hold industrial loads.

Most of these issues are economic in nature. They are not accounting issues or engineering issues. How does one attempt to analyze these issues under the traditional rate-base/rate-of-return model? What are the implications of deregulation and competition? How does the traditional model of rate-base regulation apply when only a portion or segment of the industry becomes more competitive? How should price be determined for those customers who cannot avail themselves of alternatives? How do we price for those who do have alternatives? Should a regulator aggressively promote competition where possible or move cautiously? Where will movement toward deregulation and competition find us in another decade? What will happen to such goals as reliability and universal service? Should economic efficiency be the principal driving force behind future commission decisions? How do we move from natural monopoly to effective competition? How fast do we move? Do we want to move? Will imperfect competition simply lead to increased price discrimination?

How Can Economic Theory Assist the Institution of Regulation in Resolving and Adapting to These Issues?

Economic theory can provide the decision-maker with a framework within which to analyze current issues. Many regulators will resist letting the market set the price. They may not be convinced that competition will work and will be especially concerned about the consequences if it does not generate the results that various prophets are predicting. It is incumbent upon the economist to help the regulator understand that if the necessary conditions for effective competition are in place, the market will provide the desired outcome *without* the influence of the regulator. It is also the intellectual responsibility of the economist to point out just as quickly to the regulator that deregulation of a market will not work *unless* the required structural conditions for effective competition are in place. Deregulation absent effective competition will not be an effective cure for imperfect regulation.

In summary, the regulators need a blueprint or a map to provide them with courses of action as the structures of our energy and telecommunications industries evolve more toward more competitive possibilities.

Regulation is a human institution directed by men and women who, for the most part, believe in the contract that has been struck between the utility and society: a monopoly franchise subject to public control. However, as mentioned earlier, this contract is being reexamined by the various parties and may possibly be changed in the future.

Regulators want to be fair to both sides and to act as a check against the tremendous economic and political power of the energy and telecommunications industries. They want to do a good job. They work diligently at their task against insurmountable odds and try to live by a code of conduct that will allow them to leave office with their self-respect. Their decisions will be affected by many variables that may or may not reflect economic analysis. The economics profession must be patient. Their ideas will *never* be accepted in totality but neither will those of anyone else. There has never been a time since the adoption of regulation as America's choice of social control of monopoly in which economics can play a more important role. Economic theory can and must be relied upon to aid the regulator in shaping future social policy. If economics is to make a positive contribution to the regulatory process in the future, the decision-maker must be given an agenda of pressing issues, economic alternatives for resolving these issues, and the cost and benefits of adopting a particular course of action. The economic solutions that are proposed must be presented to the regulator in clear and understandable language. It is a golden opportunity for the economist to provide this type of analysis. The future will tell whether economists heed this advice.

References

1. Associated Gas Distributors v. FERC, Nos. 85–1811, et al. (D.C. Circuit Court, June 23, 1987).

Index

Agthe, D. E., 166
Airline Deregulation Act, 32
Alchian, A. A., 22
American Telephone & Telegraph, 95–120
antitrust issues, 95–6, 99, 145–53
Averch, Harvey, 21, 111–12, 214n
Averch-Johnson effect, 21–2, 111–12, 131–2

"balancing act" of regulations, 224
Baumol, W. J., 18–19, 22, 186, 194, 204, 213, 215n, 219, 222n
Becker, Gary S., 81
Bell Operating Companies (BOC's), 99–124
Berg, Sanford. V., 189, 210, 214n, 215n
Billings, R. B., 166
Bittlingmayer, G., 161n
Boiteaux, Marcel, 20
Boland, J. J., 166, 175
Bolter, Walter, 121
Bonbright, James C., 11–12, 15, 18, 37–9, 45
Bradford, David F., 194
Braeutigam, Ronald R., 6–7, 198–9, 220
Brown, S. J., 215n, 220
bypass, 101–3, 137, 142

Carlton, D. W., 161n
Carter, James E., 17
Carver, P. H., 166
capture theory of regulation, 32, 80–3
Chamberlin, E., 220
Cicchetti, Charles C., 52
Civil Aeronautics Board, 17, 32
Clark, J. M., 12–13, 133
Clark, R. M., 167
Coase, R. H., 13, 215n
Cohen, Jerry S., 15
common carriage, 140
Consumer Communications Reform Act of 1976, 101
contestable markets, 3–4, 18–9, 24, 31–2, 219–20
contract carriage, 138, 143, 148, 153
Copeland, Basil, 4
cost based rates, 39
Cramer, Curtis, 4–5, 155–61
Crew, Michael, 25n
cross subsidization, 97, 108, 111–14, 116, 118, 120–1, 123, 138, 142–4, 169, 172, 183, 196, 230
Customer Premises Equipment (CPE), 158

Dajani, J. S., 167

de Butts, John, 98
declining block rate structure, 168
"Demsetz" competition, 218–20
Demsetz, Harold, 17, 218–20
Department of Justice, 96, 100
deregulation, 17, 93, 115–17, 123,
        135, 142, 155, 157, 161, 230
diversification, 33, 113, 116
divestiture, 99–100
Domhoff, G. William, 15
Dugger, William A., 2
Dupuit, Jules, 9

economic theory of regulation, 80, 87
economies of coordination, 210
economies of scale, 3, 6, 10, 83–4,
        97, 167–8, 186–221
economies of scope, 3, 11, 14, 83,
        121–2, 135, 186–221
efficiency, 21–3, 117, 119, 191–200
elasticity of demand studies, 165–6,
        184
electric industry
    cost based rates, 39
    diversification, 33
    equiproportional adjustment, 49–
        50, 60, 89–90
    marginal costs, 41, 45–7, 57–70,
        78, 88–90
    marginal costs of generation, 52–56
    marginal energy costs, 56
    inverse elasticity rule, 49–50, 58,
        60, 89–90
    long run incremental cost, 57–8
    revenue reconciliation problem, 48,
        69–70
    time of use rates, 56–69, 88
embedded costs, 40–1, 45–7, 60, 65,
        70, 114
Environmental Protection Agency, 2
Evans, D. S., 222n

Federal Communications
        Commissions, 17, 96–9, 116–
        20, 236
Federal Energy Regulatory

Commissions, 17, 140, 146,
        235–7
Federal Trade Commission, 118
Feldman, S. L., 177n
fixed charges, 173–4
Ford, J. L., 167
Furobotn, E. G., 22

Gabel, David, 121
Gabel, Richard, 121
Gegax, Douglas, 6–7, 212, 217–21
Gillan, William J., 52
Glaeser, Martin G., 4, 121–3, 132–3
Glaeser model of regulation, 121–2
Goldberg, V., 220
Green, Mark, 15
Greene, Harold, 17–18, 99–100
Gross, Charles A., 215n

Hanke, S. H., 168
Harden, Garnett, 84
Heckman, J. J., 222n
Hopkinson, John, 40
Hotelling, Harold, 12, 193
Houthakker, H. S., 20
Howe, C. W., 166
Huber, Peter W., 107, 109

intermodal competition, 198–9
Interstate Commerce Commission,
        17, 95–6
inverse elasticity rule, 49–50, 59–60,
        89–90

Jamison, M., 121
Johnson, Leland L., 21, 111–12, 214n
joint/common costs, 96, 112–14, 116,
        121
Jones, Donald R., 215n
Joskow, Paul R., 215n

Kahn, A. E., 17, 197, 214n., 215n
Kammerschen, David R., 215n
Keenan, Donald C., 215n

Kessell, R. A., 22
Klamer, J. M., 161n
Klass, M. W., 222n
Klevorick, A. K., 22

Lancaster, K., 20, 47
Landes-Posner measure of monopoly
    power, 123
legal aspects of regulation, 225
Lewis, W. A., 13
Liebenstein, Harvey, 22
Liebhafsky, H. H., 11
Linaweaver, F. P., 166
Lipsey, R. G., 20
long run incremental cost, 57–8
long run marginal cost, 88
lump sum transfer adjustment, 49

Malko, J. Robert, 2, 78–90
Mann, Patrick G., 5–6, 168, 179–83
marginal cost pricing, 2–3, 5–6, 13,
    19–20, 41, 45–7, 57, 60, 65,
    78, 88–90, 167–71, 181, 230
  first best marginal cost pricing rule,
    193
  second best marginal cost pricing
    rule, 193
market entry, 102–4
Marshall, Alfred, 11, 19
McChesney, F. S., 79
McGowen, William, 97
Melody, William, 121
mergers, 152–3
Microwave Communications, Inc.
    (MCI), 97–9, 101, 104–5, 110,
    125
Miller, Edythe S., 18
Milliman, J. W., 163, 177n
Mills, C. Wright, 15
Minimum Efficient Market Share
    (MES), 107–8, 123
Mintz, Morton, 15
Mohring, H., 194

Nader, Ralph, 15
Nash, L. R., 10

natural gas industry
  common carriage, 140
  contract carriage, 137, 143, 148
  deregulation, 142, 152, 155, 158–
    61, 230
  FERC order–436, 235–6
  FERC order–451, 235
  local distribution companies, 137,
    141–2, 155
  merchant function, 140
  mergers, 148–53, 156
  natural gas producers, 144
  obligation to serve, 140, 148
  open network architecture, 143,
    153
  pipeline bottleneck, 145–6, 148–52
  pipeline companies, 137–61
  purchased gas adjustment clauses,
    138–40
  take or pay provisions, 138, 140,
    155–6
  tight oligopoly, 148–53
  unbundling of services, 137, 143–4,
    148
Natural Gas Policy Act of 1978, 138,
    235
natural monopoly, 6, 10–13, 18–19,
    78, 83–7, 96–8, 141, 186–221
New Mexico Public Service
    Commission, 235
Nguyen, D. T., 25n
Nowotny, Kenneth, 2, 28–34, 214n

Occupational Safety and Health
    Administration, 2
O'Leary, Marilyn C., 7

Panzar, John C., 186, 204, 213, 215n,
    219, 222n
Parker, Alfred L., 6
peak load pricing, 20–1, 43, 65, 82,
    87–8, 171–2
Peltzman, Sam, 80
Posner, Richard, A., 15–17, 31, 80
price caps, 117–20, 124, 132, 135

price discrimination, 4, 23, 97, 108–9,
    112, 123, 132, 135, 153, 155,
    196–7, 230
Pryor, T., 107
public interest, 30–1, 79
Public Utility Regulatory Policies Act
    of 1978, 38, 40, 235

Ramsey, Frank, 22, 193
Ramsey pricing, 13, 22–3, 193–200,
    220, 230
rate base/rate of return regulation, 4,
    21, 111, 117–20, 131–4, 135–6
rate design, 58
Regional Bell Holding Companies
    (RBOC's), 99–106
regulatory process, 223
    "balancing act", 224
    legal considerations, 225
    political constraints, 225
regulatory reform, 124
residual ratemaking, 115
revenue reconciliation problem, 48,
    69
revised theory of regulation, 4, 111
rolled-in-pricing, 144
Ruggles, Nancy, 13

Saunders, R. J., 168
Saving, T. R., 22
Scherer, F. M., 107, 217
Schlenger, D. L., 172
Schumpeter, Joseph, 9–10, 12, 14
seasonal pricing, 171–2
second best problem, 20–1, 47–8, 69
Selwyn, L. L., 107
Sharkey, W. W., 5, 161n, 214n, 215n
Shepherd, W. G., 102, 104
Sibley, D. S., 215n, 220
Simons, Henry C., 16–17, 28
Smith, David, B., 7
Smolensky, Paul, 52
social contract, 220–1, 236
social control, 2, 30–2, 148, 153
Spence, M., 206
stand alone cost, 120–1, 124, 135
Stevie, R. G., 167

Stigler, George, 14–16, 80–1
subadditivity, 6–7, 158, 186–221
sunk costs, 18–19, 102
Swensen, Phillip, 2, 78–90

Takayama, Akia, 21–2
telecommunications industry
    Bell Operating Companies
        (BOC's), 99–106, 109, 115,
        123
    bypass, 101, 104
    Consumer Communications
        Reform Act of 1976, 99
    cross subsidization, 97, 108, 111–
        12, 116, 118, 120–1, 123
    Customer Premises Equipment
        (CPE), 99
    deregulation, 115–17, 123, 135
    diversification, 113, 116
    divestiture, 99–100
    facilities based carriers (FBC's),
        101, 104, 106, 108, 119
    interexchange carriers, 100–1, 104,
        107–9, 123–4
    joint/common costs, 96, 112–16,
        120–3
    local access and transportation
        areas (LATA's), 99–106, 108,
        110
    local exchange carriers (LEC's)
        100–3, 107, 109, 111, 114–15,
        123
    message toll service (MTS), 97–8
    Minimum Efficient Market Share
        (MEM), 107–8, 123
    open network architecture, 104,
        109, 113
    other common carriers (OCC's),
        99–106, 110
    price caps, 117–20, 124, 132, 135
    Regional Bell Holding Companies
        (RBOC's), 99–106
Telser, L. G., 161n
Trebing, Harry, 3–4, 17, 131–6
Tschirhart, John, 189, 210, 212, 214n,
    215n
Tugwell, Rexford G., 31
Turvey, Ralph, 168

U. S. Sprint, 101, 103–6, 110

Vail, Theodore, 95–8
vertical disintegration, 210–12
Vickrey, W. S., 24

Warford, J. J., 167–8
water industry
  costing developments, 167–74
  economies of scale, 167–8
  elasticity of demand studies, 165–6, 183
  rate design
    declining block structure, 168–9
    fixed charges, 173–4
    inverted block structure, 169

seasonal pricing, 171–2
zonal pricing, 172–3, 183
urban water pricing, 163
Weaver, C., 107
Weiss, L. W., 222n
welfare, 20, 190–4
Wenders, John, 3, 25n
Western Electric, 96
Western Union, 94–5, 103
Williamson, O. E., 20, 25n, 215n
Willig, Robert D., 18–19, 186, 204, 213, 215n, 219, 222n
Woods, Charles E., 177n

Zajac, E. E., 199, 220
zonal pricing, 269–271, 288